MW01285511

RADICAL
DOUBT

RADICAL DOUBT

TURNING UNCERTAINTY INTO SUREFIRE SUCCESS

DR. BIDHAN L. PARMAR

DIVERSION
BOOKS

Diversion Books
A division of Diversion Publishing Corp.
www.diversionbooks.com

For more information, email info@diversionbooks.com.

Hardcover ISBN: 978-1-63576-934-0
e-ISBN: 978-1-63576-897-8
First Diversion Books Edition: August 2025

Cover design by Henry Sene Yee
Design by Neuwirth & Associates, Inc.

Printed in the United States of America
1 3 5 7 9 10 8 6 4 2

Diversion books are available at special discounts for bulk purchases in
the US by corporations, institutions, and other organizations. For more
information, please contact admin@diversionbooks.com.

To R. Edward Freeman

My teacher, my student, and my friend.

&

To Sauce

I'm better with you by my side.

Contents

First Contact with Reality

Imagine being named the next CEO of your organization. What improvements would be at the top of your to-do list?

Give everyone a raise?

Install a snow cone machine in the breakroom?

Finally fire that incompetent jackass of a coworker?

You might choose to improve the company's sustainability practices, close the gender wage gap, or finally stop Trent in accounting from clicking "reply all" to every email. Picturing the good choices we would make with more power, responsibility, and resources is easy and enjoyable.

Realizing the benefits of these choices is much more challenging. We forget to imagine that our initiatives could run out of money, that the C-suite and front-line workers have different views on sustainability, or that the team will struggle to balance competing goals like quality, cost, and speed. Our good intentions blind us to divergent perspectives, likely pitfalls, and pervasive uncertainty. As a result, few of our well-intended plans survive their first contact with reality.

This kind of myopia is especially problematic when we face difficult decisions—the ones without simple, right answers. Moments of uncertainty are inflection points where we can inadvertently squander time, money, and our stakeholders' trust. Alternatively, we can capitalize on the considerable opportunity these choices provide to improve our organizations, strengthen our relationships, and become who we aspire to be.

Where can we turn for help? Despite a well-stocked shelf of decision-making books, effective guidance is in short supply. Most decision-making books conveniently skip over doubt. What they're trying to sell is a shallow version of certainty, and lingering on ambiguities seems discouraging. And so most books focus on simple decisions (Should I eat Taco Bell or Burger King?). Other books bombard us with research study after research study to demonstrate that we are not perfectly rational.

Then, after we're sufficiently demoralized and convinced that we'll never make good choices, they conclude with commonsense advice and a hopeful note.

When we try to apply the insights from all these books, we naturally experience ambiguity, confusion, and discomfort, leading us to give up too soon and start looking for the next silver bullet. Without helping people cope with doubt and complexity, the abundant (and well-intentioned) decision-making advice available today just doesn't work.

Here, I'm supposed to convince you that reading this book will change your life, make you the envy of your department, and maybe even restore your receding hairline. But remember, this is a book, not a magic lamp. After you finish reading, you'll be able to recognize that everyday moments of doubt in organizational life are terrific opportunities to move forward carefully and confidently. In the process, I will ask you to take a deep look at yourself and your relationship with uncertainty and reconsider your fundamental assumptions. The irony of writing a decision-making book that extols the virtues of uncertainty is not lost on me. We will not sit back and admire problems indefinitely; instead, the goal is to proceed wisely by training you to experience doubt as a catalyst for learning.

Over the last fifteen years as a business school professor, I've taught thousands of MBA students and executives, conducted extensive research, and consulted with scores of companies. Working with leaders in organizations from non-profits to nanotech, I've listened to and cataloged their difficult decisions. In the process, I've captured the perils and the promise of different approaches, carefully disentangling what advice works, what doesn't, and why. My good fortune has allowed me to work alongside cutting-edge thinkers in the social sciences and humanities who are passionate about improving how leaders tackle complex problems. Together, our work has uncovered the science-based practices required to help you make better sense of your surroundings and generate meaningful next steps when you feel stuck.

Whether you're a CEO or a new project manager, as an organizational leader you must balance competing interests, use limited resources to improve outcomes, and build stronger relationships with stakeholders. This is hard and important work requiring patience, curiosity, and a tolerance for uncertainty. To help you grow these capacities, I'm not going to spoon-feed you the takeaways just in case your mind drifts to your Instagram crush. After all, "The only thing that spoon-feeding teaches us is the shape of a spoon." Therefore, don't think of this book as a travel itinerary where you will always know exactly where you are and what will come next. Instead, this book is a navigation course that will drop you into unfamiliar territory (with a supportive guide) to sharpen your sensemaking skills.

Chapter by chapter, we'll build a process for tackling hard choices, so while you might feel tempted to skip ahead, reading the book straight through will better equip you to handle both the issues you might be facing right now and those you'll encounter down the road. *Radical Doubt* will help you train your perception, thinking, feeling, and free will like muscles at the gym, supporting you to become the leader, thinker, and person you want to be. And, if you have a low enough bar for what you're willing to chuckle at, you might even have some fun along the way.

1

Life in Between

YOU CAN'T WALK THROUGH WALLS. There are no doors to open or windows to climb through to get to where you need to go. Even though you're sitting alone in a large open-plan office, you feel trapped. Here's why:

You run a small consulting firm with twenty full-time consultants who help local businesses with their social media advertising. Five years ago, you took a risk to start this company after graduating from business school, never hesitating to dip into your savings to make ends meet. Thankfully, your client list has grown slowly but steadily in tandem with your reputation for high-quality work. Through all the ups and downs, you take pride in building a collegial work environment where your staff provide excellent client services and has fun—at least based on the office pranks you've been roped into.

Over a year ago, you hired a sharp consultant named Ha-Joon Kim. He graduated from a prestigious business school, and his resume detailed impressive experience in the tech sector—experience that your company desperately needed. You placed Kim in charge of the small portfolio of tech clients, and he has been very successful, starting several lucrative projects in his first six months. To acknowledge Kim's excellent results, you awarded him the firm's highest bonus at the end of his first year.

The trouble started a few weeks ago when you noticed that your helpful and eager staff turned down opportunities to work with Kim. You pressed for more information and discovered that the team sees Kim as rude and disrespectful. Employees avoid him because he berates the staff, rarely answers emails, avoids pitching in to do things for the team, and micromanages the other consultants who work with "his" clients. One of your senior consultants gave Kim feedback about his unacceptable behavior a few months ago and advised him not to burn bridges with his colleagues. He responded that *his* job is to bring in essential business. He expects the team to focus on *their* jobs—giving him more leeway and following his directions.

Although Kim is deferential and polite to you, all this avoidable drama makes you concerned about his future at your company. Other senior consultants view his insulting behavior as sufficient grounds for firing. Some fed-up staff members are even on the verge of quitting. Employees are questioning your leadership, and your public praise for the company's collaborative spirit is beginning to sound like hollow corporate-speak rather than your genuine guiding ethos. You walked headfirst into a wall today when you opened an unexpected email from Kim requesting an early promotion. To be promoted, a consultant must have been at the firm for at least three years, developed a solid book of satisfied clients, and demonstrated a strong fit with the company culture. Kim argues that he has brought in more business in the last year than the other four senior consultants and has enough leads to double revenues next year. In addition, he has received a lucrative job offer from a competitor and would like to discuss his promotion to stay. He wants to meet this afternoon and "eagerly awaits" your counteroffer.

MOMENTS OF DOUBT

Think back to your first job. Despite an impressive-sounding title like "Junior Beverage Dissemination Specialist," you probably spent most of your time picking up the coffee orders, entering data, working the cash register, sorting files, and generally doing the grunt work before you were given more complex tasks. Maybe as you've progressed in your career, you've had the opportunity to manage others, allocate budgets, give presentations in front of important groups, and make critical decisions.

As most leaders in organizations progress in their careers and gain more authority, influence, and responsibility, they encounter moments of doubt, like what to do about Kim—a star performer who is a jerk. Yet they find they are unprepared to meet these moments. Different types of decisions are distributed unequally across organizations. Usually, toward the bottom of hierarchies, you encounter technical tasks that are relatively easy to evaluate because they have clear right and wrong answers. Building spreadsheets, assembling PowerPoint slides, scheduling, and emailing customers are all important tasks, to be sure; however, because they are highly structured, many people can complete them or be quickly trained to do so. Part of the point of clearly defining a task is so that it won't matter which intern or new graduate is ultimately responsible. The more structured a task, the more people can execute it; thus, the organization is less at risk if any one of those people leaves.

At the top of organizations, individuals can have much more leeway in approaching decisions. For example, Jason might show off his expertise by quickly quashing contrary perspectives. Mirabelle might seek the counsel of anyone in the hallway to avoid taking personal responsibility. And Kevin is probably still stuck analyzing the problem, trying to get it *just right* before anything ever actually gets done. We see these various (and frustrating) approaches by senior leaders because some decisions are not simple. They don't have a clear "right" answer. Therefore, they allow for a specific leader's values, relationships, and decision-making approaches to impact the organization significantly. These choices simultaneously present opportunities to improve things or make them worse. A survey of corporate executives confirms that senior leaders see difficult choices without clear answers as among the most common and challenging decisions they encounter at work.[1]

These moments of doubt involve multiple conflicting goals, high stakes, and high uncertainty.

CONFLICTING GOALS: Complex decisions usually involve multiple facets or issues that a decision-maker must notice and then choose how to address. When responding to Kim's promotion request, a decision-maker needs to consider the impact on future profits, company culture, relationships with clients, employees' well-being, and one's reputation as a leader. These choices require integrating expertise from different domains like finance, strategy, operations, compliance, and human resources. They involve working through human elements such as interpretations, communication, relationships, and values, just as much as the traditional business elements of balance sheets, financial projections, and key performance metrics. These decisions are called *multi-criteria* problems, unlike more straightforward problems where leaders optimize for a single metric like market share, profit, or customers' sanity. Multiple criteria make decisions much more difficult because we struggle to know what to prioritize or whether to prioritize at all.

HIGH STAKES: In the opening example, employees are on edge because Kim's rudeness violates basic norms of decency, and people are distressed about the company's ability to continue to serve tech clients. Once you have decided whether Kim will have a job or not, your company's ability to attract tech clients will need rebuilding, as will the larger team's trust and confidence in you. Whatever you choose will have tangible consequences on the lives of the people you care about, including their relationships with each other and with you. No matter what you choose, and even though there are no simple answers, these difficult decisions have strategic, financial, organizational, relational, and personal consequences that matter.

HIGH UNCERTAINTY: These hard choices don't come with all the necessary information. We don't know if Kim is willing to change or capable of changing his behavior. How upset will the other consultants be if you keep him around? How easy would it be to replace him? Accurate predictions are ephemeral because you don't know how different groups, such as your tech clients, administrative staff, new hires, and the partners at the firm, will evaluate and react to your decision. Not all uncertainty can be easily erased with more analytics, focus groups, surveys, and generative

AI. Deeper questions about how critical environmental factors will change and about "unknown unknowns" make facing uncertainty inevitable. The experience of doubt can make it more tempting to give up, take the rest of the day off, or convince ourselves that we're making progress when we're actually just scrolling through the latest adorable cat videos.

In moments of doubt, our imagination fails to guide us forward. We find ourselves staring blankly at a wall, debating which path to take at a crossroads, or squinting through the fog to anticipate where exactly we might end up if we fire Kim, give him another chance, or something in between. Yet, on some level, most leaders know that for the sake of their teams, organizations, customers, suppliers, shareholders, and their own careers, greater responsibility means that rather than running from moments of doubt, they must find ways to see through the fog and tackle that uncertainty head-on. Let's look at what we know about how people tend to make these kinds of difficult choices.

RIGHT-ANSWER-GETTERS

The short answer is that people tend to simplify the decision to feel like they have the right answer. In school, we learn that being smart means repeating what the teacher tells us, not making mistakes, and getting gold stars. Over time, we associate the feeling of not knowing the correct answer with feeling inferior or stupid. Trying to be a "right-answer-getter" when we experience doubt and uncertainty leads to counterproductive patterns that result in regretful choices. These patterns prevent you (and me) from effectively making difficult decisions.

When most people encounter a complex, multi-criteria decision, they are apt to confidently prioritize a single feature of that situation, choosing profit, culture, or personal reputation as *the* most critical feature. They base their choice only on this one consideration, ignoring all the others, and usually highlight their priorities with phrases that fast-forward time like, "At the end of the day," "When push comes to shove," or "The bottom line is . . ." Then invariably, their teammates, bosses, friends, and social media critics push the rewind button and point out that any decision built around only one consideration would cause unforeseen difficulties. For example, when someone prioritizes culture in the decision regarding

Kim, they generally neglect to consider how the company should protect its tech consulting revenues. Similarly, when people argue to promote Kim, they fail to consider ways to retain the frustrated team members. We often treat complex problems like simple ones until we are confronted with the remainders.

Decision-makers also make assumptions about uncertainties that conveniently transform their preferred choice into the correct answer. For instance, we don't know Kim's likelihood of leaving the company. People leaning toward promoting Kim exaggerate the risks of letting him go. "Oh, he'll definitely sue the company if we don't promote him, and then we'll go bankrupt!" In contrast, if they are leaning toward firing him, they minimize the risks to the company's revenue. "Nah, we'll be fine; Kim is easily replaceable." Like the weary programmer who recasts every bug as a feature, people quickly refashion any doubts and ambiguities, not as opportunities to think more carefully but as reasons their answer is correct. To recapture the feeling of getting a gold star, we put unquestionable faith in our initial intuition. But in novel situations, those very intuitions can betray us.

FOR WANT OF A SIMPLER WORLD

When facing doubt, most of us are driven by our intuitions—defined as immediate reactions without being aware of thinking.[2] For example, when choosing what to do about Kim, we might remember the time our CFO screamed and threw a stapler at us and, as a result, have a strong intuition that we should fire Kim. Or that one time we abandoned a project too early, and our competitors succeeded with our idea, and we now feel anxious and conclude that we should stomach Kim's working style to avoid falling behind again. Intuition is our memory of the past and motivation in the present, compelling our imagination of the future.

An influential line of research argues that relying on intuition is the default feature of decision-making, particularly in complex situations. According to this social-intuitionist view, when making difficult choices, individuals don't weigh the pros and cons but rather look for reasons to support their first gut reaction.[3] In a famous set of studies on moral dumbfounding, participants read scenarios designed to elicit an intuitive response to harmless yet morally repulsive behaviors. They read about scenarios like a woman who eats a disease-free cadaver and biological siblings who have consensual sex using multiple forms of birth control. (I know this paragraph just took a sudden turn, but bear with me; there's a point here, and it's not just the fork in the cadaver.)

After the participants read about these aberrant situations, researchers asked them to explain why they thought the actions were right or wrong. As you might expect, participants had quick, strong, negative reactions to these examples. However, the experimenters challenged participants' reasoning. If a participant said it was wrong for the cannibal to "cut other people open like cantaloupes" because she could get sick, the experimenters would reply, "Well, she didn't get sick, so why is it wrong?" Other participants would say, "Incest is just wrong because people could have unhealthy children," and the experimenters would reply, "Well, the siblings used several methods of contraception. Why is it still wrong?" When pushed repeatedly, participants fell back on statements like, "I don't know why it's wrong, but it just is!" The researchers argued that if participants had thought through the facts, they should have been able to give well-thought-out and defensible reasons for their choices. Instead, participants intuitively reacted and looked for reasons only when prompted. This foundational study concludes that we treat our intuition as our decision and then use reasoning to pass off that initial reaction as a well-thought-out reflection.

Before this work gained recognition in the early 2000s, many decision-making scholars ignored the role of intuition in our choices; they assumed that people were like dispassionate judges, rationally weighing and considering all the evidence. For the last two decades, research has focused on intuition's starring role in our decision-making and downplayed when we're likely to be more thoughtful and careful. Swinging the pendulum so far in the opposite direction has troubling implications for our ability to face moments of doubt.

Make no mistake: intuition is a valuable and powerful guide for many of our choices, specifically if we operate in environments like those where our intuition was formed. If we go to our favorite Italian restaurant on Thursday nights and decide what to order based on intuition, we will likely be delighted. If we're given accurate previews of our options, such as watching people at the neighboring table enjoy the burrata, our intuition is probably a good proxy for how we'll feel when we order it. Yet, if intuition never cedes the spotlight in our decision-making, then I can't help but wonder, What's the point of an education? At worst, education becomes a way for people to dress their incomplete intuitions in fancy jargon, allowing them to argue for any position rather than providing a process for refining, adapting, and elaborating on their instincts.

If we can only find ways to dress up our intuitions in more polished reasoning, we're out of luck because when we face difficult choices, we are in unfamiliar circumstances. Our instincts are less likely to be useful when the experiences and expectations they are based on don't hold. We might have a mistaken intuition that the foreign-looking person on the street is dangerous, that the woman on the team is uninterested in playing golf with the men, or that the ShamWow on the infomercial will work just as well to clean up our own mess. When our intuitions are based on a map that doesn't fit the territory, blindly following our hunches can lead us off a cliff.

These troubling implications aren't confined to ordering at a restaurant or shopping by way of infomercial. As a species, we have existential issues to address, such as slowing climate change, reducing income inequality, preserving functioning democracies, working toward an increasingly just and fair society, and extending freedom and opportunities to more people. And despite what social media algorithms might encourage, all these challenges require forming new intuitions and refining existing ones by *learning*, not just reacting quickly based on what we already know.

Giving intuition the starring role in all our choices would be the equivalent of studying how the body works and saying, "The liver is the most important organ, and everything we do is driven by how our liver functions." Of course, the liver is essential (please take care of yours), but so are our hearts, brains, lungs, and other organs with names longer than one syllable. Health emerges from how all our organs work together. Good choices emerge from how our intuition and reason join forces. Our models of human behavior need to account for the full range of human experience rather than holding only one kind of behavior up as the dominant and most important strategy. Assuming that people are primarily rational or intuitive leaves out the compelling variety of responses we see when we look around and the fascinating ways these systems work together. And more important, painting most people with the same broad brush makes it harder to help those who want to make better choices. If we believe that most decision-makers are ruled by their initial reactions in complex situations, it is harder to help leaders effectively regulate their responses. Thankfully, in addition to our common sense, cutting-edge research from neuroscience helps us move beyond simple explanations of our choices. Let's take a look at the surprising science of when we are more likely to have simple, intuitive reactions in complex situations, and when we are more likely to be more thoughtful, careful, and selective.

THE BRAIN'S TRIO

Nowadays, you can't write a book or article that draws on psychological research without dropping in some reference to neuroscience to dazzle readers. Psychologists name-drop brain regions like celebrities at a Hollywood party. Whether it's about the frontal lobe, amygdala, or hippocampus, people love to hear the latest gossip about the brain. My dorsal parietal lobe will also shamelessly jump on this bandwagon. Did you hear that the more we learn about the brain, the more we appreciate its incredible ability to anticipate our future?

A foundational premise of neuroscience is that our brains constantly and seamlessly assemble our experiences into predictions, large and small, about the world and how it works. These expectations form the basic structure of our mental maps, including predictions about the stability of the sidewalk when we run across it, how our Peruvian chicken will taste when we take the first bite, and how our self-deprecating humor will come off in a job interview. Based on our experiences, our brains instantaneously stitch together expectations, allowing us to predict that specific actions will have specific results and that certain cues are more likely to co-occur with other cues. For example, when a ball is dropped, we expect it to fall down, not up; when a magician shows us an empty box, we expect that it will stay empty unless we see someone go into it; and when we call to cancel our cable service because the bill rivals a mortgage payment, we don't expect to hang up paying more for a premium sports package.

Most of the time, our brain's ability to immediately weave together an accurate mental map of the circumstances is astonishing. No other brain in nature has yet rivaled the human brain's awe-inspiring ability. But sometimes we encounter a disparity between our mental maps and our surroundings. As a result, we are surprised when we are confronted by something we didn't expect (Oh, no. Cousin Eddie is leaving his kids with us for Christmas!). We can also be surprised because something we expected didn't happen (Who knew that frozen orange juice concentrate futures would fall? I bet my fortune they would go up!). When the world we encounter is different from the world our brains anticipated, our pupils dilate, our eyes widen, our pulse quickens, and—if you are a fellow millennial—in these moments of surprise, you might find yourself blurting out, "*Wait, what?*"

Scientists have identified a trio of interconnected circuits in the brain that help regulate your behavior in both predictable and surprising situations.[4] These three systems stitch together our expectations to create our experience of certainty and doubt.

These systems help you:

- *Pursue* the things you value
- *Protect* yourself from physical and social dangers
- *Pause and Piece-Together* clues in the environment when you don't know what to do.

The *Pursue System* propels us to seek and approach objects, people, and experiences where we anticipate a reward. This system involves brain regions like the left prefrontal cortex[5] and the ventral striatum,[6] which are active during reward-seeking behavior. The Pursue System primarily runs on dopamine, the neuromodulator that makes anticipation feel good and helps us get up and seek something delicious, delightful, and desirable. The aroma of freshly baked chocolate chip cookies, time alone with your crush, being a drunken idiot with your best friends, scoring the game-winning basket at the buzzer, figuring out the perfect comeback to an insult, losing yourself in service to a higher calling, and scrolling to see how many people liked your Instagram post of breakfast are all things we expend time, energy, and effort to get more of because our brains predict these actions will feel good. When your Pursue System is active, you feel more certain and are more likely to be the adventurous, novelty-seeking, confident, and reward-driven version of yourself. "Step 1: Build stuff. Step 2: ??? Step 3: Profit!"

In contrast, the *Protect System* helps you fight, flee, or freeze when you interpret something in your environment as risky, dangerous, or socially threatening. It involves the amygdala, hypothalamus, adrenal cortex, and autonomic nervous system.[7] Researchers have identified that some diagnosable anxiety disorders are related to an overactive Protect System,[8] causing some people to have agoraphobia (fear of going outside), mysophobia (fear of germs), triskaidekaphobia (fear of the number 13), or claustrophobia (fear of being stuck in tight spaces with a Santa).

Even if you don't have a diagnosable anxiety disorder, you have fears that trigger the Protect System, like accidentally offending your friend's grandmother by making an ill-timed joke, letting down someone who took a risk to help you, or being asked to give a thirty-minute speech with no preparation in front of a crowd of ill-humored and overcritical clowns. (That was a terrible, horrible, no-good, very bad day. I don't want to talk about it.)

When you make excuses to avoid going bar-hopping with your friends, pray for the meeting with your boss to be canceled, or avoid the family drama by skipping Easter dinner, that's the Protect System kicking in. It revs up our sympathetic nervous system, causing our hearts to pump faster, our pores to open in preparation for exertion, and our muscles to flood with hormones like adrenaline and cortisol to get us running, yelling, and swinging our fists to keep us safe from clear threats.

If all we had were these two systems, it would make sense that our responses to difficult choices would involve some form of approach or avoidance. We can see traces of these reactive systems at work in people's initial responses to Kim's promotion request. Some decision-makers distill the complex situation in ways that clarify the benefits of promoting Kim and evaporate the risks. As a result, their Pursue Systems are more active, and they choose to promote him. In contrast, others sort through the complexity and pull the worst-case scenario to the top of their minds.

Subsequently, their Protect System is more active, and they choose to fire Kim.[9]

Making quick decisions by primarily relying on the Pursue or Protect Systems is incredibly advantageous when we encounter situations with unambiguous signals. For example, when we learn about a new restaurant serving the perfect bánh mì sandwich, and we drop everything to get in line. Or when we return from a hike to find a grizzly bear in our tent devouring our perfect bánh mì sandwich, and we drop everything to run away. Without the approach or avoidance responses catalyzed by certainty, our ancestors wouldn't have been able to move from the savanna to the C-suite.

Moments of doubt, however, generally contain stimuli we want to approach and avoid simultaneously. So, what do we do in those situations?

When things are unclear, the third member of the brain's trio, the *Pause and Piece-Together System*, gets to work. It produces our experiences of uncertainty and doubt. It recruits brain regions, like the right prefrontal cortex, hippocampus, dorsomedial thalamus, and anterior cingulate cortex,[10] to regulate conflicts between and within the other two systems. We may want to approach and avoid the same stimulus (Should I invite Uncle Simon to the wedding? He'll bring an expensive gift but he'll also offend everyone he talks to). We can also feel doubt when there are two things we want to approach (I'm so torn, should I vacation in Hawaii or the Bahamas?) or two things we want to avoid (How can I avoid trying too hard to be cool while also not trying hard enough?).

Neuroscientists have collected considerable evidence over the last fifty years about our Pause and Piece-Together System and how it regulates our intuitions when they conflict.[11] In one study, researchers compared a group of participants with damage to their Pause and Piece-Together regions to a group with healthy systems. Both groups were asked to complete a gambling task that required participants to balance the benefits of an immediate reward with the risks. Participants with lesions in their Pause and Piece-Together System were more likely to take risks in the laboratory gambling task[12]—in the words of rock band Journey, "paying anything to roll the dice just one more time." What's more interesting, though, is that the amount of risk participants took was proportional to the volume of their brain damage. Meaning that the more impaired a participant's Pause and Piece-Together regions, the more they made intuitive (and, in this case, risky) decisions because they could not regulate their immediate impulses.

The relationship between the Pause and Piece-Together System and self-regulation comes into focus when neuroscientists temporarily paralyze or enhance specific brain regions to learn more about their function. I should also mention that they do this with consent, care, and considerable supervision. When scientists used a safe and painless low-intensity electric current to enhance the Pause and Piece-Together regions, participants performed better in tasks that required regulation of their instincts to avoid frustrating errors.[13] These participants also demonstrated more attention and memory[14] of relevant risks.[15] In contrast, participants made more impulsive short-term decisions, like cheating for immediate gain, when researchers stimulated the Pursue System and suppressed the Pause and Piece-Together System.[16] Indeed, when the Pause and Piece-Together System is not working as it should, people are at higher risk for substance abuse, depression, and generalized anxiety disorders.[17] When we cannot regulate our intuitions, we cannot effectively address moments of doubt.

Neuroscientists conclude that the Pursue System "is more adept at constructing determinate, precise, and unambiguous representations of the world. Thus, it automatically fills in any gaps in the available information, often prematurely or incorrectly." The results of these studies suggest that our experience of certainty is often driven by our Pursue System activity (and our Protect System activity, as we'll see later). The Pause and Piece-Together System is essential to our experience of doubt because it is "more adept at constructing and maintaining fluid, indeterminate, vague, and ambiguous representations, enabling it to temper or 'inhibit' premature interpretations."[18]

Experiments such as these demonstrate the first critical benefit of doubt (and in the coming chapters, we'll encounter several more). The brain leans toward constructing unambiguous mental maps that help us intuitively and confidently pursue clear rewards and protect ourselves from clear threats. But when things are uncertain and complex, when we feel stuck between conflicting interpretations, the Pause and Piece-Together System can help us examine and regulate our initial inconsistent intuitions and can open the potential to be more thoughtful and intentional in our choices. It regulates our approach or avoidant behavior,[19] as if saying, "Hey, watch out! Tread carefully; we don't have a single, clear mental map of this situation. We're in less predictable territory."

By recruiting our attention, coordinating various brain regions, recalling things from memory, or deliberating about what we know, we can observe, learn, and refine our mental maps to figure out what to do when we're stuck and unsure. Thus, doubt is a powerful signal that we need to build new intuitions and refine existing ones.[20] Pausing and piecing together is one way we make the unfamiliar more familiar. In short, our intuitions are essential to our choices, but we don't have to live at the mercy of our initial reactions—thankfully, our intuitions can be educated.

In neurotypical human brains, our Pursue, Protect, and Pause and Piece-Together Systems work collectively to help us choose when to approach cautiously or fight strategically, enabling us to avoid the pitfalls and surgically extract the prizes when we face moments of doubt. This general overview of the brain's trio provides a useful and sufficient departure point for our purposes, so don't worry; the worst is over. I'll stop name-dropping brain regions now.

YOUR FIRST STEP INTO A LARGER WORLD

Every hero gets beaten up; that's part of what makes them a hero. Or at least that's what I tell myself when nursing my bruises. The protagonists of our favorite movies, shows, and books stumble, make embarrassing mistakes, and fail to demonstrate essential skills at the story's start. Then, usually with the help of a mentor, they slowly learn to see the world differently and build the skills to thrive in their new surroundings. In *Star Wars*, Luke learns to control the force from Obi-Wan and Yoda. At the beginning of *The Devil Wears Prada*, Andy can't tell the difference between Versace and Old Navy but eventually pulls together the finer details of high fashion with coaching from Nigel. In the movie *Knives Out*, Marta learns to outwit the family trying to steal her inheritance (and, yes, for those who noticed, it is possible to love *Star Wars* and director Rian Johnson, but maybe just not in the same movie).

Like the heroes in our favorite stories, we can build the skills to make difficult decisions by learning how to engage our Pause and Piece-Together System when facing doubt. Decision-makers with experience have learned to engage doubt differently. In one study, researchers compared military officers with different levels of experience, some captains (less experienced) and some generals (more experienced), who made decisions about uncertain and complex battlefield scenarios.[21] They were instructed to look over the information, ask questions, build tactical strategies, and provide a rationale for their choices. A group of judges then evaluated their recommendations (without knowing if a captain or general made them). The results show that the experienced decision-makers asked questions to understand critical uncertainties rather than ignoring them or assuming the most favorable conditions. They also perceived the "same" situation as more complex than the less experienced decision-makers and saw more obstacles that could derail their plans. Finally, the generals' strategies were more detailed and flexible, containing multiple contingencies anticipating battlefield changes. Together, these patterns show that experienced decision-makers relied on more data to *test* their intuition, proactively looking for ways they could be wrong. As we've seen, more novice decision-makers were more likely to assume the best case would occur and focus primarily on information that confirmed their intuition. In uncertain situations, *experts don't treat their intuition as their decision; they treat it as a hypothesis.*

Similar patterns are evident when observing expert entrepreneurs, who notice more complexity, identify more unintended outcomes, and attend to the long-term consequences of their choices more than novices.[22] Expert nurses collect twice as many data points when making uncertain diagnoses than novice nurses.[23] Expert lawyers scan the courtroom more frequently to learn how to adapt their arguments.[24] Expert writers spend more time revising their initial drafts than novice writers.[25] Expert teachers are more likely than novice teachers to think about learning from the perspective of their students and adapting their lessons in realtime.[26] Expert crime scene investigators are less confident than students about their first impressions,[27] and expert firefighters imagine and rehearse a broader range of potential wildfire scenarios, allowing them to be resilient in the face of an unpredictable fire.[28] These studies suggest that even when they don't know what to do, experts notice more complexity than novices, who may prematurely simplify the problem and react quickly to that loose, often inaccurate, sketch. Ironically, in unfamiliar situations, experts don't act like "right-answer-getters" but work to make *better answers.*

Additionally, experts don't take a dismissive view of the risks; instead, they pay attention to information that can help them anticipate and prepare for things that can go wrong. They hold their intuition as a hypothesis and learn to improve it. Then, based on their more detailed mental map of the situation, experts build more nuanced, flexible, and comprehensive strategies that help them increase the odds of achieving their intentions and decrease the odds of being derailed.[29] All of this suggests that experts pause and start piecing things together rather than rushing headfirst into action or prematurely abandoning the project. Like geographers who never find themselves lost, only doing fieldwork accidentally,[30] when experts face moments of doubt where they have no reliable mental map, *they start mapping.*

ONWARD

Okay, enough setup already. Let's get down to business. The burgeoning research on expertise and the neuroscience of uncertainty gives me hope that we, too, can make the transition from being "right-answer-getters" to "better-answer-makers." Under specific conditions, we can build our capacity to learn, adapt, and effectively face moments of doubt. For the last fifteen years, I've seen this growth firsthand in my students and executive participants as they practice these skills, observe others, and get feedback. After careful and intentional practice, they are strikingly better at noticing complexity, holding their intuition as a hypothesis, drafting more careful and thoughtful strategies, and productively engaging with colleagues who see things differently.

To help you develop these skills, I've organized this book into four parts that build upon each other. It's hard to appreciate the details of part IV without understanding part I's basics. Parts I and II will provide a multi-faceted toolkit for tackling difficult decisions. Specifically, in part I, "Losing Your Bearings," we must unlearn some common myths that prevent us from engaging doubt. We'll learn where our choices come from and introduce multiple perspectives about what makes a choice "good." In part II, "Wayfinding," we introduce research-tested mindsets and practices that help us create novel solutions, work effectively with others to improve our decisions, and prepare to act based on what we know and will learn. Together, these skills will help you move forward wisely when you feel unsure.

Parts III and IV unpack common obstacles to applying the toolkit described in the book's first half. Specifically, in part III, "Sidestepping Obstacles Along the Way," we introduce stumbling blocks, such as knowing when and how to accommodate others' goals, avoiding blame when things go wrong, and addressing conflicting standards so that we can prevent being derailed by these pervasive impediments. Finally, in part IV, "Facing the Obstacles Within," we'll dig into common ways we self-sabotage our learning, such as regulating our strong emotions and overcoming "analysis paralysis." We will detail the most promising strategies to free ourselves from the challenges we all carry with us.

Radical Doubt is based on my research, consulting, and teaching with thousands of MBA students, executives, and organizational leaders. I've cataloged ten common moments of doubt that leaders encounter with increasing frequency as they rise to higher levels of influence and authority. For example, how should we proceed when norms at our global headquarters conflict with norms in the country where we've just expanded operations? How should we handle situations where our product or service has unintended negative effects, like when social media platforms are used to spread disinformation? There are many ways that doubt and uncertainty manifest at work. So, each chapter in this book begins with a prevalent moment of doubt that derails leaders and then digs into the most up-to-date science to help us understand why people stumble, what we know about resilience, and how to apply it.

In each of these instances, smart, hardworking, and respected people disagree about what to do and how to move forward. That's what makes them "moments of doubt" and why they are essential to discuss, debate, and decide. I argue that no matter how these moments initially appear, a common set of skills, tools, and mindsets can help us avoid pitfalls and maybe even feel excitement for the potential these moments provide. As we review these topics, I'll rely on our most replicated research insights, hopefully in a mildly entertaining fashion (as long as you, unlike my teenaged kids, can survive my dad jokes). In the appendix, I've collected helpful tools and exercises so you can apply these insights in your own life. Individually, the lessons in each chapter aim to inoculate you against a specific point of failure. Collectively, if you can master the skills introduced across chapters, they will help you become shatterproof.

And finally, an astute reader might wonder on which page I've buried *the answers* to these decisions so they can skip to the good part. To build your capacity to make the most of hard choices, I may tell you how my students or research participants perform on similar decisions in the coming pages, but I won't tell you *the answer* or even *my answer*. My goal is to build your ability to think about and tackle these problems. If I tell you what I would do and pretend it's the only correct answer, that will undercut your efforts (like a personal trainer who does the squats for you). When you feel impatient for things to fit together or crave immediate clarity, think of that sensation like the burn at the end of your last set at the gym. That's the part where you're actually getting stronger. I hope that by the end of this book, you will be more confident when facing uncertainty, know how to create better responses when there's no single "right answer," and occasionally, when needed, be able to walk through a wall.

I

LOSING YOUR BEARINGS

2

Update Your Mental GPS

IMAGINE BEING OFFERED a promotion at your dream hedge-fund job (I know you probably don't dream of working at a hedge fund, but just play along, all right?). Given your outstanding performance over the last year, you are offered a chance to lead the office in London. It's no secret that the London office has been struggling lately, and the executive team believes you are the perfect person to inject energy and fresh ideas. Taking this opportunity will put your career on the fast track.

Your mother calls to tell you that your father has been diagnosed with an aggressive form of cancer, and the doctors say he has about a year to live. You are devastated. Your parents have sacrificed a lot to give you a shot at a life they never could obtain. You know you would not have had the same unique educational and career opportunities without their long hours at work, diligent saving, and unconditional love. You have a special relationship with your father, who has been a constant source of support and dad jokes. Supporting your parents through this challenging time would be hard when you're all the way in London. A single phone call has put your life on an unforeseen detour.

Your father doesn't want you to change course. He wants you to go to London and not worry about him; he says you can talk on the phone all the time and visit on holidays. He's happy knowing you are living your dream and is just thankful that he "doesn't have to see a dermatologist because they make *rash* decisions." Seeing you succeed at work makes him feel proud and at peace with his life. Although she hasn't said so explicitly, you can sense that your mother wants you to stay.

What would you do?

———

Most of us want to be the kind of person who cares for our family *and* is successful at work. Here, in this moment of doubt, we feel forced to choose. Is it more important for me to be with my family or to fulfill my parents' dreams about my career? We often find that it is challenging to satisfy multiple, deeply held personal values. Choosing one option over the other feels like choosing which essential organ to remove from our body.

To address moments of doubt when our personal values conflict, we need a better understanding of where our choices come from. Even if we've never considered it, we all have an implicit answer to the question, Why do people do what they do? This simple yet surprisingly tricky question has vexed philosophers, psychologists, and people stuck at the DMV for centuries. Kicking the tires on our answer to this question is critical to improving our decisions because our answer shapes how we approach and make all kinds of choices, including choices with multiple goals, high stakes, and uncertainty. But the way most of us answer the question actually makes it harder to achieve our intentions.

IS CHARACTER A GUARANTEE?

We take personality tests to determine which jobs to pursue, who to date, and what wines, coffees, and mattresses suit us best. In our personal lives, we read our horoscopes to know whether a Gemini is compatible with a Sagittarius. In our professional lives, we take assessments like the Myers-Briggs Type Indicator (MBTI) to become more aware of our tendencies so that we can work effectively with the Extraverted, Intuitive, Thinking, and Judging type (ENTJ) on the team, who sucks up all the air in the room and jumps to conclusions.

The underlying view in these assessments, quizzes, and tests is that our character and personality are constants that make us distinct from others and are, thus, the ultimate sources of our unique preferences and choices in moments of doubt. Character traits like extraversion, dominance, and warmth are supposed to be fixed dispositions that apply across a spectrum of situations. In this chapter, I'll use character, personality, and traits synonymously. The results of these assessments are abstract descriptive phrases such as "Min is reliable," "Sadiq is an introvert," "Johnny is open to new experiences," and "Jack is a psychopathic clown." We tend to navigate our relationships by using simple descriptions of others' motives, values, and character, like those examples. In authoring these descriptive statements, we are like an over-zealous film editor, creating a brief montage about a person from select, memorable snippets of our interactions. We make heroes, villains, extras, and plucky sidekicks out of people whose actual behavior is much more complicated and harder to typecast. We then expect these simple statements to help us predict what Min, Johnny, Sadiq, and Jack will do across situations and over time. Well, good luck! Min is supposed to be reliable at work but when she's not on the clock she's capricious about which dates she shows up to. Is Johnny really supposed to be adventurous all the time, whether at home, traveling abroad, or choosing from a bourbon menu for the first time? You mean to tell me that Sadiq is supposed to be an introvert on and off the soccer pitch? And would any of us be surprised to learn that Jack is running for Congress?

We treat these character traits as guarantees when we hear or say claims like, "Highly authoritarian people support violence against the government" or "Prosocial individuals recycle." Let's call this view the *Deterministic View of Character* because just as gravity determines how fast something will fall, a fixed character is supposed to determine our decision-making. The Deterministic View of Character is the most common view about where our judgments come from, leading most of us to believe that knowing someone's character allows us to forecast their future decisions accurately. We put the deterministic view to work in our office gossip, book clubs, family reunions, recruiting coffee chats, and dating profiles. Yet few of us have skimmed the resume, checked the fine print, and verified the evidence.

HOW MUCH DOES CHARACTER DETERMINE OUR CHOICES?

To assess the evidence favoring the Deterministic View, we must take a quick diversion to understand how researchers typically measure these traits and their predictive value. When measuring character traits, researchers generally ask participants to rate their level of agreement with short statements like, "When people make jokes, I feel compelled to laugh even if the joke is not funny." Participants indicate their level of agreement by selecting a number on a scale, where higher numbers typically indicate more agreement. Researchers then average the responses to several similar statements to create a single number to compare individuals.

For example, your average might be 4.5 out of 5 on the "social graces" scale, while mine would be a 1.2, implying that I have less social grace than you (it's obviously true). Scientists can then use our scores to predict other behaviors that are related to having social grace, such as the number of dinner parties we attended in the last three months, the number of times we confused our salad forks and dessert forks, or our likelihood of being thrown out of a monster truck rally.

Across thousands of studies, there is a small, statistically significant correlation between character traits and choices. But what exactly does, that mean? Researchers calculate a measure called a "correlation coefficient" to gauge the degree to which two variables are related. Take two variables, like (1) the number of drinks you have at a party and (2) how attractive you think you are; a correlation measures the amount that those two variables are related. For instance, how many drinks would it take before you see yourself as a twelve on a ten-point scale? You can think of a correlation kind of like a slope of a line. Remember when you thought you would never need to know $Y = MX + B$? M is the slope; it's the amount of change in Y for every change in X. Unlike a slope, correlations only range from −1 to +1. A positive correlation indicates that an increase in one variable is related to an increase in the other. A negative correlation means that as one variable rises the other will fall. Calculating a correlation helps researchers measure exactly how much social grace you need before having tea with the king or how much more attractive you think you are after each drink you consume. Generally, in social science, researchers think of correlations of around 0.1 as small, correlations around 0.3 as moderate, and correlations greater than 0.5 as large.

When scholars examine the strength of various character traits like openness to experience, extraversion, prosociality, guilt-proneness, self-esteem, and hundreds of others, they find that the correlation between different traits and behaviors is usually less than 0.2, and very seldom higher than 0.3, suggesting real and yet relatively small effects.[1] Even for a rare correlation of 0.3, which is as strong as they come, it would mean that for a specific sample of participants, the character trait would explain only about 9 percent of their behavior, which means that 91 percent of it wouldn't be explained by the character trait.

If we care about answering the question, Why do people do what they do? then the evidence collected over the last fifty years suggests that character traits have a far smaller impact on our choices than what the Deterministic View promises. That means people who score high on extraversion can go to a party and be quiet. ENTJs can be empathetic and good at listening, and Hufflepuffs can also be studious and cunning. Meta-analyses, or research reviews that report the total results of hundreds of similar studies, corroborate that the impact of character traits on behavior is small at best.[2]

All in all, the evidence paints a very different picture than what the Deterministic View of Character promises. Instead of traits like being superstitious always leading to superstitious behavior, we see that sometimes these traits matter a little more than random chance (knock on wood), but still, a lot less than expected. The evidence also shows that it would be wrong to say that character traits don't matter at all; it's just that their impact is much more modest than we tend to believe.[3] Despite what many people think, when making hard decisions like choosing whether to stay with our ailing father or to take the job in London, our character is not going to magically make our choices. At best, these measured traits are like one ingredient in a complex recipe, one of many subtle influences on our choices.

Some psychologists argue they never claimed character and personality were invariable,[4] but when scholars and the media talk about character and personality-based results, they tend to exaggerate them. Who wants to read that honesty is only correlated with cheating at around −0.2? Or that extreme authoritarians are merely 10 percent more likely than average to overthrow the government? It is undoubtedly a thrill for researchers to publish a statistically significant finding. Still, the small effect sizes are not newsworthy for the rest of the world, so, unfortunately, they generally don't get reported. People don't want to hear that the personality assessment they just paid $500 for is only 9 percent better at predicting their job success than a monkey throwing darts at a target.

So, the next time you read or hear a strong claim for the predictive value of character traits, look at the fine print and ask how large the correlation coefficient really is because, to date, the research record doesn't support anything close to a guarantee.

GETTING THE RABBIT INTO THE HAT

We've all enjoyed watching a magician defy gravity, saw an assistant in half, or make a tiger appear in inconvenient places. If "illusion" is seeing evidence for things we know can't be true, then "delusion" is believing things are true despite contradictory evidence. If decades of psychological evidence paint the same modest picture of character traits, are we deluded when we believe the Deterministic View, or do we see an illusion? If character's impact on our choices is so small, why do we think it is so big?

First, we think other people behave more consistently than they actually do. We may see people in similar routines, so we don't notice how differently they behave at home, at work, or at the swingers' club. "Wow, who knew that Kate was so cutthroat on the volleyball court? She was so laid-back when we visited the coffee joint." We are convinced that character explains our choices because we create brief montages about people from a small and biased sample of information. We achieve this illusion partly by selectively forgetting or ignoring information about people.[5] Consider the acclaimed TV show *Breaking Bad*, which follows the descent of cancer-stricken chemistry teacher Walter White into the meth kingpin Heisenberg. The show creator and writer Vince Gilligan said, "Walter White . . . makes this active decision . . . to become a criminal, to become a villain. . . . The character starts off as a protagonist and gradually becomes the antagonist."[6]

Spoiler Alert! Walter does some evil things, such as letting his partner Jesse's girlfriend die of a heroin overdose, hiring neo-Nazis to kill a witness in prison, and destroying his relationship with his wife and son. Yet many fans see Walter as the "good guy" and remain loyal to him no matter what lines he crosses to make money and achieve dominance. Just google "Walter White did nothing wrong" and kiss three hours of your life goodbye. For a fraction of the audience, Walter wasn't bad; it was the world around him that was broken. The critical point is that when assessing someone's character, we selectively remember things consistent with our initial assessment. If we think that Walter is a good person, we are more likely to remember that he helped Jesse in the past, wanted to support his family, and made a lot of money to do so.

We are more inclined to see character as determining our actions because we tend to ignore, forget, or downplay information about people's complexity.

Second, we think character is deterministic because we focus on extreme cases where traits can have a larger effect. For example, suppose you score extremely high on a neuroticism scale. In that case, your trait is more likely to predict your rumination about that crooked pile of paper on your colleague's desk than someone who just leans slightly toward that direction. The interplay of genetic, environmental, and physiological differences can cause a person to have a more extreme trait. In a fascinating body of work, researchers at the University of Pennsylvania show that the size of a person's amygdala (a key brain region for processing emotions, especially fear) relative to the population's predicts how that person responds to other people's fears.[7] Psychopaths (estimated to be about 1 percent of the population) have smaller than average amygdalae. Therefore, they are less likely to register and respond to someone else's fear, allowing them to lie without remorse, harm others, and eat a slice of pizza crust-first. In contrast, people who become quickly and deeply connected with others' emotions (called hyper-empaths) have relatively larger amygdalae, making them more sensitive to others' fears. Hyper-empaths are more likely than average to undergo risky surgery to donate their kidney to a stranger. Suppose the combination of your genes and environment causes you to have an extreme neurophysiological characteristic, like a larger amygdala; in that case, how you score on a related measure would be more predictive of your actions across situations. Similarly, character and personality may help diagnose disorders outside of the "normal" range of behavior, but by definition, most of us are in the normal range, where traits are not ironclad predictions. We think that character determines our choices because we pay attention to and generalize from extreme cases where physiological or genetic differences lead to more consistent behavior. Oh, and for both our sakes, you can stop pretending to be neurotic now.

Third, we prioritize internal or character-based explanations for others' actions. We explain the behavior of our colleagues, family members, fellow citizens, and Jake from State Farm, based on their personality, character, and internal motives.[8] In contrast, we tend to explain our own behavior based on the situations we find ourselves in. For example, when explaining why a colleague is perpetually late to meetings, we might say that "He's disorganized" or "She's not respectful of other people's time," but when explaining our own lateness, we're more likely to point outside of ourselves and say, "My alarm didn't go off, traffic was insane, and Mercury is in retrograde." We underestimate how much external causes impact someone else's behavior, making their character seem like a more significant driver of their choices.

And finally, at the risk of making things even more complicated, our simple stories about others impact how we treat them, subtly encouraging them to live up to the roles we've assigned. For example, when a teacher sees a student as advanced, that teacher is more likely to pay attention to that student's answers, give her more time to answer questions, and assign her more challenging work, all of which might change her performance in school and help make her advanced.[9] We treat people as we imagine them, which sometimes causes them to act in line with our sketches, confirming our original view. This self-fulfilling prophecy applies to adults just as much as children. For example, studies show that you perform better when your manager has high expectations of you.[10] When we end up eliciting certain behaviors from others based on how we imagine them, we think that we've found a more predictable personality. Yet, we miss our role in creating that consistency.

We love the certainty that our simple illusions about others provide. Participants in one study preferred this predictability so much that they were willing to give up money to work with a consistent partner rather than with an erratic one.[11] The hidden cost of our penchant for predictability is that we are surprised when people show us that they are more complicated than the simple stories we curate, such as when the girl who is not supposed to play chess defeats all the boys, or when the man who is supposed to be racist ends up showing exceptional kindness to his Hispanic neighbors, or when a gay athlete wins the world's strongest man competition. When it comes to the strength and endurance of the Deterministic View of Character, we are content to sit back and be amazed by the simple stories we craft about others, deluded by illusions of our own making.

THE STAKES

Okay, so what? Am I just making glaciers out of ice cubes, oceans out of puddles, and mountains out of . . . well, smaller mountains? Maybe it's not a big deal that we cling to simple stories about ourselves and others, particularly if we're not always wrong. Isn't a tiny predictive value better than no predictive value at all? Before we talk about how the Deterministic View of Character erodes our ability to make the most of hard choices, let's see why this isn't just some innocuous foible of human thinking, but rather a real threat to our society.

Here's a sobering fact: Acceptance of political violence in the US is rising. People plotted to kidnap the Michigan governor; a man in Texas killed a woman and injured her husband because they voted for another political party; in my hometown of Charlottesville, Heather Heyer was murdered and many others badly injured as they stood against white supremacy. Currently, only 1.5 percent of Americans have been involved in violence against the opposing political party. Yet, today, 9 percent of Americans overall and 13 percent of Republicans say that some form of violence is necessary if political leaders fail.[12]

It seems like a hazy memory, but as a child of the '80s, I can recall growing up with friends on both sides of the aisle and being much more concerned about whether they defeated Bowser in *Super Mario Bros. 3* than whether their families were Republicans or Democrats. Now, those cross-party friendships are harder to maintain because we think people's political choices are central to their character. This division is reflected in increasing political polarization[13] and dwindling marriage rates across party lines, shrinking from 30 percent in 2016 to 21 percent in 2020.[14] Similarly, Democrats and Republicans are choosing to live in increasingly politically segregated neighborhoods.[15]

One factor (admittedly out of many complex historical, political, and social factors) for this increase in political polarization is that we've come to see liberals and conservatives as having fundamental character differences. Moral Foundations Theory (MFT) is a psychological theory that argues that individuals use five innate moral foundations to form their intuitions about what makes something right or wrong.[16] The five foundations are care, fairness, loyalty, authority, and sanctity. Specifically, liberals are said to have innate traits that cause them to prioritize fairness more than conservatives. On the other side of the aisle, conservatives are thought to rely more on loyalty, sanctity, and authority than liberals.

MFT aims to call attention to and normalize differences between groups in the hope of greater tolerance and better communication. There's preliminary evidence that speaking across party lines is improved when messages are framed using the appropriate moral foundation.[17] Yet the story isn't so simple, and the differences between liberals and conservatives are not as stark as initially reported. A recent meta-analysis across eighty-nine samples and about 225,000 participants worldwide confirms correlations between people's responses to the moral foundations' questions and their expressed political leanings.[18] To be clear, so far in this chapter, we've only talked about the small relationship between self-reported character traits (how people respond to questions) and their actual behavior. This meta-analysis examines the relationship between two self-reported variables: people's answers to questions about which moral foundations are important to them and their answers to questions about where they fall on the political spectrum. These studies did not examine actual political behavior, which, based on decades of research, we would expect to have even lower correlations.[19] According to the findings, people who indicated that they are more conservative on the political spectrum also indicated small negative correlations with the moral foundations of care (−0.17) and fairness (−0.19), and small-to-moderate positive correlations with loyalty (0.25), authority (0.31), and sanctity (0.39). Even for sanctity, which has the highest correlation, only explains about 15 percent of what people report about their political affiliation.

These small correlations mean we are all more complex than MFT promises. For example, in some situations, liberals can care about authority and not care as much about fairness.[20] One just has to look at housing, tax, and education policies in Democratically controlled states like Washington and California to see the gap between the fairness liberals espouse on surveys and the unfair policies they vote to maintain. Similarly, try publishing cross-disciplinary research in an academic journal, and you'll see how caring politically liberal researchers really are and how much they can focus on authority and loyalty, quickly rejecting ideas that don't fit within their own worldview. Similarly, sometimes conservatives can care about fairness. Like all the other character measures, individuals vary considerably; people can change which foundations are relevant in different contexts and at different times.[21] Saying that liberals and conservatives have different stable traits masks the considerable variation within individuals, groups, and regions.

Recent research argues that it's not an individual's innate moral foundations that cause them to identify with a specific political party but rather the opposite. Identification with conservative or liberal political parties influences the moral foundations individuals use to describe and justify their views. This "top-down" explanation better aligns with observed differences across countries; for instance, liberals in France don't talk and act precisely like liberals in Guatemala because specific political parties use the moral foundations differently in their rhetoric.[22]

The point here is that despite its admirable motives to promote dialogue and understanding across party lines, MFT can inadvertently reinforce the idea that the people on the other side of the aisle are fundamentally different from us. While the research does show consistent small to moderate differences between self-reported moral foundations and what people say about their political views (again, remember, not their actual behavior), it is too easy to take these findings and turn them into guarantees about the character of the people we disagree with. "We care about fairness, and they don't" or "We care about the sacredness of our institutions, and they don't."

If political parties have fundamentally different dispositions, finding consensus is downright impossible. People might think, "If you care about this value and I don't, and neither of us can change our minds because we are born this way, then let's agree to disagree and fight it out by gerrymandering voting districts and raising more money to win elections." MFT, at its worst, could be used to justify and fuel the political divide rather than seeing people as complex and fully human. Call me naïve, but if we stand any chance of reducing partisanship in the US (and it may be a dwindling chance), it's not going to be only because we clarified and entrenched the differences between liberals and conservatives. We must also reaffirm our shared commitment to the democratic process that holds this country together. We must remember that we can change our minds and see the world similarly.

The danger in MFT and the Deterministic View of Character it is based on is that they both lead us to believe most people are simpler than they are and preclude changes in our behavior. If you attribute people's unacceptable actions to immutable and unchanging traits, what can they do? Get a character transplant? In contrast, if we make room for people to change their minds, we might have a chance of humanizing the other side and finding enough temporary, shaky, common ground to live together without resorting to violence.

WHAT THE WORLD ALLOWS US TO BE

If the Deterministic View of Character doesn't get us as far as we hoped in understanding the question, Why do people do what they do?, and it prevents us from seeing the complexity and variation in people's actions, then what other options do we have? Frustration and disappointment with the low predictability of character-based explanations have caused some scholars to argue that the whole endeavor should be abandoned. The philosopher John Doris wrote, "Divesting ethical reflection of an empirically discredited psychology of character will facilitate emotional, evaluative, and deliberative habits that are more defensible, more sensitive, and more conducive to ethical desirable behavior."[33] Translated from nerd-speak: if we want a better understanding of why people do what they do, we need to look elsewhere.

In the mid-1960s, psychologists started to articulate a different perspective to understand people's choices. It's the idea that situations, not character, determine our behavior—creatively named "situationism." In this view, in the right context, a quiet person can become gregarious, a good person can do evil things, and bitter enemies can find common ground. According to situationism, to paraphrase the Joker from *The Dark Knight*, "[People] are only as good as the world allows them to be."

Situationism was ushered in by social psychologists such as Stanley Milgram, whose famous Obedience to Authority Experiments in the 1960s put participants in circumstances where they had to choose whether to disobey immoral orders from an authority figure.[24] Participants came into the lab at Yale University and were told they were part of an experiment on memory and learning. They were instructed to apply increasingly painful electric shocks to another participant in a different room to help those subjects memorize random word pairs. This memorizer was in on the experiment and, unbeknownst to the real participant, wasn't actually being shocked. The confederate made many planned errors and ultimately begged to be let out of the experiment. Surprisingly, Milgram and his team found that around half the participants ignored the confederate's objections. Instead, they obeyed the authority's orders and continued to deliver what they thought were painful electric shocks to another human being despite his screams of protest. In subsequent conditions, when the researchers changed the salience and proximity of the authority or the confederate, they saw changes in obedience rates, leading them to believe that the nature of the situation is a powerful determinant of people's actions. Scholars have replicated these results in different countries at least fifteen times,[25] including a recent replication in 2017.[26] Milgram's doctoral student returned to the original participants and gave them a series of personality tests to see what character traits would predict their behavior. Ultimately, he and Milgram believed they didn't find character-trait data worth publishing, further cementing their view that *situation* was more potent than *personality*.

The power of situations doesn't just apply to charged choices like obeying immoral orders but also to more mundane decisions. Another commonly cited example of situationism is the Good Samaritan Study.[27] Researchers instructed seminary students at Princeton University to give a talk on the parable of the Good Samaritan from the Bible. The parable is a story about the virtue of taking the time to help a homeless person. Researchers gave some seminary students plenty of time to walk across campus before giving their sermons, while others were given very little time. On their way to give the sermon, all the students encountered a poor homeless person who, in reality, was an employee of the experiment. The confederate asked the students for help, re-creating the exact situation from the parable. The results showed that the students who were given more time were more likely to stop and help than those who were late. One tardy seminary student even stepped over the "homeless" person to avoid being late to give a sermon about the importance of taking the time to help others. The researchers also measured the participants' religiosity, which did not distinguish who chose to help—although the sample size was small.[28] The strength of the situation (being late or not) caused participants to be more "goal-directed," making it harder for the seminary students to notice and empathize with the confederate who asked for help. The Good Samaritan Study and the Obedience Experiments show that we're not always aware of a situation's influence on our choices; therefore, the situations we find ourselves in can overwhelm our intentions.

More recently, researchers have found that people are more likely to cheat in dark rooms than in rooms with bright lights,[29] more likely to make harsh moral judgments when they are physically clean,[30] and more likely to cheat when no one is watching[31] or when other members of their group behave unethically.[32] When researchers look at the predictive power of situations, they find that the correlation centers around 0.39, sometimes slightly greater than character and sometimes not.[33] For example, a meta-analysis examining the impact of character and situations on unethical behavior at work found that individual character traits, such as a person's level of manipulativeness, had a slight positive correlation to unethical behavior (0.12). Other demographic variables like education level, age, and gender had no impact. Situational features like the organization's ethical climate and whether the company enforced its ethics code had about the same level or slightly more of an effect on reducing unethical behavior (−0.21 and −0.33, respectively).[34] In other words, both personality and situation have real but relatively small effects on our choices.

When making difficult decisions, situationism argues that we'll default to what's happening around us and do what context pushes us to do. When choosing whether to take the promotion or stay with family, we may default to the incentives around us in the office, choosing to go to London when our career and annual bonus are dangled in front of us and staying home when our mom lovingly pinches us in the living room. Yet situationism cannot explain why some people in the same situation make different choices. For example, why did some participants disobey in the Obedience Experiments even when commanded to continue? Why did some seminary students stop to help even if they were late? Why do some people refuse to cheat or jump off bridges even when they see their friends are doing it? Sometimes, people overcome "what the world allows." To understand when that is likely to happen, we must look beyond personality and situation.

THE MIND'S MAPS

For most of the twentieth century, psychologists tried to find a way to describe human behavior through laws that resembled physics, capturing the relationship between stimuli and objective behaviors while doing their best to shut out anything that smacked of squishy subjective experience. Eventually, in the late 1960s, scholars like Jerome Bruner kicked down the door and ushered in the use of concepts like perception, cognition, and mental representations. The third answer to the question, *Why do people do what they do?* foregrounds the role of our mental representations and meanings. We construct the world around us in such seamless detail that it's easy to confuse our subjective interpretations with objective reality. Scholars have many different words for these interpretations: schemas, construals, appraisals, theories, causal attributions, mindsets, narratives, and meaning, to name a few. No matter what they are called, these are all fluctuating *states* of mind, not stable *traits*. We'll refer to these changing interpretations as mental maps. And like any map, they depict relationships that define who we are, including our relationships with others and our surroundings.

One famous example of a mental map is a *growth mindset*, a concept pioneered by Carol Dweck at Stanford University. A growth mindset is a set of beliefs about your abilities and that they can change and grow depending on your actions (If I keep practicing my steer roping, I'll become a better rodeo clown). In contrast, if you have a *fixed mindset*, you believe that your abilities are unchangeable (No matter what I do, I'll never be able to stay on that bull). According to Dweck, "In different situations, your mindset can change. . . . Mindsets are just beliefs. . . . They're powerful beliefs, but they're just something in your mind, and you can change your mind."[35] Dweck and her colleagues have shown that mindset makes a difference in most choices that require effort, and the correlations range between 0.27 and 0.34, depending on the specific effortful behavior in question.[36] Similarly, in a meta-analysis of trust, trait-based trust was found to only correlate with trusting behaviors at 0.26. In contrast, perception-based trust (e.g., Do I trust this person in this situation?) was correlated to trusting behaviors at 0.65.[37]

As another example, when people think of themselves in relation to others—"I'm part of an important family," "I'm my father's daughter," or "I belong to a team of champion rodeo clowns"—they are less likely to cheat and act with narrow self-interest.[38] Specifically, in one study, 27 percent of the participants who thought about themselves as autonomous individuals cheated when given a chance, but only 6 percent of the participants who thought about themselves in relation to others did, showing that the specific details of our mental maps direct our choices.[39]

To understand the impact of mental maps on obedience to immoral orders, I went back to Milgram's shock experiments in my dissertation. I obtained the original audio files of several experimental sessions and coded patterns in each participant's speech to learn how they interpreted the situation as it unfolded. When looking at the speech of obedient and disobedient participants, I found clues that suggested differences in their mental maps. Specifically, obedient participants were more likely to focus on narrow details of the task and ask questions like, "How fast should I read these word pairs?" whereas disobedient participants were more likely to focus on the broader impact and future consequences of pushing the buttons on the shock generator. They would ask more questions like, "What's going to happen if he gets hurt?" In addition, I found that participants perceived their agency differently. Disobedient participants were more likely to use the subjective pronoun "I," indicating that they saw themselves as agents in the situation with some power to choose. In contrast, obedient participants were more likely to use the objective pronoun "me," suggesting that they saw themselves more as the object of the experimenter's intentions, with less agency to stop. Participants' age, gender, religion, political affiliation, and education level were not predictive *at all*. The way participants made sense of an unfolding situation, precisely what they paid attention to, and what they believed about themselves—all of these things were highly predictive of whether they were ultimately (dis)obedient.[40]

To be as accurate as possible, researchers isolate one specific feature of our mental maps and measure its impact on our choices. For example, researchers examine single features like whether our interpretations are concrete or abstract, whether we see ourselves primarily as individuals or related to others, and whether our thoughts reflect specific beliefs like a growth or fixed mindset. When researchers measure a single aspect of our fluctuating interpretations, they can explain as much behavior as when they measure the strongest situations and character traits.[41] But when researchers simultaneously look at multiple aspects of our mental maps, their ability to predict behavior increases. For example, in one study that simultaneously manipulated more than one type of belief, researchers explained more than 50 percent of the variance in people's choices, which is a high level of predictability for psychological studies.[42]

The brain constantly goes "beyond the information given,"[43] to extrapolate, assume, fill in, stereotype, surmise, and predict what will happen to precisely me in precisely this environment. We're not always conscious of these assumptions, but these momentary interpretations of our social and physical environment shape our actions and reactions. The variation and consistency in our meaning-making can explain the variation and consistency in our choices,[44] including when we're likely to make similar choices across different situations and when two different people are likely to make the same choice.[45] For most people, most of the time, the specific nature of their squishy subjective experience significantly influences their immediate behaviors more than their situation and their innate character traits. If we want to capture the benefits of doubt, we can't rely only on our character, or on the situation; we must learn to recognize and regulate how we perceive, interpret, and think.

UPDATING THE BRAIN'S GPS

For most of us, examining, refining, and updating our mental GPS provides the greatest opportunity to make better choices and achieve our intentions. Consider how effective therapy works. Therapy involves patients talking about their thoughts and feelings, including what they assume, see, and feel. Then, a qualified therapist helps the patient become aware of their interpretations and gently prods those mental maps to make them more productive. For example, if you are afraid to commit to a relationship, your therapist may inquire about your history and help you see patterns of thinking that get in the way. ("Let's explore why you keep rescheduling our sessions?") If you are afraid of spiders, a therapist might work with you to find ways of diminishing that fear by controlled exposures that allow you to interpret the situation and your reactions differently. ("That wasn't so bad! If I don't bother it, it won't bother me.") Therapists may also roleplay and practice with patients to help them build the skills to manage their emotions and act in ways that are consistent with their updated mental maps. Hundreds of effective psychological interventions, ranging from signs encouraging hotel towel reuse to educational interventions for underachieving students, work by changing how people interpret themselves, their relations to others, and their sense of where they are.[46] Studies have shown that writing about trauma is one of the most evidence-based ways to overcome it.[47] Writing about your experience forces you to make sense of what happened, redrawing the map of where you've been, where you are, and where you might go. Our most successful interventions to change behavior involve updating our mental GPS to help us better perceive, interpret, and cope with our surroundings.

To preclude this argument from being taken to extremes, I'm not claiming that updating our mental maps has the same effect on everyone all the time. In extreme cases where genetic and environmental factors have a larger role, updating how we think may be more challenging. In addition, when someone is in a difficult situation with fewer degrees of freedom, such as being trapped in poverty, changing their mindset might open fewer possibilities than for someone with more resources. I'm not suggesting that we can easily overcome neurological disorders or put a positive spin on systemic injustices by just choosing to think differently. But while solutions to those deep-seated challenges require changes in social systems, personal skills, and even brain chemistry, they must also include changes in thinking to be sustainable. In different circumstances and for different people, their ability to change their beliefs and interpretations might be expanded or constrained.

Still, for most people, most of the time, the details of our mental maps provide the most reliable route to understand, explain, and exercise control over our choices.

MAKING CHARACTER COUNT

In this chapter, you've been patient as we've reviewed three ways of answering the question, Why do people do what they do? We've looked at the surprisingly sparse evidence in favor of the most accepted answer—the Deterministic View of Character—and two other answers: situationism and mental maps. We've seen that while all three of these work together to produce our choices, we generally have the most control over how we perceive and interpret our surroundings.

So, what exactly does all of this have to do with moments of doubt?

Let's return to the choice at the start of the chapter, page 3. In this decision, where you're forced to choose between your values of being a person who spends time with their dying father and being a newly promoted hedge fund manager, we might think that our innate character will determine our choices. The Deterministic View of Character allows us to just tell ourselves that we are a "good person" and avoid or discount the work of figuring out how our actions can reflect our intentions. "I'm a good husband; I don't need to do my fair share of anything around the house." "I know I'm a good person, so it's not scamming when I trick retirees into sending me Target gift cards," or "I know I'm not a racist; I don't have to speak up about that offensive joke my coworker just made." Plenty of people who have done terrible things in the world—from price-gouging lifesaving drugs to genocide—can more easily excuse those acts because they believe they are innately good and, therefore, they can't possibly do anything wrong. To no one's surprise, research shows we are all prone to overestimating our morality. Most of us believe that much of the goodness in the world starts with us and radiates out to our family, friends, and people who follow us on Instagram.[48] By seeing our choices as resulting from our innate and unchanging good character or from the hidden features of our situation, we underestimate or outright avoid the effort to make our actions match our aspirations, ultimately leading to choices that fall short of our intentions. If the Swiss psychiatrist Carl Jung was right when he said, "I am who I choose to become," the Deterministic View of Character and situationism take that choice largely out of our hands.

When making hard decisions, like when your personal values conflict, seeing our goodness as innate and unchanging can make us *passive*, exactly when we need to be *active*. We shouldn't think of character as only a *predictor* but also as a *project*, something to be accomplished through our future actions. (See appendix tool 1.) No matter what you choose, in moments of doubt, it will take additional effort to become the person you aspire to be. For example, if you decide to forgo the promotion and stay with family, you can't spend your days playing video games and wasting time, telling yourself, "I know I'm the kind of person who cares about my dad; he knows we're good." If you take the promotion, you'll have to follow through by networking, building skills, and staying current on the trends in the industry. And if you choose to try to have both of those things, then you'll need to be extra clear on how to spend time at work and how you will help your parents. If I want to be a good son and employee, both need to show up on my mindscape when making a choice, and both goals need to stay at the top of my mind as I decide how to spend my time. Thus, to make better choices in moments of doubt, the best place to start is to take the time to evaluate and improve our mental maps.

Our answer to the question, Why do we do what we do? impacts how we make choices and where we spend our time, effort, and energy. By sharpening our thinking, we are more skeptical of simple explanations of others and ourselves, more open to situational determinants of our actions, and more aware that the ephemeral ways we think and feel shape our choices. And understanding our mental maps allows us to exert a degree of control over our decisions. To make complex, uncertain, and high-stakes choices requires perceiving, interpreting, and behaving in ways that help us become who we aspire to be.

3

No Shortcuts to Utopia

YOU RUN A POPULAR DATING WEBSITE that matches hopeful romance seekers based on their responses to an in-depth questionnaire. Your company's mission is to facilitate a user's hooking up with as many weirdos as needed until they settle for their least-worst alternative. As your marketing team rephrased it on the website, "Unlock the happiness of finding your soulmate."

Your website and apps capture the daily online behavior of millions of hopeful match-seekers. Over the years, you have amassed a treasure trove of data from their profiles, selected matches, communication patterns, location data, and the sites they visit before and after yours. You use this data to optimize the recommendations you present to each user. As a result, your site has one of the highest customer satisfaction ratings of any service. Competition in online dating, however, has recently increased, with several new apps siphoning specific groups away. For example, some new sites target younger, attractive users; others target religious users; and others are aimed at pig farmers who only want to complain about their exes. Unfortunately, your new registrations and overall revenue dropped about 10 percent compared to last year.

As luck would have it, you are approached by a data aggregator. This company buys data from several sources and repackages it to create a more complete picture of consumers. The aggregator then sells the data and the insights they mine from it to other companies who want to target and better understand specific demographics, like Gen Z college graduates who prefer not to label their relationships but will go to dinner with anyone to get a hot meal. The aggregator wants to buy information about your users because it would help them answer questions like: "What kinds of ads do customers respond to when they are on a romantic high?" "What kinds of purchases are people likely to make when their friends start dating?" and "What types of coupon deals would be most effective after leaving someone at the altar?" Many companies would be eager to understand how the dating market shapes the market for their goods and services.

In some cases, customers might benefit by saving on products and services they want, but in other cases, they might pay more for things they might not need (Do I really want to use this Groupon for a couple's massage by myself?). You would only sell anonymized data, so individual users would not be tracked; only patterns across groups could be identified. And you're well aware that other popular websites sell user data to aggregators for a healthy profit.

Given the size of your customer base, the data aggregator's initial offer is $3 million a year. This timely cash infusion would help diversify your revenue stream and allow you to stay ahead of the growing competition. Legally, you are covered because your users accept a privacy agreement specifying that your company owns any data your services generate. Nothing about selling data is mentioned explicitly in the contract. But as you know, no one reads the fine print before hastily accepting the terms and conditions. While the laws in European countries give users more control over their data, the US law currently favors companies. As a result, many North American customers wrongly believe they own their personal information, and some may wish to be informed explicitly about the potential data sale. You worry that calling any attention to selling the data would further stall new registrations.

If you don't say anything, it will be virtually impossible for anyone to know you are selling the data. Much of it will be used in "behind-the-scenes" algorithms for pricing and advertising, so the odds of someone tracing the data back to the company are very low. In addition, you are unsure how your employees will feel about the situation; some may object, and others may not care. On the one hand, you want to preserve customer trust and prevent anything that could drive users to your growing list of competitors; on the other hand, you see considerable benefits in working with the aggregator.

Would you sell the data?

———

This type of choice pits a general rule (obtain informed consent about how customers' data is used) against a set of outcomes (greater profits for the company). Often, we feel doubt when deciding between sticking to the well-worn trail of social norms or stepping off the beaten path to walk directly toward more favorable consequences.

Most of the time, when breaking a rule leads to negative outcomes (like jail time or fines), or when following a rule leads to good outcomes (like better reputations and relationships), we don't need to think much about our choices. But when rules and outcomes point us in opposite directions, we find ourselves stuck and scratching our heads to determine which path to take. Before our scalps are relieved, things will get a little itchier. Relying on rules and outcomes are two different ways to know whether we are making good choices, but as we are about to see, they are not the only ways.

SWITCH YOUR LENS

Who knew customers wouldn't like Crystal Pepsi, New Coke, 3D TVs, and Segways? Executives and investors who lost millions didn't realize that WeWork, Theranos, FTX, Quibi, Fyre Festival, and Woodstock '99 would be such dumpster fires. Why do smart, well-trained, hardworking people make decisions that result in such disappointing outcomes, like the final season of *Game of Thrones*? A key source of error in our everyday choices is the gap between the world we imagine and the world we encounter. We imagine our investment in a startup will lead to doubling our money but encounter a founder who is lying about their technology. We imagine making the world better by being an evangelist for cryptocurrency but fail to imagine how our choices can evaporate billions of dollars. I imagine more than three people reading this book; alas, it's just you and me. Bad investments, failed ideas, and critical errors result from our pixelated and blurry imagination.

The way we imagine the future is intimately connected to our Pursue and Protect Systems. For example, when pursuing a new product launch, it's easy to focus only on the potential for success and to forget to look around and see what customers think. Similarly, when we are motivated to avoid a process change at work, it's easier to focus on all the reasons it won't work and fail to notice anything good about the project. As we've seen before, when we're highly motivated to Pursue or to Protect, our mental maps are sparsely detailed, as if we're using a zoom lens to focus on our destination, and everything in between is blurred out. Yet navigating unfamiliar territory is precisely when we need to engage our Pause and Piece-Together System and switch to a wide-angle lens to better notice the contours of the terrain, including the obstacles we may trip over. Imagining with discipline helps our mental maps better reflect the landscape we'll encounter as we venture forth.

In the last chapter, I made the case that people's mental maps are critical to understanding why they do what they do. When experts can't rely on their existing mental maps in uncertain situations, they start mapping and looking around to understand their current circumstances. If the goal is to see further so that we can think ahead and chart a more careful path in moments of doubt, then what exactly should be on our radars?

To answer this question, we'll examine the lessons and the liabilities of moral philosophy—the study of what makes a choice good. Philosophers and psychologists (predominantly from Western traditions) have carved and polished four lenses highlighting how we can and do judge choices—principles, consequences, character, and relationships.

Whether deciding to follow the rules, maximize benefits, invest in new technology, or even how to end a once-beloved TV series, these lenses suffuse our imaginations with light and shadow, helping us to more clearly perceive where we are and more deliberately conceive where we should go next.

LENS #1: PRINCIPLES

If you're feeling bad about a decision you've made that didn't turn out according to plan, take heart. At least you're more competent than a baby. In fact, you can do a lot of things babies can't even dream of yet. For example, you can brush your teeth correctly, greet strangers appropriately, and form orderly lines when waiting (unless you grew up in India, China, or Russia, in which case you learned how to navigate a disorderly throng of people). So how do billions of humans learn these various complex practices? Thankfully, our parents, siblings, friends, and teachers taught us *rules* that guide our behavior.

These socially accepted rules are so important that they are essential to determining whether a choice is considered "good" or "right." These rules can be implicit and taken-for-granted norms such as "don't make unnecessary conversation in yoga class," "don't ask for ketchup at a fancy steakhouse," or "don't mention that Uncle Rohit sprays his hair on from a can." Rules can also be explicit, such as when we see signs reminding us not to speed in a construction zone, read laws that prevent the disclosing of confidential health information, and receive instruction to use "oatmeal raisin" as a safeword when engaging in some racy roleplay.

Some communities believe their rules are divinely inspired, such as the Judeo-Christian Ten Commandments or the Islamic Hadith. Other rules, such as the UN Declaration of Human Rights, result from human reason. We'll use the term "principles" as a general term for the wide-ranging social expectations, norms, rules, policies, and laws intended to guide our daily behavior. Principles can *promote* specific actions (Honor thy father and mother) or *prohibit* other actions (Thou shall not covet your neighbor's wife's motorcycle) or some combination of the two (Do unto others as you would have done to you unless you're a sadomasochist, in which case, "oatmeal raisin!"). Regardless of their specific content or level of detail, all rules make specific actions permissible or impermissible. Therefore, if your choice is consistent with that principle, it is judged as "good."[1]

You might not realize it, but dozens of these social principles are shaping your behavior right at this very moment. For example, you're reading this book forward (and not backward), you're probably sitting down (not hanging from the ceiling), and you're staying clothed the entire time. Unless, of course, you're a three-month-old baby.

But while we're dutifully following these rules, let's stop and notice the absence of something else. When using this lens, the consequences of a choice are rendered invisible. Indeed, they are assumed to be mostly irrelevant, meaning that some choices are morally forbidden (or morally required), no matter the benefits and costs. For example, if we believe that killing is forbidden no matter what, then it would be wrong to go back in time and kill baby Hitler to prevent World War II, no matter how many lives you would save.

Applying the principles lens to the dating-website questions at the start of this chapter, we might notice a norm around providing informed consent. Selling your customers' data without their knowledge would violate that norm and thus be wrong. Another relevant principle would be to protect the interests of your employees. In light of that principle, selling the data to increase revenues and secure employment for your workers would be considered good.

There are several strengths of using a principles perspective. First, it can economize on thinking; having clear rules like "don't lie," "don't cheat," and "don't steal" makes getting along in social groups easier. Clear rules help people act quickly and intuitively. Additionally, rules help coordinate our behavior; therefore, the more people that follow a rule, the greater the benefits of that coordination. Imagine the resulting disaster if only half of the drivers on the road chose to pay attention to traffic lights. Coordinating our actions within our communities is so ingrained that people pick up rules, even when they are not explicitly taught.

A second strength of the principles lens is clarity—i.e., reasons based on principles tend to be better signals of intentions. For example, imagine after deciding not to sell your user data, you held a press conference, stood in front of a gaggle of reporters, customers, and employees, and declared,

"After careful thought, I have decided not to sell our customers' data because I fundamentally believe in protecting privacy." Let's also imagine that there are a few researchers around, and they pass out little cards and have your audience rate how ethical they think you are. Now, let's rewind the press conference. You show up to the same podium, the same audience, and proclaim, "After careful thought, I have decided not to sell our customers' data because I fundamentally believe that the long-term costs would outweigh the potential benefits."[2] Again, the researchers pass out the same little cards and tabulate the results. You don't need to rewind the tape a third time to see that the first statement leads to higher morality ratings. Clearly articulating the general principles that shape our choices signals what we value. Our audience feels they can better predict our behavior, increasing their trust in us and their perceptions of our morality.[3]

While the principles lens has some clear strengths, just like the other lenses we will peer through it also has weaknesses, highlighting some things and obfuscating others. First, a view of morality based only on principles can lead to gaming the rules. For example, when I was eight, I was grounded because I was probably being a jerk to my sister. I wasn't allowed to watch TV for a week, yet the very next day after school, my mom found me in the living room with the TV on, facing the window, rocking out to the *Teenage Mutant Ninja Turtles'* theme song. (If it's now stuck in your head, you're welcome.) When my mother reminded me that I was not to watch TV for a week, I tried to convince her that I wasn't technically violating the terms of my punishment because I wasn't looking directly at the TV; I was only watching the reflection in the window. She thought about it for a minute, and I lost another week of TV. A principles lens can lead us to try to find loopholes, caveats, and ambiguities in the letter of the law when the spirit doesn't get us what we want.

The second weakness of the principles lens is that blindly following rules, laws, norms, and orders can sometimes make the world worse.[4] For example, in the *Mahabharata* (the ancient Indian version of *Game of Thrones*), the venerable warriors and advisors, Bhishma and Drona, support a cruel and corrupt prince because they believe they must serve the crown, no matter who wears it. Beloved family members and all of society suffer as these statesmen enable a corrupt prince to use the throne to benefit himself. Bhishma and Drona were motivated primarily by their abstract duty to the throne, not to any specific individual. Tyrants can take advantage and control others by getting them to follow the rules and not think too hard about whether doing so is still a good thing. Sometimes, blind obedience to specific rules, laws, and norms can perpetuate harm. Over-reliance on the principles lens can cause us to narrow our focus on our moral purity at the expense of our impact on others. We assume that it is more important to follow the rules and be "morally clean" than to break a rule and potentially bring about better outcomes for others. This focus on one's moral purity can lead to rationalizations like, "I was just doing my job, mopping floors on the Death Star; it doesn't matter that I helped support the Empire's system of oppression."

This myopia isn't confined only to our moral purity. Research confirms that when people's actions are based on a strongly held principle, such as the duty to serve the throne, we are less able to imagine conflicting consequences. In one study, participants were asked about controversial moral issues like promoting premarital condom use, forcefully interrogating terrorists, and condoning capital punishment. For each issue, the researchers measured the strength of the participants' beliefs in principles by asking them how much they agreed with statements like, "Forceful interrogation of terrorists is wrong, even if it is effective in getting suspects to talk." Then, the researchers asked participants to estimate how likely the specific behaviors were to lead to positive outcomes. For example, how likely is it that encouraging condom use reduces teen pregnancy? The stronger a participant's principle-based view was against an act (in this case, teenage condom education), the less they believed that any positive outcomes would occur. The more participants endorsed the belief that premarital condom education was morally wrong, the less they believed that condoms effectively prevented pregnancy and STDs. A weakness of using only a principles lens is that it obscures contrasting consequences.[5]

Finally, while we've seen that principles are harder to uphold when there is complexity, the principles lens doesn't offer guidance on what to do when one set of rules conflicts with another. This idea is illustrated perfectly by Jaime Lannister's quote from *A Clash of Kings*, a book in the *Song of Ice and Fire* series. "So many vows . . . they make you swear and swear. Defend the king. Obey the king. Keep his secrets. Do his bidding. Your life for his. But obey your father. Love your sister. Protect the innocent. Defend the weak. Respect the gods. Obey the laws. It's too much. No matter what you do, you're forsaking one vow or the other."[6] This quote leads to one more weakness in the principles lens. There is an inherent ambiguity in how we interpret and implement rules. Even when we agree on which rules matter most, we may interpret and apply them differently; for example, Jaime's interpretation of "Love your sister" is . . . unconventional.

Principles are essential for social groups to coordinate their beliefs about acceptable choices and actions. We should be thankful to our parents and teachers for passing them on to us. In moments of doubt, a clear benefit of principles is that they are general, abstract guides for making good choices. But that strength is also a weakness. A principles lens may not adequately consider the specifics of the situation; thus, depending on the circumstances, laws to obey traffic lights, prohibit premarital condom education, and protect customer data privacy—and even rules created with good intentions—can end up being incomplete, counterproductive, conflicting, unfair, or unjust.

LENS #2: CONSEQUENCES

The second lens from moral philosophy defines a "good" choice primarily by the consequences or outcomes of an action. Most people have heard aphorisms like "the greatest good for the greatest number" or "the ends justify the means," which are expressions that can be traced back to a branch of moral philosophy called "consequentialism."[7] Philosophers such as John Stuart Mill and Jeremy Bentham viewed English society in the 1800s as obsessed with enforcing antiquated rules and norms. They argued that people should pay more attention to the harms and benefits of their choices. Whatever choice maximized happiness, utility, pleasure, or welfare should be considered best. Mill and Bentham aimed to unshackle people from their blind obedience to orthodoxy by urging them to ask, "Does this choice create more good?"

To accurately assess the resulting pleasure and pain, consequentialists turned decision-making into a complex multivariate calculus. They argued that to make good choices, one must weigh the duration of pleasure and pain, their intensity, certainty, proximity, purity, fecundity (or how likely they are to lead to other pleasures and pains), and the number of people impacted.[8] By carefully crunching the numbers, we could identify which actions were *really* good and which only seemed good because of tradition. In this view, no actions are intrinsically right or wrong, just right or wrong because of the net positive outcomes they create. It's important to note that this lens requires the calculus to be agnostic and impartial to your own interests. When you are focused on harms and benefits only to yourself, that's called "egoism." If you can't think of another person who embodies that philosophy, well, then I hate to break it to you. . . .

Regarding the decision at the start of this chapter, a consequences lens would focus our attention on the outcomes of selling the data. We would attend to the good we could achieve with the additional money; for example, will our customers' lives be better because of services that use this data? We would try to determine if selling the information produces more positive outcomes than harm for society. In addition to more tangible financial results, we could also think about social consequences related to our company culture, our ability to attract top talent, and any potential for negative press.

The first strength of this consequences lens is that it provides clear guidance when outcomes are easy to measure and predict. For example, we can more easily decide when to change insurance policies, sell our shares of a stock, trade in our used car, refinance a mortgage, invest in solar panels, and time our naps to optimize our beauty sleep when we can plug the costs and benefits into a spreadsheet or calculator.

A second strength is that a consequences lens may even offer a way to think about the origin of some rules. For example, the Jewish philosopher Maimonides argued that some religious dietary restrictions have their roots in keeping the body healthy. Prohibitions against eating pork in the Jewish and Islamic faiths may come from the observation that pigs eat anything they can get their snouts on, including waste, leading the people who ate the pigs to get sick. In this way, attention to consequences provides a way to create and adapt various rules.

But let's not gloss over the "cons" in consequences. First, because it aims to be agent-neutral, a strict version of consequentialism means there is no room to give special consideration to oneself and one's family and friends. Consequentialists believe we should maximize the *overall* good, not just what's good for ourselves and our close connections. Self-sacrifice, or even sacrificing one's kin for the greater good, is considered praiseworthy. In contrast, a principles lens allows for special considerations because different obligations govern different relationships. For example, I have special obligations to my family, the University of Virginia, the City of Charlottesville, and the United States of America that differ from my obligations to the Byrde family from Osage Beach, Virginia Tech, the Agrestic subdivision outside of LA, and the population of Laos. A consequences lens asks us to be neutral to our own situation, which seems to contradict how humans are wired to think and feel. If someone is willing to harm their own family and loved ones to help strangers, most of us would keep them at a safe distance.

Another con is that focusing on consequences permits acts that seem immoral from the principles lens, such as killing innocents. It doesn't matter how harmful an act is to some as long as it is more beneficial to some others. This criticism is illustrated by a famous example called the "transplant case."[9] Should you kill one innocent person who has come to the hospital so that you can use their organs to save five others? Murdering one person to save five seems permissible under a consequences lens but doesn't square with most people's intuitions about the sanctity of human life. We can use consequences to rationalize atrocious acts if we can do anything as long as it benefits more people than it harms.

A third weakness is that while the logic of consequences is helpful to think through, it may also be impossible to apply fully, particularly in highly uncertain choices.[10] How can we know what the exact duration, frequency, distribution, and fecundity of pleasure and pain of our choices will be ahead of time? Let's suppose that pleasure and pain can be measured accurately on a single scale, for example, in units of goodness over seconds, which we'll call a Clooney (named after either Amal or George, you choose). Could we ever be confident enough in our math when deciding whether to date Ben over Matt because a relationship with Ben would produce 15.6 Cloonies of net pleasure per hour versus only 13.8 for Matt? If you're not a math genius, don't worry, it's not your fault. Even if we could agree on an accurate measure of pleasure and pain, a large body of research consistently shows that we have a hard time predicting what will actually make us happy because of common errors in our memory and imagination.[11] While we can and should take the time to think through the outcomes of our actions, even then, there will still be things we don't know and can't predict with the certainty that consequentialists covet.

Finally, the consequences lens is relatively silent on how we should accurately weigh different types of good.[12] How do we compare various benefits if we can't measure goodness in Cloonies? Is the pleasure of sipping a Dark and Stormy on a black-sand beach equal to watching your daughter score the game-winning goal after a season of losses? Is the satisfaction derived from snuggling with the love of your life the same as removing twenty-four tons of CO_2 from the atmosphere? Who decides the hierarchy and exchange rate of different types of "goods," and is it even possible?

When making difficult choices like whether to sell your customer data, consequentialism is adamant that decision-makers take an abstract, dispassionate, and neutral view of the necessary calculations. But shouldn't we care about the outcomes that affect us directly? If we don't consider the impact on ourselves, who will? When trying to make good choices, how should we consider ourselves?

LENS #3: CHARACTER

A man is speeding in a rainstorm, gets into an accident, and kills an innocent bystander on the road.[13] The driver is speeding home to hide cocaine from his parents. How much blame do you think this driver deserves for the death?

Another group of volunteers is told to imagine the same scenario, except the driver is racing home to hide an anniversary present for his parents. As you might expect, the cocaine-hiding driver is blamed more for the exact same outcome because he is seen as a bad person with a worse character than the driver racing home to hide a last-minute purchase of Edible Arrangements. The character lens from moral philosophy directs our attention to character and motives to identify good choices.

Specifically, this lens emphasizes the personal virtues (or forms of excellence) and character traits that shape and are shaped by our choices, as we saw in the last chapter. In Western philosophy, attention to virtues is grounded in the work of Aristotle.[14] He taught people to cultivate virtues like courage, justice, temperance, and fortitude. Chinese philosophers such as Mèngzǐ (Mencius) and Kǒng Fūzǐ (Confucius) highlighted the importance of character traits like loyalty, benevolence, harmony, and love.[15] No matter where the list comes from, virtues are considered consistent dispositions. Possessing a virtue means being a specific type of person who notices, expects, values, feels, chooses, acts, and reacts in ways consistent with a particular trait. For example, it's not enough to be honest because it leads to better outcomes. A person who embodies the virtue of honesty chooses to be honest because they desire to be an honest person. I know it sounds like the world's most tautological tongue twister, but the point is that from the character lens, good actions result from the motivation to be a specific type of person. In this view, integrity is a particularly important virtue because it helps us find connections among our different identities, roles, and responsibilities, rather than being a faithful person at church on Sunday and a deceptive person when smuggling drugs across the border in a shipment of Bibles on Monday. This lens helps us to think ahead to the reputational results of our choices and defines good choices as those that allow us to achieve the virtues we desire.

One contemporary way to think about virtue is brand; individuals and organizations who manage a brand ask themselves, "How is this action consistent with who we aspire to be?" They are actively trying to achieve a particular reputation and coherence in their actions. Poor brand management is about only presenting the veneer of having commendable values, faking concern, or doing things that you don't really care about to gain the benefits of having a good reputation. Think of the social media influencer who posts about the latest social justice cause but then does nothing else.

Better brand management, however, is about actually living and demonstrating the values you espouse, particularly when no one is watching. For example, the company Patagonia cares deeply about the planet; they also put their money where their mouth is by reducing waste and using renewable energy and recycled materials in their products, making high-quality products so that customers don't have to buy as much, and donating a portion of their profits (and their whole company) to help protect the environment.

In the data-selling case, a character-based lens would focus our attention on our reputation, our brand, and the values we aspire to as an online dating company, including how we want to be seen by others and how we want to see ourselves. Then, depending on those values, we may lean toward selling the data if we want to be the most tech-savvy dating site in the world, or we may not if we want to be the most trusted.

The character lens captures something important about the human experience; we cannot help but make sense of others' behaviors by creating identities and descriptions for each other. Even from an early age, when we meet people for the first time, we quickly assess their level of warmth, competence, and morality.[16] In the last chapter, we saw that the short montages we create about people are not as accurate as we'd like to think. But, despite their inaccuracy, these descriptions still have a powerful impact on who we choose to spend time with. For example, we want to spend more time with Ling because we've heard great things about him from Sasha, whom we trust. And we don't share food with Estelle when we go out because she is always rude to the waitstaff, and we don't know what they might do to get revenge. Identifying cheaters, free-riders, liars, malignant narcissists, and villains increases our chances of survival; evolution has helped us to be vigilant and maybe even hyper-sensitive to their potential presence.

Critics of a character lens counter that what makes a choice good is not only about what kind of person you are.[17] A person without virtues can do good things. I'm done giving **spoiler alerts**! If you haven't seen *Breaking Bad* yet, go watch it already, or at least skip to the next paragraph.

At the end of the series, Walter White tries to take a step toward redemption by destroying the meth he has produced, giving money to his family, and freeing his accomplice. Some would argue that Walter's general lack of virtue doesn't negate the "goodness" of those acts.

As discussed extensively in the previous chapter, the most severe criticisms of this tradition have come from psychologists and philosophers who point to both the surprising flexibility and the low degree of consistency in character traits and virtues. Like the previous two lenses, principles and consequences, the character lens also says little about what to do when virtues conflict. For example, when being a good daughter conflicts with being a good employee, virtue ethicists say it takes practical wisdom to figure it out.

From this perspective, a good decision allows us to achieve the character we desire, to become good parents, philosophers, stewards of the planet, and CEOs. But not everyone agrees that making good choices means we should gaze so intently at our navels.

LENS #4: RELATIONSHIPS

In the 1970s, psychologist Lawrence Kohlberg studied how children's thinking about morality develops as they mature.[18] He gave participants (ranging from toddlers to teens) a series of moral dilemmas with questions like, "Is it permissible to steal a lifesaving drug to save someone in your family who will die from an illness?" and asked the kids to explain their choices. Hopefully, he also gave the children some free therapy afterward. Next, Kohlberg and his team categorized the children's answers into six stages of moral development. They defined stage one as focused on punishments and rewards and the sixth and final stage as using abstract moral principles. When tabulating the results, Kohlberg found a quirk in the data. He noticed that boys were more likely to respond to the drug-stealing scenario with answers like, *It's wrong to steal the medicine because stealing is wrong.* In contrast, girls were more likely to say things like, *Stealing the medicine would be wrong because you could go to jail, and you wouldn't be able to look after your family.* Some girls in the experiment didn't accept the dilemma because of the lack of social context, asking, *Well, why couldn't I ask my neighbors for help?* Kohlberg coded these responses at lower levels, leading to the curious result that boys demonstrated a higher level of moral development than similar-aged girls because they used more abstract logic.

However, in the 1980s, psychologist Carol Gilligan, Kohlberg's research assistant on the original study, described the results with a technical-scientific term—"bullshit."[19] Instead of being morally inferior, she saw the girls' responses as a different way of thinking about morality—one that foregrounded specific relationships, empathy, and an ethic of care for others. From this perspective, as social creatures, an essential determinant of what makes a choice good is how it shapes our ability to get along with the specific people we care about and live with. Similarly, the philosopher Simone de Beauvoir has argued that people's (specifically women's) embodied experiences, intimate relationships, and social situations are largely neglected in moral philosophy in favor of abstract, independent, and contextless moral reasoning.[20] Our connections with those with whom we work, play, eat, and share a bed impact our survival and happiness more directly than abstract, generalized strangers. Therefore, much of our everyday morality is about addressing issues that arise in those socially situated, flesh-and-blood relationships. Who gets stuck with the middle seat? How will we split the last piece of cake? Whose career gets priority? In terms of the relationships lens, to make good choices, people should be focused on "meeting the needs, fostering the capabilities, and alleviating the pain and suffering of individuals in attentive, responsive, and respectful ways," rather than on abstract moral principles or distant consequences.[21] Indeed, in Gilligan's view, the highest level of moral development isn't the use of abstract moral principles but rather the ability to create connections between what's good for the self and what's good for others.

For the dating data case, using the relationships lens would highlight your particular obligations to employees, customers, and shareholders in deciding whether to sell data. You would need to learn what it means to care for each of these groups and how your choice would impact your ability to continue caring for those relationships.

While it might be obvious to us, researchers have recently shown that information about social relationships changes how people judge choices.[22] For example, participants rate actions like "not feeding someone" as less morally problematic when a restaurant owner refuses to feed a customer who can't pay, compared to a mother who refuses to feed her hungry child. When given a specific relational context, people change the severity of their moral judgments based on the expectations and obligations governing those relationships.

There is considerable diversity and nuance within feminist perspectives on morality and ethics. Yet many of these scholars are united by the belief that traditional moral philosophy has an illusory and counterproductive fetish for impartiality. As human beings, we are born "always already" entangled in a web of social relationships. Therefore, we cannot help but rely on our connections and shared experiences when deciding what to do. The relationships lens is valuable because it directs our attention to the critical connections that impact our well-being and expands the way we think about ourselves—from individual autonomous agents to enmeshed in relationships that simultaneously sustain and constrain us.

Critics argue that too narrow a focus on relationships can quickly devolve into tribalism by biasing us in favor of our close connections at the expense of impartial consequences or rules. Caring at the expense of other considerations can be a slippery slope, leading to nepotism, cronyism, feudalism, bribery, in-group bias, and, ironically, maintaining the good ol' boys club.[23] Other critics argue that relationships is not a distinct lens but a type of virtue ethics, with care being the critical virtue.[24] Not all relationships should be maintained and nurtured—the ethics of care has not yet helped us to effectively make sense of and address stifling, adversarial, and abusive relationships.

Finally, as you might expect by now, just as we've seen with the three other lenses, this lens says very little about what to do when obligations, relationships, and caring conflict.

SHORTCUTS TO UTOPIA

In learning to make good choices, we've looked at four different lenses and tried to summarize hundreds of years of ethical debate to identify *what makes a choice good*. In this process, I've admittedly left out considerable nuances. Yet even the simple shapes I've blocked in with broad brush-strokes allow us to identify these lenses' relative strengths and weaknesses and notice that the discipline of moral philosophy has largely ignored moments of doubt.

One way I make sense of these competing approaches is to see that they focus our mental maps on specific ideal types. Figure 1 depicts a grid with two axes; the horizontal axis depicts our breadth of focus. At one extreme, we have a narrow, primarily internal focus on ourselves. On the other end, we have a broader, primarily external focus on others; in the middle, there is some degree of focus on both. The vertical axis represents

Figure 1

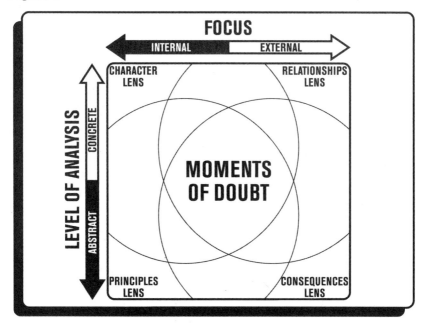

the level of abstraction. At the top, we have an increasingly concrete, immediate level of analysis, and at the bottom, we have an increasingly abstract and distant level of analysis.

Each of the four main lenses from moral philosophy recommends a stylized way to make sense of a good decision anchored toward each corner. For example, the character lens is focused primarily on the self in more immediate and concrete terms. "If I copy these answers from my classmate's quiz, will I be a cheater?" The relationships lens is also immediate and concrete but expands its breadth of focus to those we are connected to. "How will my choices impact my relationships with Arthur, Bill, Charlie, Percy, Fred, George, Ron, and Ginny?" In contrast, a principles lens is more internal and abstract. Specifically, a central guideline of the principles lens is that we should act so that our personal motives can become a universal law. Finally, the consequences lens suggests we think about the pleasure or pain generated by our choice abstracted from our own time and place. "What are the harms and benefits to everyone but me?"

Specific communities may have built consensus on how to approach and justify specific choices to each other; for example, if you're a Christian, other Christians will accept your choices if they align with God's laws. If you're an economist, other economists will accept your choices if you can show your calculations about the marginal utility gained. If you belong to a fraternity, your brothers will judge your choices based on how they strengthen the bonds in the group (and the availability of beer). In addition, there could be certain situations where these lenses are more or less useful (honestly, we don't know yet). For our purposes, what is important to know is that moments of doubt occur at the intersection, where there are competing ways to think about what is good.

Additionally, our stakeholders will interpret our actions (or lack thereof) through one or more of these lenses. If we sell our customers' data, some users will rely on the principle of protecting privacy and be upset with our choice. "How dare you sell my data and take advantage of my broken heart by selling me more singles' vacations?!" Others—like some investors and employees—will focus on the consequences, like increased revenue, and be supportive of our actions. "Who cares what happens to customer privacy? It's our job to make more money! Also, when will I be getting a raise?" Others might be ambivalent because they're happy that the company is doing better but not thrilled about how the data is used. So, which lens provides the "right" answer?

The history of moral philosophy has been a quest to find the secret code to making good choices.[25] Philosophers have hoped we could find a shortcut to utopia if they could isolate the hidden grammar of ethics and rally society around that universal standard. In this quest, philosophers have reduced the complexity of difficult decisions to one of these lenses and argued that their way of seeing the world is *really* the best way.

This race to definitively prove which lens is "right" has taken precedence over exploring interconnections among these traditions. As evidence, in a survey of nearly a thousand university philosophers, 32 percent said their personal beliefs leaned toward the principles lens, 31 percent chose some form of consequentialism, and 37 percent chose character and virtue ethics. Unfortunately, relationships and care didn't make it onto the survey. Most scholars who study, write, and teach moral philosophy continue to choose one view and remain adamant that the other views are not just different but lesser.[26]

Each of these traditions also has weaknesses, so in complex situations, a decision built solely on one of them will ultimately give rise to considerations from the other lenses. For example, advocating for abortions based only on the benefits to society raises questions about principles (Who has rights and what are they?). Arguing to outlaw gay marriage based on the technicality of laws raises questions about consequences (What are the impacts on couples that are already married?) and character (What kind of society are we?). Like the proverbial blind men who encounter an elephant and try to describe it by latching on to only one body part, each lens isolates a specific part of morality, holds it up as the essence of making good choices, and argues against the other views.

FOUR TICKETS TO PARADISE

What might be less evident to philosophers and more apparent to people who work with elephants is that despite being quite far apart, the tail and the ear are connected. What's true of elephant parts is also true of these ideal types of thinking. No matter where our mental maps start, we can find connections to the other three lenses. For example, in my business school courses, sometimes I'm lucky enough to get a student with a previous philosophy degree. This student may proudly declare in class that they make all their decisions using a set of guiding principles. If I ask this student why they prioritize one principle that is in tension with another, ultimately, they appeal to a character trait or desirable consequence. The same is true for a student who sees herself as a consequentialist. If you ask her why she thinks that returns to shareholders are more critical than the company's reputation, she talks about rules, norms, or relationships. "We should maximize shareholder value" (a principle for those keeping track). This situation has been replicated in the lab with similar results.[27] So, while we might identify with one or another lens in the abstract, research shows that we use multiple lenses in practice.

People switch back and forth among these perspectives depending on the information presented. That's why it seems like moral philosophers have become obsessed with trolleys lately. It's not because they have a passion for tying people to train tracks (well, not all of them). It's because the trolley problem[28] shows that when presented with an abstract dilemma to pull a lever and divert a train from killing five people tied to the tracks and instead kill one person, people are more likely to act consistently with a consequences lens and pull the lever.[29] Still, those very same people make the opposite choice if the decision is made more personal and involves physically pushing one person off the bridge to stop the trolley, an action that violates a deeply held principle. "Um, I was taught to keep my hands to myself in preschool, and I'd rather not be the one to push a person to their death. I'm not even sure pushing this person will stop the train, so no thanks, I'd let the train do what it's going to do and take a flight next time." Apparently, when presented with abstract situations where harms and benefits are pitted against each other, we rely on consequences. Still, when the same choice is made more personal, we switch tracks and rely on principles.

We're also learning that we don't rely on a single lens at a time. For example, in a recent project, my coauthors and I asked participants to read a series of sixteen stories in which we varied information about the four lenses within each story: character, consequences, principles, and relationships. In some stories, the protagonist had positive motives; in other stories, he acted for selfish reasons. In some stories, the protagonist's actions led to harms; in others, people gained benefits. Therefore, one story had positive information about consequences, relationships, character, and principles, another had negative information about all four, and the other fourteen contained all the permutations in between. After reading each story, participants rated the morality of the protagonist's actions. By looking at the responses of hundreds of participants, we calculated the relative impact of each type of information on participants' ultimate moral judgments. The results showed that no single lens explained all or even a majority of their judgment, which means that participants used information from all four lenses to reach their conclusions. The relative weight of each type of information changed depending on the specifics of the scenario. Sometimes, participants prioritized consequences more; other times, they prioritized character, but in each case, they used information from multiple lenses to reach a more nuanced judgment.[30]

FROM BLACK AND WHITE TO HD

Consider how an RGB TV set combines three colors (red, green, and blue) to produce more variety and detail. By turning all three colors on simultaneously, we get white pixels; by turning them all off, we get black pixels; and by changing how much each color is activated, we get 16,777,216 combinations in between. While some scholars might want to continue searching for a shortcut to utopia by isolating the essence of morality (Damn it, why can't you see that the red pixels *really* are the most important?!), I want to argue for the benefits of complex, adaptable systems. Paradoxically, a system with multiple components allows for more control, just as an RGB TV produces so much subtle color variation with just a few inputs. That variation is valuable in complex and dynamic environments because different ways of thinking about the "good" allow us to notice and react to more fine-grained information. Multiple lenses mean we have a moral sense that cannot be easily reduced to simple rules, calculations, or universal heuristics. This adaptability can provide the potential for learning, careful action, and conscientious responses.

Our multi-faceted morality can allow moral progress or stagnation, depending on how we use it. Innovation and progress result when people can cope with the complexity of their environment and make things better for themselves and others—in all the rich ways of describing "better," including principles, character, consequences, and relationships. For example, it was illegal and immoral in medieval Europe to desecrate dead bodies. If curious doctors in fourteenth-century Italy hadn't started dissecting corpses to see what was inside, we wouldn't have gained knowledge about the human body that has saved countless lives ever since.[31] This adaptability also allows us to see others who are different from us as fellow humans, conferring rights and responsibilities on each other so that we can live more peacefully. "Maybe we should treat people of color as equal citizens? Perhaps gay people should be allowed to get married?" Our choices differentially allocate harms and benefits, cohere or not with different moral principles, shape our virtues and vices, and alter the nature of relationships in which we are enmeshed. In contrast, adaptability can also be a tool for stagnation when we overly simplify our beliefs relative to the complexity of our environments. For example, when we focus on only what we want to see, ignore the larger risks of our actions, lend a deaf ear to dissent, or kick the can down the road, we take shortcuts at the expense of long-term survival. Thus, our choices cannot achieve their intended impact; instead, they plant the seeds of our unintentional demise.

When different moral standards conflict and we experience doubt, an opportunity arises to switch from autopilot to awareness by pausing and piecing together. Tensions within and across these lenses signal areas where we should tread carefully and choose intentionally. By noticing these tensions and building a more detailed mental map, we can choose who we want to be and the kind of world we want to help create. When used together, each lens allows us to get a clearer picture of our situation, sharpening the image from grainy black and white to a deep and rich HD.

When making decisions in which rules and outcomes conflict, we need to scan the social context to understand how other people will make sense of our actions, what they judge as good, and how they might respond, all of which can ultimately constrain or confirm our choice. Instead of defaulting to our favorite definition of the good and ignoring others, we can take the time to understand the situation using insights from each of the four lenses of moral philosophy to identify a broader range of potential enablers and barriers to our choices. (See appendix tool 2.) By becoming more aware of competing standards, we can be more intentional about which standards we will affirm, which we will not, and which we will work to change. We shouldn't rely only on our minds to learn about the social context. For example, when deciding whether to sell our user data, we can and should engage with employees and customers to learn about their concerns, share our own perspectives, and iron out the details of how the data could be captured, stored, and accessed to remove and minimize any privacy threats. When you imagine in more detail with more discipline, you "expand the number of undesirable consequences you envision so that you can expand the number of precautions and mitigation strategies you will take."[32] In moments of doubt, observing and learning can help you make better choices by shrinking the gap between the world you imagine and the world you encounter.

II

WAYFINDING

4

Dis-solving Problems

YOU RUN A REGIONAL HEALTH INSURANCE COMPANY based in the Southwest US. (Why can't you hold on to a job for more than one chapter?) Recently, your state legislature proposed an amendment that would limit the rights of transgender citizens. The new law defines gender as only male or female and removes gender identity from the list of protected classes such as race, age, ethnicity, national origin, veteran status, and disability. The rationale provided for the law is to simplify the definition of sex used by the government and save the healthcare sector millions of dollars in compliance costs. But it also allows insurance companies to refuse to pay for a variety of medical procedures for transgender individuals, including cancer treatments. The proposed law has sharply divided your state (and the country), causing many businesses to threaten to leave if the law passes.

As a smaller insurer in the area, these changes impact you directly. You could refuse service to some clients, but you don't want to. If the law passes, you could save about $250,000 in annual legal paperwork. It was easy for you and your entire leadership team to decide against making any policy changes to discriminate against trans community members. But it's been difficult to decide how much to speak out against the bill. Unlike other companies, you cannot credibly threaten to leave the state or move your headquarters. More importantly, even if you could, you don't want to disrupt your customers' lives.

Several employee groups encourage you to speak out and donate company funds to oppose the law. Based on the HR team's latest assessment, about 70 percent of your employees would approve of publicly opposing the law, while only 30 percent of your customers would. Many of your customers simply don't care about this issue. Publicly fighting the law might gain you a few new customers, but given the demographics of your state, probably not many. On the other hand, you won't lose too many customers either because, for them, leaving your insurance company for another option is costly and time-consuming. You want to avoid the risks of damaging your relationship with employees and tarnishing your reputation in the larger community. You also worry that elected officials could retaliate and make your life difficult if you don't support their bill.

It seems that doing something and doing nothing will upset different groups. You feel stuck between Dwayne Johnson and that old pull-out couch that hurts your back.

What could you do?

FOREIGNER AT HOME

When I was growing up, riding the school bus was like flying across the globe. Home and school were two different worlds with very different rules. At home, I was too "American" for my parents and friends who had immigrated from India recently. I didn't have an Indian accent since I was born in Chicago, but like most Midwesterners, I learned to pronounce all my vowels like a pirate with a sinus infection. I watched American TV shows, listened to American music, had crushes on American girls, and played too many video games.

But at the same time, I was too Indian for my American school friends; my lunchbox was filled with unrecognizable food. I smelled like cumin, garlic, and spices my friends had never sniffed before. I didn't look like your average kid from the suburbs. I was a skinny, brown kid with glasses too big for my face—picture Steve Urkel dressed as Fievel from *An American Tail*. My non-Indian friends didn't have a frame of reference to understand my family other than Apu from *The Simpsons* or Babu Bhatt from *Seinfeld*. No matter where I was, I felt like I was forced to choose: Am I *really* American or *really* Indian?

I've been called a "coconut" (someone who is brown on the outside and white on the inside) and an "ABCD," which stands for "American-Born Confused Desi," or an Indian person who has lost their sense of culture and identity in America. I remember watching Bollywood movies where the main villain was an Indian who grew up abroad and lost his traditional values. He ate meat, was rude to his elders, renounced his religion, disrespected women, and was always drunk for some reason. Is that what will become of me? I wondered.

Like Gogol Ganguli from the book *The Namesake*, I didn't want to give up either the "American" or "Indian" parts of myself, yet I had difficulty finding ways to express both. I deeply resented the pressure to choose to be only one or the other. Research shows that many children who sit at the border of different communities (multicultural, nonbinary, multiethnic, and multiracial) struggle and feel pressure to trade off one of their identities for the other. This pressure can lead to increased stress, anxiety, and depression, resulting in an increased rate of suicide for children raised at the boundary.[1]

But, perhaps surprisingly, people who don't fit neatly into one group or another also have more resources for creativity. They can draw from a broader range of stories, traditions, practices, relationships, and recipes.[2] When young adults find ways to integrate their multiple identities, they can avoid the psychological risks of feeling like they don't belong anywhere. Just as it doesn't make sense to ask if a mouth-watering fusion dish like tandoori chicken burgers is *really* a burger or *really* tandoori chicken, or if Mexican ravioli are *really* Italian or Mexican, it doesn't make sense to always prioritize one aspect of yourself over another. Fusions are simultaneously both, and make no mistake; they are fricking delicious!

In the previous chapter, I introduced the idea that when confronting moments of doubt, we can use the four lenses from moral philosophy to see more complexity, identify more relevant criteria, and proactively avoid errors. However, we might worry that multiple criteria make it harder to make good choices because knowing how to deal with conflicting goals is difficult. We might believe that good decision-making is fast decision-making, and looking for conflicting goals will unnecessarily slow us down. The psychological challenges and opportunities faced by people with multiple identities are like the challenges we all face when confronting difficult decisions with multiple conflicting goals. We can feel anxious, nervous, or stressed when we feel forced to choose and imagine disappointing our customers, employees, friends, or parents, all of whom we care about deeply. Integrating different decision criteria (and different identities) is possible. It's just not easy.

TRADEOFFS

Usually, when decision-makers face a difficult choice, a conventional bit of advice is that they should be ready and willing to make tradeoffs. For example, one decision-making advisor counsels, "Look at decision-making as optimizing between tradeoffs to achieve a given objective. In other words, you'll almost always have to give up something to get something else. Purposefully choosing and embracing one tradeoff over another provides a framework to make better—and less stress-filled—decisions."[3]

A tradeoff is a decision where you believe you must accept more of attribute A for less of attribute B because you can't have both A and B simultaneously. Usually, in corporate strategy examples, we're referring to things like cost, quality, speed, flexibility, customization, and scalability. If we're talking about dating, your friends might tell you that you must trade off kindness, intelligence, and attractiveness. If you're lucky, you might get to choose two of the three, but you can't find someone who has them all. (Don't listen to them; you can. Well, I did.) In the opening example, framing the choice as a tradeoff would require you to pick sides between the group of employees and customers who oppose the law and those who support it.

Making tradeoffs assumes scarce or constrained resources. When we believe we have limited time, money, and attention, our decision-making shifts toward protecting those resources in the short term, and we become less attentive to other relevant considerations.[4] Recall that the Protect System makes us more sensitive to threats and easily distracted by the certainty of imminent dangers.⁵ Beliefs about scarcity can activate our Protect System and nudge us toward fleeing, freezing, or quickly choosing the first alternative instead of trying to find creative options. Indeed, framing decisions as a tradeoff is one way to manage this unwelcome psychological discomfort.

Historically, tradeoffs were prescribed to combat the illness of indecisiveness. In the late 1960s and 1970s, many US companies were large conglomerates like RJR Nabisco and Teledyne, with multiple divisions and products, making everything from cookies to cigarettes. They focused primarily on expansion, not efficiency. Ultimately, the organizations' lack of clarity, focus, and consistency doomed them to fail because they were slow, wasteful, and uncompetitive. Framing decisions as tradeoffs became a practical way to help executives make hard choices, and now many leaders think that making tradeoffs quickly is a sign of expertise and discipline. For example, companies like McDonald's learned to focus their operations on price-sensitive consumers, leading to practices that reduced costs and increased efficiencies, like using frozen hamburgers. People don't go to McDonald's to get a fresh, never-frozen, mouth-watering burger because we assume we can't have both high quality and low prices. The notion that making tradeoffs is always required for good decision-making has been extended so far that it's starting to wear thin. Does this medicine cure all decision-making maladies? Are there any boundaries to this rule of thumb?

Tradeoffs don't automatically appear in nature like rocks, rivers, or trees; they are ways of perceiving and framing situations, a product of how we understand the world around us. Saying that a tradeoff *must* be made implies at least two different actions. First, it could mean we must pick one option because we don't have an alternative that satisfies all our preferences. This is the most common interpretation. However, less often acknowledged is that we could revise our options to create better alternatives that satisfy competing values. For example, sometimes we must choose between Korean barbecue and tacos, and sometimes we can have Korean barbecue tacos. It depends on what restaurants are nearby, what ingredients we have in our pantry, our access to resources like money, a car, or a delivery service, and our imagination. If no local restaurant serves them, we could stop at the Korean barbecue restaurant and then pick up freshly pressed tortillas at the Mexican restaurant and make our own tacos at home. Conflicting criteria don't mean we should default to making a tradeoff. They can inspire us to create something new.

Decision-making scholars have over-emphasized the first interpretation (either/or) and downplayed the second (creating new options). Sometimes, we need to choose one available alternative even if it doesn't satisfy as many of our criteria as we would like, particularly when we don't have time, resources, or the capacity to create new options. The problem is that many decision-making gurus and executives assume making tradeoffs is the starting place for every decision. Like the over-prescription of drugs we once thought could do no harm, we're starting to see the side effects of this advice.

VICTORY HAS DEFEATED YOU

What would happen if you automatically made a tradeoff in every choice? If you quickly and consistently choose one set of values or relationships over another, you'll bear the cost of sacrificed relationships, ideas, and values. Imagine that your life partner always traded off your desires for their job. They have a work dinner when you want to try the new Colombian restaurant on the corner. When your friends want to go bar-hopping, they're too busy answering emails. When you're in the mood for some afternoon de-light, they're in the mood for an afternoon of de-partment meetings. Most of us would find this kind of life unsatisfying and unsustainable. Building a life where you can achieve more of your dreams and be a good partner, parent, sibling, child, and leader is possible. Most people aspire to balance multiple identities because we know that repeatedly trading off one meaningful relationship for another can cause irreparable damage when you're served with emancipation papers, pink slips, and divorce papers.

Similar risks show up for organizations. We can kill our brand to maximize shareholder value if we consistently trade off profits for quality. Companies that "offshored" their production to save costs are now "re-shoring" that same production to boost quality and regain lost market share. GE has brought some appliance manufacturing back to the US to build a more skilled workforce and avoid unpredictable transportation costs. Similarly, if doing what we are currently good at is always more important than trying new things, then like Blockbuster refusing to work with Netflix, we're just waiting for our business model to die. To be clear, I'm not arguing that organizational leaders should never make tradeoffs. Instead, I'm arguing that they should reconsider their default setting. Rather than starting with the assumption that tradeoffs are the norm and then making them at every opportunity, maybe try to avoid tradeoffs first, and then only make the tradeoffs if we *must*.

When a tradeoff cannot be avoided, leaders can implement choices in ways that minimize any harm and relational damage. For example, when raising product or service prices to pay a living wage to staff, owners can help customers better understand the cost they bear and why. Indeed, some restaurants that have done so have reported more loyal customers, and their satisfied employees also provided better service to those customers.[6] In these cases, leaders should work to improve the situation for those stakeholders whose interests are not fully met so they don't continue to get the short end of the stick in the next round of decisions.

Framing difficult decisions as tradeoffs helps people make choices quickly. But repeatedly trading off the same values can extract a high cost when the consequences of ignoring other vital considerations come back to bite us. When customers start buying from a competitor, when the cost of environmental disasters can no longer be externalized, and when a breakup text dampens your promotion celebration, making tradeoffs becomes a strategy that helps us make the immediate decision at the expense of the larger dream.

PROBLEM DIS-SOLVERS

Finding ways to avoid tradeoffs may sound good in theory, but what does it look like in practice? Let's examine reforestation, a carbon capture strategy essential to slowing the rise in global temperature. Currently, reforestation involves planting trees in nurseries, placing them in bags, and having volunteers walk long distances to dig holes and plant seedlings one at a time.

Obviously, planting trees after a wildfire is a time- and resource-intensive process, and forestry services face a tradeoff between cost and speed. The faster we need to reforest an area, the more people, greenhouses, time, and money are required. A company called Mast Reforestation, based in Portland, Oregon, has come up with a way to reduce costs and increase the speed of planting trees.[7] The company uses eight-foot-wide drones with a fifty-seven-pound payload of specially formulated tree seeds and nutrients to reforest land six times faster than standard practices. The drones can currently reforest forty acres in a day. By combining drone technology with best practices for growing trees, Mast Reforestation substantially decreases the cost of reforesting an acre, proving to be a vital tool in the fight against climate change.

In contrast, when a company leans toward a tradeoff for a particular stakeholder group, it leaves itself open to threats from competitors willing and able to reimagine that tradeoff. For example, suppose one company continually trades off employees for shareholders. In that case, some employees can find better work at a company that cares about attracting and retaining the best talent. If a company constantly squeezes its suppliers, those suppliers will work with other distributors as soon as possible. If one company doesn't offer a sustainable product, some customers will find a producer that does.[8] In each of these cases, when executives assume that fast decision-making is good decision-making, they may leave lucrative options on the table. Instead, to dissolve tradeoffs, we need to take the time to learn about our stakeholders' preferences, the limits of our resources, and where we have degrees of flexibility. When researchers examine successful negotiations, they find that offers made later in the negotiation tend to be more creative and satisfy more competing requirements than initial offers. Over time, both parties learn about each other's preferences, degrees of freedom, and goals, which they use to generate more creative ideas that grow the pie rather than cut it into smaller and smaller pieces.[9]

In moments of doubt, taking the time to learn about our situation and map the terrain more carefully is an investment that helps us generate more nuanced and creative options, dissolving tradeoffs that others find unsolvable.

Avoiding tradeoffs requires creativity. If you search online for images related to creativity, the results look like kindergartners were asked to draw a picture of an acid trip. You will see squiggly rainbow lines coming out of peoples' heads, clouds, arrows, and lightbulbs—lots of lightbulbs. (Yes, I stole one for the cover of this book.) The lightbulb has become *the* icon of creativity because we tend to focus on the "ah-ha moment" that feels like flipping a light switch. The lightbulb is an apt metaphor for creativity, but for reasons that have nothing to do with the illuminating moment of creative insight.

On February 3, 1879, Mosley Street in Newcastle, England, became the first street in the world to be lit with incandescent lightbulbs. "Oh, look, Nigel, all that horse shit is still there in the dark!" Today, it's hard to imagine a world without lightbulbs even as concern about light pollution intensifies. Yet the lighting of Mosley Street and the electric revolution it ushered in was not the product of a single moment of insight but of decades of innovation and diligent, creative practice. Today, hundreds, if not thousands, of great books and articles describe helpful creativity strategies like the kind that led to the ubiquity of the lightbulb.

For our purposes, I'll summarize three broad approaches that are most relevant to generating creative options when making difficult choices: (1) generating and comparing multiple options leads to better thinking, (2) recombining existing elements leads to novel alternatives, and (3) revising and refining options can better align our intent and impact.

GENERATING MULTIPLE OPTIONS

Despite the fake news propagated in many third-grade book reports, Thomas Edison did not invent the lightbulb; the invention can't be attributed to a single person. For decades before Edison, dozens of inventors, scientists, and hobbyists experimented with electricity to create a lasting light source. Early lightbulbs only lasted for a few minutes to a few hours. To increase their durability, inventors tested hundreds of filaments (the thin, flexible material that electric current passes through to generate light). Materials like tungsten, platinum, carbon, cotton, and bamboo were compared to each other to find the best candidate. In short, these inventors generated a variety of options and compared their relative performance to learn what would work best. Similarly, we make better decisions when we generate and compare multiple alternatives.

Think about the last time you had to buy a smartphone, laptop, camera, or another tech device. There are a mind-boggling number of options that we need to compare and contrast. We might not even know all the features and differences. What's the difference between RAM and CPU? How are those things different than storage? When we ask the teenaged salesperson, Kyle, he looks back at us with silent resignation as if we've just insulted his young life's work. We might start off thinking that we want the laptop model that looks cool, and then when we're in the store, we realize we need a model with longer battery life or a better warranty. Comparing options might lead us to think about things we hadn't considered before, like the repair cost.

When we compare different alternatives, we can discover things about our preferences, resources, and potential impacts that we might not have thought about before. Comparing multiple options can reveal implicit assumptions in our thinking; thus, our decision-making is improved when we make those assumptions explicit and reflect on their appropriateness.

But unlike buying existing products, when making difficult choices, we must generate multiple options before comparing them. As we've seen, it's natural for ideas to pop into our minds as we encounter a difficult decision. But instead of just running with those initial ideas, it's essential to take the time to generate options that don't come to mind so easily. Edison reportedly tried thousands of different materials when working on the lightbulb, seeking out tropical plant experts who might know of some durable fibers that he could experiment with. In contrast, today, decision-makers can easily fall into a "ready, fire, aim" approach, not taking the time to find and generate multiple options but moving quickly and efficiently in precisely the wrong direction.

We can generate more ideas when we take the time to ask questions that open possibilities before asking questions that shut them down. For example, researchers in one study showed that when people ask, "What *could* I do?" instead of "What *should* I do?" they generate more alternatives.[10] *Could* opens possibilities, and *should* narrows them down. Unfortunately, we tend to ask the *should* question too early; we generate and evaluate ideas simultaneously until we get to an option we like. To get more variety, separating idea generation and evaluation is essential. You never know if a kernel of an idea you reject early could be part of a valuable solution when adapted somehow. Creativity requires being intentional about gathering multiple diverging perspectives and evaluating them later to converge on the best way forward.

One way to generate multiple options is to use questions to trigger new ideas.[11] Questions like, "How could we benefit the least-well-off stakeholder?" and "What might our heroes do in this situation?" can encourage us to look beyond our initial gut reaction. For example, suppose you changed your goals from making the fastest or most profitable decision to making the most sustainable one or the one that would make you proud. These questions work by forcing us to consider things beyond our initial intuition. Here's a list of some sample questions:

- What could you do if you had no constraints?
- What could you do that might cause the least harm?
- What actions could preserve important relationships?
- What could you do that would satisfy the most commonly held principles or rules in a novel or unexpected way?
- What actions would you be most proud of?
- What could you never do?
- What could you do to avoid tradeoffs?

If we applied some of these questions to the decision about addressing the transgender healthcare law at the start of this chapter, we might generate a diverse set of initial ideas like:

- Don't openly support or oppose the law.
- Talk internally about opposing the law, but not externally.
- Financially support organizations opposing the law.
- Pick a side to support or oppose.
- Engage in non-profit community work.
- Give employees the ability to designate funds for legal advocacy.

- Provide a benefit or discount on insurance to all or some of your customers.

- Meet with transgender groups to better understand the impact of the law on them.

- Join or start a coalition of businesses to oppose the law.

- Find a way to legally protect your company from government interference.

- Support your state legislature.

- Craft a statement that lists your reasons for your decision.

- Meet with customers to understand how they think about the proposed law.

- Ignore the law.

- Use your expertise in healthcare to increase awareness about available services.

- Increase company support for trans employees and customers.

- Provide more coverage for trans customers and employees than your competitors currently do.

- Have employees who oppose the law talk with customers who don't.

- Make a personal donation to fight the law, not using company funds.

- Do nothing.

At this stage, we might have negative, positive, or ambivalent reactions to some of the ideas on the list. Understanding your response to different alternatives can help you refine your values and get a clearer picture of how to achieve them as you articulate why you think specific options are more or less likely to work. Whether purchasing the latest gadgets like a Wi-Fi-enabled water heater, smart stepladder, and Bluetooth septic tank or choosing how to move forward in a difficult situation, generating and subsequently evaluating multiple options is critical.

RECOMBINATION

The incandescent bulb is made up of three main technologies: a filament, a vacuum tube, and a source of electric current. The original filament-based arc lamp was created forty-four years before people got lit on Mosley Street. Batteries that stored sufficient electricity were available seventy-nine years earlier, and vacuums had been invented two hundred thirty-four years prior. Some historians will quibble with those exact dates, but it's safe to say that each component technology existed for *decades* before the lightbulb. The lightbulb's creation occurred by recombining existing technologies into more novel forms.[12] Indeed, all innovations *recombine* existing concepts, tools, and practices to produce something novel and valuable.

Recombining insights today from different fields led to a new visionary eyecare breakthrough. Dr. Silver, an optometrist with previous training in physics, has invented a liquid lens for glasses. This thin optical lens can be adjusted with a knob in realtime, just like focusing a pair of binoculars. With liquid lenses, there is no longer a need to go to the optometrist and sit through thirty minutes of being asked, "Which is clearer, one or two?" We all know they both look the same and that they're just screwing with us! Instead, liquid lenses can cheaply correct vision in populations that do not have access to eyecare, potentially billions around the globe. Silver works with Dow Corning and plans to develop and give away billions of adjustable liquid lens glasses. This innovation would not have been possible without recombining knowledge from both physics and optometry.[13]

Recombining ideas allows us to benefit from competing values. One of my favorite examples comes from the behind-the-scenes footage from *The Lord of the Rings*. I enjoyed the movies, but I loved watching the footage of the talented set designers, costume makers, and miniatures teams even more. According to the "Taming of Smeagol" video in the *Two Towers* DVD boxed set, there were heated arguments in the early stages of production about who would animate the computer-generated character Gollum, leaving director Peter Jackson to make a hard choice. Historically, keyframe animators would pose the character frame by frame like a digital stop-motion puppet. However, the newly created motion capture group also coveted the precious opportunity to animate

Gollum because they could re-create realistic movement more cheaply and quickly by having actor Andy Serkis wear tracking dots. Apparently, these competing approaches led to disputes at Weta Digital, with both teams arguing that they should be given the job. If he believed that good decision-making was fast decision-making, Jackson could have just picked one of the well-qualified teams and moved on to the thousands of other pressing decisions he had to make. Instead, he asked the teams to work together. They realized that using motion capture for larger body movements and keyframe animation for more fine-grained facial and hand gestures created the most believable overall performance. Without recombining the best of motion capture and keyframe animation, the Academy Award–winning work that brought Gollum to life (and death) would have been impossible.

When recombining options in novel and useful ways, we can use two specific strategies: rebricking and bundling.

Rebricking

As another example of recombination, LEGO celebrates how customers take LEGO bricks from different kits and make completely different creations out of them. You can stack pieces from the *Titanic* kit to build an iceberg, the kit for a *Star Wars* Imperial AT-AT to make a Rebel X-Wing, or turn the kit for the Real Madrid stadium into the FC Barcelona stadium (I can't guarantee your safety if you do, but I'm just saying it's theoretically possible). LEGO calls it *rebricking*, rearranging your building blocks to form something unexpected and new. Despite not using any LEGO bricks, the lightbulb provides an example of rebricking. Inventors broke the lightbulb down into a few essential parts, like a glowing filament and some kind of contained gas, to prevent the filament from oxidizing. Then, they tried putting those pieces together in different ways—multiple combinations of filaments and other gases (including argon, nitrogen, ethyl alcohol, and no gas at all) to optimize the amount and duration of the light produced.

The same principle can be applied to your options when making difficult choices. Returning to the choice about the transgender law, let's say that you want to address your employees directly and talk about the law. Rebricking would mean breaking down that option into its constituent pieces and rearranging them to maximize the benefits and minimize risks. When discussing the situation with your employees, you must decide "who, what, where, when, why, and how." For "who," it could be you; you could also bring an employee representative with you, an HR official, or a trans employee with a different perspective on the law. For "what," it could be sharing your perspective, posing questions to a panel, and sharing divergent viewpoints. For "when," you could do it during work hours, hold a virtual session, or schedule something after work. Each of these choices sends very different signals to your employees and contributes to the success of your idea. Holding the session during work hours would signal how important the issue is to you and the company. On the other hand, you could do more damage if the conversation comes across as hurried and haphazard. By breaking the option down and rebuilding it intentionally, aligning each element to your intended goals, you increase your odds of satisfying multiple criteria, such as supporting marginalized groups and building trust with those who don't prioritize the issue.

A typical business deal might have degrees of freedom in cost, quality, time, effort, communication levels, transaction frequency, inputs, and volume, each offering an opportunity to minimize risks and increase your intended impacts. Whether turning the Death Star into the Millennium Falcon or optimizing your engagement with employees, rebricking allows you to break an option into its components and build it back up into something more consistent with your intentions.

Bundling

Marcellin Jobard, Frederick de Moleyns, John W. Starr, Henry Woodward, Alessandro Cruto, Moses G. Farmer, and Alexander Lodygin were some inventors who created commercially viable incandescent lightbulbs before Thomas Edison. So why do so many third-graders credit Edison with this invention? Because in addition to the lightbulb, Edison and the Menlo Park mafia built a larger system to make the lightbulb readily available. They designed a conduit system for electricity, created the first electric meter, and built the first power plants. All these supporting inventions helped make Edison's lightbulb the dominant one. Like Edison's system, which brought together multiple components, a second strategy for recombination is to bundle options to reinforce the benefits and reduce negative impacts.

For example, returning to the decision about the transgender law, you could speak with your employees, send a letter to your customers, make a personal donation to an organization working to oppose the law, and provide increased support and resources for trans employees and customers. In short, you could pick "A" from your list of options, but if you picked "A" and also did "C," "E," and "F," you could mitigate some of the risks of only choosing "A" and reinforce some of the benefits. A bundle of actions can help you address multiple goals because it's unlikely that any one act will satisfy all the relevant criteria.

Ensuring the set is held together by an overall strategy and assemblage of values is essential when bundling actions. Otherwise, you risk being a hypocrite by saying one thing to one group and something else to another group. For example, an ineffective bundle would be saying, "We support our transgender community members and will work to oppose the law," to your employees, and "We don't get involved in political issues" to your customers. Bundling works best when there is a clear connection across the actions in the bundle that reinforces the outcomes you are trying to create.

USING THE MAP TO REFINE YOUR OPTIONS

After generating multiple options and recombining (by rebricking and bundling), you may settle on a few alternatives that you believe will most likely help you achieve your intentions. Next, we take our best options and hold them up to our list of issues from each of the four ethical lenses: principles, character, consequences, and relationships. The goal is to identify the most significant remaining risks ahead of time and use those risks to improve your alternatives. Looking for weaknesses in the original system of incandescent lights led to innovations like the fluorescent lightbulb when factories needed cheaper, longer-lasting lamps during World War I. When customers became increasingly concerned about sustainability, companies invented LED bulbs.

You might look at the alternatives you have generated and see that one remaining risk is that your current action doesn't say anything about how the company will spend resources to oppose the law. So, you can refine your plans to be more explicit about your reasons. In addition, you might notice that a portion of your workforce and community don't want you to get involved, so you need a better justification about why you are taking the time and effort to address this issue. As you hold up your options to the list of issues and explicitly look for weaknesses, you will see that there are things you can add, refine, and improve to address these concerns.

Picture yourself as a navigator tracing your preferred path on a map and looking ahead for obstacles, errors, and dangers. We, too, can use the relevant issues from each lens to simulate and anticipate the most likely pushback, misunderstandings, and concerns. For example, tracing out your preferred path can allow you to identify if you have enough supplies for the trip, where to camp safely, and to adjust when you encounter specific obstacles. You might cycle through this process before feeling confident enough to start testing and implementing your choice.

Moments of doubt ask us to consider creating new paths that are not obvious at first. This takes creativity and perseverance to generate, recombine, and refine options. Because we tend to believe that good decision-making is fast decision-making, we treat option creation as a *single point in time*, a flip of a switch, when it's actually a process. Just as it took decades of disciplined experimentation by hundreds of people to create the lightbulb, it takes time and effort to generate and refine alternatives when confronting moments of doubt. The upside of creating new options is avoiding trading off the things you care about.

The downside is that it takes time and perseverance. The inventor of the Dyson vacuum, which basically uses a controlled tornado to improve suction, reportedly created 5,127 prototypes before finding the one that worked. Similarly, scientists in labs spend their entire careers trying to find a novel medicine, a new bacteria, or a gene. For some, that investment in creating novel solutions is worth the time and effort; for others, it's not. We might give up after trying one prototype or conclude that something is impossible after failing a dozen times.

But if sound research has shown that these innovation practices can spark creative insight, why do some of us give up so quickly and choose to stay in the dark?

CONFRONTING WHAT THE BRAIN WANTS TO AVOID

Executive: I think these creativity practices will help my team, but how do I deal with the fact that my company doesn't have the time or patience to generate new ideas? They want me to get things done yesterday.

Me: What happens when you try to apply these tools at work?

Executive: Well, as a leader, my team expects me to have all the answers. We are an efficiency-focused organization; we calculate the hourly cost of each meeting. I will get blamed for wasting thousands of dollars to brainstorm and generate ideas that don't get used. Honestly, it's easier for me to just stick to our normal ways of doing things and avoid the eye rolls my team will give me. By the time I'm promoted out, someone else can deal with the mess.

Over the years, I've encountered several leaders who want to innovate and avoid tradeoffs, like this candid executive, but don't use creativity practices because they are wary of being seen as less of an expert and tired of fighting organizational pressures that favor quick and sloppy decision-making. When leaders face pressures to maximize metrics, cross off tasks on the never-ending list of things to do, and believe they'll never make everyone happy, they abandon their attempts to create novel alternatives. The roots of this problem lie in the discomfort of stepping into the unknown. That discomfort is the Protect System activating. Organizational systems, processes, incentives, and cultural assumptions can either alleviate or aggravate those discomforts. For example, organizations have routines, like hour-long meetings. Being creative doesn't always neatly fit into that time frame, so people are less likely to arrange and attend longer meetings with more amorphous goals and deliverables. "Hmm. I don't think I can be the smartest person in this meeting. Request declined."

The idea that good decision-makers are fast decision-makers is so ingrained in us that some leaders would rather seize the immediate reward of moving forward boldly than take a little more time to explore, learn, adapt, and increase their chances of success. We might think these executives should demonstrate more self-control to stick with the challenge when things inevitably get difficult. After all, self-control is supposed to help us stay in line with our overarching goals despite distractions. We're supposed to demonstrate self-control when we focus on our tasks, avoid doomscrolling, and reduce our exposure to addictive foods, games, and people.

But when we look around, instead of self-control, we see that people who face uncertainty, particularly tasks involving creativity, can give up quickly. To explain these fumbles, pivots, falls off the wagon, snafus, and lunges for the marshmallow in front of us, psychologists have described self-control primarily as a battery with a finite set of resources. This implies that once we deplete the energy in the battery, we need to refill it before we can continue drawing it down for other demanding tasks. We'll call this idea the battery model of self-control for short.

Evidence for the battery model involves dozens of studies demonstrating that difficult tasks like eating radishes instead of chocolate,[14] suppressing emotions,[15] making an attitude-inconsistent choice,[16] or doing something exhausting[17] all decrease performance on subsequent tasks that require self-control. Studies like these helped make the battery model dominant and the source of much advice about enduring difficult tasks. Yet, surprisingly, new evidence is draining support for that once-powerful view.

FROM DEPLETION TO DESIRE

While the battery model was intuitively appealing and easy to understand, some researchers noticed it didn't stand up to further scrutiny. For example, where exactly is this battery in the body, and what exactly is the "energy" that it uses? No one could find it or see it. Experiments revealed it wasn't blood glucose,[18] lack of sleep,[19] or neurons becoming fried.

In addition to being unable to find the "battery," laboratory tests started to generate results that the battery model couldn't explain (for example, when people were *motivated* to complete the difficult task like eating radishes, or making a difficult choice, the drop in performance disappeared in the subsequent self-control tasks).[20] Furthermore, when researchers gave participants quick breaks that allowed them to watch a favorite television show, smoke a cigarette, pray, or affirm one of their core values, their seemingly depleted "batteries" became instantly replenished. Their performance in subsequent tasks returned to baseline. One research team said, "Increased task motivation, perceptions of vitality, and beliefs that self-control is unlimited can all attenuate the depletion effect."[21] This new data raises the question of whether it makes sense to talk about self-control as a battery if it can be recharged almost instantly. So, if self-control is not a battery, what is it?

To better understand the updated way to think about self-control, we need to return briefly to our friend, the Pause and Piece-Together System—the brain system that is active when we encounter something unexpected, the one that regulates conflicts within and across the Pursue and Protect Systems. When this system is active (as it often is during creative tasks), it can also increase anxiety because it has circuitry directly connected to the amygdala, the fear and threat center of the brain. Basically, extended activation of the Pause and Piece-Together System also puts the Protect System on standby just in case you realize that you need to flee or fight your way out of the current predicament you're making sense of.[22] Research has shown that as people spend more time Pausing and Piecing Together, they become increasingly attuned to negative signals and stimuli. That's why neuroscientists say that exercising cognitive control "is intrinsically aversive."[23] Longer durations of pausing and piecing together can increase your risk in some situations, making you more susceptible to threats or causing you to forgo other life-sustaining activities like searching for food. Instead of getting stuck in this state, the brain has a built-in system to make you periodically look around and reevaluate your strategy. In short, it's as if the more time our scouts spend exploring and noticing the new surroundings, the more nervous their accomplice becomes, placing the key in the ignition and revving the engine in case things get out of hand and they need to make a quick getaway.

Instead of a hardwired battery, the current thinking is that natural selection has favored a model of flexible self-control.[24] This flexible system helps people balance persistence in the current uncertain activity with the potential payoff of switching to something new. When generating multiple ideas, comparing alternatives, mapping new territories, or trying out different combinations, our chances of distraction increase as the current task feels more difficult. It's as if the brain is saying, "Hey, this is hard. Are you sure you want to continue? Maybe we will find more dopamine if we check out something over there?"

For example, when we've been working on our term paper, doing our taxes, or trying to find a way to dissolve a tradeoff, it becomes more tempting to check our social media feed to see who liked our post (and more importantly, who didn't), stop by and chat with our hilarious coworker, or start watching video after video on how to braise short ribs. Similarly, in relationships, we all hit a period when things get complicated, and we can choose to address that difficulty or look around for someone else. We might think, "I'd rather not learn how to argue more effectively with my current partner. I'll log onto eHarmony and see if I can find someone who won't squeeze the toothpaste from the middle."

When our brains ask us to reevaluate our current path, and we see more immediately rewarding options elsewhere, we need a compelling reason to stay the course.

KEEP YOUR EYES ON THE PRIZE

To avoid giving up on our creative efforts or any efforts under conditions of uncertainty, we need to find ways of also triggering the Pursue System while we are in the middle of learning. Our mental maps must feature some dopaminergic rewards we care about, like money, friendship, admiration, gratitude, competence, helping others, or world domination. We can even learn to find the challenge itself rewarding: "This is so hard, but it's so awesome!" I can really feel the burn!

Neuroscientific studies suggest that this is exactly what people with a growth mindset do when confronting a challenge. For example, when they go for a run, people with a growth mindset about running trigger a small dopamine spike when they put on their shoes, again when they make it to the next telephone pole, and again when they laugh in conversation with their friends, which, like a series of breadcrumbs on a trail, carry them to the bigger dopamine reward at the end of the run.[25] In contrast, individuals with a fixed mindset about running are more likely to wait for the dopamine at the end of the run, increasing the odds that they find the actual running aversive. (I'm not a good runner, and I never will be! Wait, am I running away from running? Help!) As a result, they are more likely to get distracted and give up when something else with a higher expected dopamine spike comes along their path. "I don't need to finish the run; I'll stop at this Korean barbecue taco truck and have a second breakfast."

Self-control is related to our ability to suppress or inhibit distractions; psychologists now think that ability is connected to our motivation. The current research on self-control suggests people don't drain their battery and lose the ability to control themselves. Rather, they prefer to indulge in more enjoyable pursuits where the dopaminergic payoff is more immediate and certain, after exercising self-control. This new model suggests that dips in self-control are driven by reluctance, not fatigue.[26] The longer we pause and piece together the harder it can be to see the next breadcrumb.

When we change the diagnosis, we should change the remedies, too. It's not so much that we need considerable rest and time to recharge the battery; indeed, depending on how we "recharge," we might not return to the task.

When the brain inevitably asks, *Are you sure you want to continue?* we need to create the next enticing breadcrumb in response. For example, feedback and praise are reinforcers to promote continued self-control under challenging situations. As another example, when gamblers are given intermittent rewards, with random payouts, where spikes of dopamine are harder to predict, they don't get tired of gambling even when they have been at the craps table for hours betting their kids' college fund on a hard six, because the intermittent rewards help keep the promise of a big payday just around the corner. We all can think of examples that fit this motivation model of self-control, like the single father who works two jobs and still makes time to help his kids with a science project because he's motivated to support them. Think of teachers who teach for hours on end because they enjoy interacting with their students, and the marathoner who finds a second wind and runs faster as she spots the finish line.

The current evidence supports the idea that self-control is potentially unlimited when fueled by high motivation. Like for the inventor who tries the thousandth prototype because she imagines changing the world every time she starts over, the scientist who imagines saving millions of lives when the experiments don't work, and the artist who focuses on the joy of painting despite what the critics say, sustaining our creative efforts is inextricable from our motivation. We may attach dopamine to different things, but if those things aren't a part of our mindscape when we pause and piece together, our ability to deal with distractions drops. We're more likely to switch to other tasks that promise a more proximate reward. Periodically thinking of our motivational breadcrumbs helps calm the Protect System and encourages the Pause and Piece-Together System to help create enough focus and flexibility to achieve our goals.

By sharing the motivation model of self-control, I don't intend to make tired people feel guilty or encourage a culture of workaholism. My goal is to help you understand how your self-control works so that you can use it strategically. While self-control may not function as a battery, the impact of sleep and rest on learning is becoming more apparent, and in that domain, we know that pushing the boundaries can be detrimental to the quality of your work. If pursuing our goals is like a hike, then I'm not saying that we shouldn't rest as much as we need to keep our bodies in shape for climbing. I am saying that we should understand how our motivation and self-control work together to avoid giving up on the hike altogether when it inevitably gets challenging and we just happen to spot a shortcut.

Conveniently, findings from creativity science combine nicely with the motivation model of self-control. Without using the same words, creativity researchers show that individuals and organizations can sustain creative efforts by promoting the Pursue System's activation and limiting the Protect System. For example, participants in a lab who report feeling good because they listen to their favorite song, watch a standup comedy routine, or enjoy a tasty snack perform better on divergent thinking exercises and other standard creativity tests than participants in control conditions.[27] Similarly, positive moods increase the number and type of creative outputs, even when researchers measure creativity in different ways.[28] In one study, researchers had pairs of participants engage in a creative bargaining task. To succeed, they had to share information and develop an innovative solution. Participants in a positive mood were more likely to succeed at the task. These findings have been replicated outside the lab as well.[29] When researchers asked members of project teams to reflect daily on their progress and asked them questions about their moods, they found that positive moods were correlated to the number of creative ideas about their projects, even though they were not instructed to write about creativity.[30] In general, the more relaxed and optimistic we feel, the more we can associate disparate ideas that can lead to innovative solutions. That's why people report having moments of insight in the shower, bathtub, or bed. Don't move, honey!—I'll be right back. I just need to jot down my next startup idea!

In contrast, when people's Protect Systems are activated, the flexible thinking that creativity requires is more challenging to maintain. Sure, sometimes negative moods can signal that something needs to change and can motivate us to find better solutions,[31] but social, financial, and emotional risks generally heighten amygdala activation and make it harder to sustain cognitive control. We become certain that the obstacles will block our way forward. Research confirms that individuals and teams are less creative when the boss doesn't like to hear bad news or the team is not a safe place to be candid.[32] When your boss asks for your ideas but never takes them, tells you the answer she wants before asking for your input, shuts down ideas because "we already tried that once in 1993," and celebrates results over efforts, we all feel a little less able and less excited to dip our toe into the unknown. Like the candid executive who felt unsupported in being creative at work, we might worry that we will be seen as a failure if we try to practice creativity. We find ways to minimize those negative emotions by ignoring the problem, focusing on something we already know how to solve, kicking the can down the road, and sometimes framing the problem as a tradeoff that we can quickly make and move on.[33]

So, what does all this talk about self-control and motivation mean for our ability to generate and refine ideas when facing moments of doubt?

First, we must accept that motivation naturally waxes and wanes. Anticipating ups and downs can help us weather inevitable storms. For example, when generating ideas, I might have difficulty concentrating; instead of interpreting that difficulty as a signal that the task is unimportant and that I should do something else, I could see it as a natural part of the work and know that the feeling will pass. Setting the expectation that creativity requires a different method from normal operations can help people anticipate, interpret, and manage any unexpected Protect System activity. When we're asked to do something new and challenging, and our pulse quickens or our breathing becomes shallow, some of us might interpret our body's reaction as threatening and find ways to exit stage left. Others might interpret those same physiological signals as a sign that they think the task is an opportunity to push themselves.[34] When we anticipate negative physiological responses, we can reduce the chance of being hijacked and derailed by them. Similarly, knowing that motivation changes means we don't have to anxiously wait for that "ah-ha" moment to begin creative work. When ideas don't come rushing forth, people who practice creativity well don't take it as a sign that they're not good at the task, just that it can be hard for everyone to get started. As any person in a creative role will tell you, "Inspiration is for amateurs; the rest of us just show up and get to work." When we start to feel less motivated, having a clear short-term goal or task can help us move in the right direction.

Second, when making hard choices or encountering any activity that requires dealing with uncertainty, we need a clear reason for *why* we are confronting that uncertainty. We need to articulate, see, and experience the dopamine motivators that will help us pursue improvement rather than give up when a shiny something-else comes along. This can mean clarifying your purpose, connecting with relationships that matter, identifying the skills you want to improve, being the first to pull something off, proving someone wrong, or doing something small that needs to be done.[35] But there are limits to this strategy. If we spend too much time imagining these benefits, we can also give up on our goals when our imagination substitutes for the real thing. The relationship between the task that needs to be done and the reason why we're doing it is critical.[36] That link needs to show up periodically in how we think about and experience our efforts.

Third, when you inevitably feel fatigued or look around for something to switch to, provide yourself with small dopamine rewards to get back to the task, and be sure to watch out for bigger derailers that prevent your return. Examples of small rewards are enjoyable conversations, snacks, being outside, seeing the faces of the people you care about, and connecting back to the positive impacts of your task. These rewards must be intermittent, making it hard for your brain to anticipate and become desensitized to them over time. Be sure to create and take advantage of clear rest stops, but be careful not to turn those rest stops into off-ramps.

Finally, when engaging in the creative process, guard against signals that can trigger the Protect System. Threats from negative social judgment, penalties for out-of-the-box thinking, lack of gratitude for creative or risky efforts, red tape, dealing with office jerks, and a lack of constructive feedback kill motivation with a thousand little cuts. Organizational leaders must be vigilant for these derailers and remove obstacles that make it more likely that the team will abandon creative challenges or will only explore safe territory.

When making difficult decisions it can be tempting to quickly make a tradeoff and move on with your life. Whether you're deciding how to handle a situation where employees and customers disagree with each other or finding ways to integrate more than one of your identities, avoiding tradeoffs in difficult choices requires overcoming several common misconceptions. First, we tend to think that good decision-makers are fast decision-makers and thus—to look and feel "good"—make more tradeoffs than necessary. Second, we assume that creating options happens at a single point in time, not during a process that takes investment; therefore, we avoid the work of creating alternatives that can help us dissolve tradeoffs. Third, we think our self-control is like a battery and underutilize our motivation to help us persevere through the difficulty of creative tasks. There are no simple rules of thumb to generate creative alternatives, such as *always trade off X for Y*. Instead, you must carefully understand your situation, including your degree of freedom and the resources available to you, be willing to generate ideas, and work with others to improve them. (See appendix tool 3.) When the paths in front of us take us to places we'd rather avoid and force us to become people we'd rather not be, we don't always have to default to the options in front of us. Sometimes, but not always, we can blaze our own trail home.

5

———

Addicted to Feeling Right

YOU WORK FOR A DIGITAL EDUCATION COMPANY that creates online games for schoolchildren to help them learn math, reading, and science. Your employees are passionate about using technology to ignite children's love of learning. Your team of six developers has been with you since the beginning; they are like your family, and you've always taken good care of them.

Recently, your team finished studying the usage patterns across all your games to learn how to make them more effective and enjoyable. The team discovered that students play for longer and more often when your games make digital rewards more engaging, frequent, and random. The bright lights, sounds, and animations keep children glued to the apps. Kids play almost twice as long (and learn more) when the games use rewards that resemble intermittent gambling payouts. The team suggests optimizing these rewards across all your games and making them the default setting. In addition, their analysis shows that it's critical to impress teachers, parents, and students in the initial twelve-week trial period because once a school district selects an app vendor, the odds of switching are relatively low. By showing that students play longer and learn more from your games than competitors, you stand a better chance of increasing adoption and thus might be able to give your team raises.

However (because there's always got to be a complication), one of your developers, Jean, sends you a somewhat concerning set of research articles. The research shows early childhood exposure to gambling can change brain development. Specifically, the changes in the number and sensitivity of their dopamine receptors make it slightly more likely that students will take risks in adolescence and adulthood.[1]

Jean is unsure if these concerns are overblown, but she wonders if you should consider these findings when changing your game designs. For example, could the specific rewards designed in your games impact the development of children's brains, increasing students' eventual risk of gambling, drug use, and unsafe sex practices? Additionally, the largest segment of your user base comes from homes of lower socioeconomic status. According to recent government reports, this group is already at a higher risk for several types of addiction.

Of course, many factors determine whether someone becomes more risk-seeking, and your games are only one small experience in a child's life full of exposures. Also, it's not like you're directly increasing children's risks of becoming addicted to harmful substances like junk food and opioids. You're using these features to motivate them to learn math and reading, which can boost their odds of loving learning, graduating college, and getting better jobs.

You also think about your own children and how you monitor their screen time and set boundaries for the types of content they're allowed to view. You know that some kinds of technology can be addictive, and you believe that parents are responsible for determining what's suitable for their kids. So, you're unsure if this is a problem you really need to worry about. There are thousands of children across the country whose risk-seeking behavior may or may not increase slightly versus six people in your office you care deeply about who will likely lose their jobs if you can't sign up more school districts.

Does this even count as a moment of doubt? Would you apply the reward features to the app?

In this type of decision, you are asked to think about an issue that seems small and innocuous on the first pass, yet on a second pass, the adverse effects are more noticeable. For example, if every app made by anyone used addictive features and children used those apps all day, their risk for other addictions would increase.

Our everyday life abounds with relatively harmless practices when conducted on a small scale, but they become problematic with increasing frequency. For example, drinking one beer is not usually a problem, but drinking fifteen in one night is a life-or-death issue. If one person eats a steak for dinner, it's no big deal, but if everyone eats steak every night, we could not sustain the environmental impacts. Similar concerns exist for driving a gasoline-engine car, eating sugar, gentrification, repeating jokes, checking social media, not donating to charity, and reposting a questionable news story.

In choices where small harms can scale, it's easy to identify things as clearly right and wrong when we look from one distant horizon to another. Still, when we look down at our feet, we find ourselves standing on a gradient, seeing subtle, incremental changes that make it challenging to determine precisely where things cross the line. Yet we must draw the line somewhere. When small harms are scalable, we can experience doubt about when and where to stop. And we see examples of these makeshift guardrails when people declare rules like, "I can have pork but not beef, and only on Thursdays." "To help the environment, I will recycle and buy solar panels, but I won't give up my Aston Martin DB9." We might think that our reasons for drawing these lines are purely personal and not the business of others like our parents, the village elders, the clergy, courts, your team, the king, or the mafia don. But we'd be wrong. Let me tell you why.

REASON-GIVING

Three-year-olds (unlike babies) can do some marvelous things. They can say about nine hundred words. They can learn to take turns when playing Candy Land. Three-year-olds can stop you dead in your tracks and hold you hostage when they slowly uncap a Sharpie pen near your new white sofa. They can tell it like it is when they tell you that your nose is big, that your ears are hairy, and that you compensate for insecurities through humor. Another interesting thing happens around thirty-six months, making children even more lovable and (slightly) easier to live with—they learn to ask for and give reasons.

To learn more about why this happens, researchers asked three-year-olds in an experiment to work with a partner to place different items in a zoo. Some items were things you would expect to see, like reptiles, ice, flowers, cages, and overpriced snacks. Others, like a piano, were unconventional. Children gave fewer reasons when choosing where to place the conventional items like the ice (near the polar bears, duh),[2] but more reasons when discussing where to place the unconventional items because they didn't share a perspective on where a piano should go. By the time children reach age seven, they become much more adept at giving and assessing the quality of reasons. Children also start to separate good reasons from bad ones and prefer to interact with peers they consider reasonable.[3] These studies show that reason-giving requires young human brains to recognize what others see and know is different from what they see and know.[4]

Experiments like these suggest that reason-giving has evolved to help facilitate cooperation. To assess this hypothesis, researchers compared children in two conditions. In the competitive condition, only one child would be rewarded for completing the task. In the cooperative condition, both children would be rewarded if they completed the task. Five- and seven-year-olds produced more reasons and engaged with their partners more in the cooperative condition. In the competitive condition, there were fewer total reasons given.[5]

These studies show that children and adults give reasons to influence how others see the world in order to coordinate their actions. We do this because our actions can surprise others. Imagine the nightmare of living with someone whose behavior you could not predict or understand, such as the roommate who makes meth in the bathtub, the officemate who cooks leftover garlic salmon in the breakroom microwave, or the manic first-time shopper at Costco who buys buckets of ranch dressing. As people make sense of surprising (even disturbing) behaviors, their interpretation of those actions shapes their subsequent emotions. When we realize that our roommate is buying buckets of ranch dressing to donate to the food bank, we breathe a sigh of relief. On the other hand, if we believe that our roommate is experimenting with meth production to start the "Uber for blue sky delivery," we get anxious about our safety. Positive interpretations of surprising behavior generally lead to positive emotions. Negative interpretations lead to anger, anxiety, resentment, and frustration. Reason-giving helps us to make our choices and actions more intelligible and predictable to others, to bring our interpretations in line with theirs, and to reduce the chance they view our decisions negatively.

Indeed, when we can't give *good* reasons for our choices, there are social consequences ranging from eye rolls (when we explain that we are late to the party because our three-year-old took two hours to put on their shoes) to jail time (when we explain we left that three-year-old at home to finish drawing their Sharpie mural on the couch). Giving better reasons for our decisions improves our relationships with others and can minimize punishment for harm. Reason-giving is such an essential part of being a social species that anticipating giving reasons to others doesn't just change what we say about our choices; surprisingly, it changes how we make them.

YOUR BRAIN ON ACCOUNTABILITY

Imagine that you must choose between two concerts you could see tomorrow night. One is a reggae show, and the other is a folk music band. You like them both equally. However, next week, your friend Marcie will be in town for a merger and acquisition meeting, and she's a big fan of reggae legend Peter Tosh. Will anticipating your meeting with Marcie—and the stories you could tell her!—make it more likely that you will choose to see the reggae concert? If you were like the volunteers in the following experiment, then it would. Researchers asked college students to choose a punishment for a classmate accused of cheating. Some students were told before making the decision that they would explain their decision to a student honor court representative. Others were told they would explain their decision to the professor who brought the charge. The students recommended harsher punishments if they expected to meet with the professor.[6] Knowing that we will have to give reasons for our choices to a specific person or group before we make a choice changes our decisions.

We see this same effect when managers feel more accountable to shareholders, doctors to drug companies, politicians to major donors, and teachers to their principals. Likewise, when MBA students are instructed to be ready to explain their choices to another student, their thinking shifts toward their audience.[7] The same pattern has been documented for insurance agents,[8] telecommunications workers,[9] and professional auditors.[10] In each case, anticipating giving reasons to a specific person or group shifts our thinking more in line with what we imagine our audience wants.[11] But we don't always know whom we'll have to give reason. So what happens then?

When decision-makers don't know their audience, research demonstrates that they prepare more effectively, think in more complex ways, take multiple perspectives, and are more likely to criticize their own views.[12] For example, when they didn't know the opinion of their evaluators, auditors wrote more thorough justifications for their audit choices. They were more likely to qualify their conclusions to cover their bases and recognize both the strengths and weaknesses of a particular recommendation.[13] Knowing that you will have to give reasons to someone but not knowing the audience's view is a generally effective strategy for removing decision-making errors from lack of attention, effort, or self-awareness.

Our decisions aren't just influenced by information about *who we are accountable to*, but also by *what we are accountable for*. Specifically, holding people responsible for their decision-making process rather than only their outcomes changes their choices. When researchers asked purchasing managers to justify not only the final decision but also the process they used to make their selections, they subsequently spent more time and effort diligently analyzing competing products.[14] Similarly, when negotiators are rewarded for sticking to a prescribed negotiation process, they are more likely to notice compatible interests with their counterparts than negotiators who are incentivized to win the deal.[15] In some laboratory situations, telling powerful people they must explain their decision-making process reduces their selfish behavior.[16] In short, just like not knowing who you are accountable to, accountability for the *process* can promote learning and more careful consideration.[17]

Knowing that we will have to give reasons to others changes what we pay attention to and decide. When we don't know who we are accountable to but know we will still have to give reasons to someone, we tend to be more prepared, be more open to learning, and think more carefully and thoroughly. In these situations, our goal is to make a good decision that is justifiable to our audience. In the studies we have described so far, whether deciding on the punishment of a classmate, the amount of a client's money to invest, or how thorough to be in a research, people know they will have to give reasons to someone *before* they make their choice. What happens when they find out they must give reasons *after*? Whether it occurs before or after a choice, learning that we must give reasons should have the same impact on our thinking, right? Nope. Not at all.

SHIELDS UP

On December 21, 1954, a group of people in Oak Park, Illinois, waited outside in the freezing cold to be escorted beyond the galaxy by alien saviors. The Seekers believed a flood would destroy most of the western US the following day, so they were waiting to be saved from the impending deluge. The group's leader, Dorothy Martin, believed she was receiving prophetic messages from planet Clarion. In anticipation of their departure, several group members quit their jobs, ended meaningful relationships, and gave away their prized possessions. Unsurprisingly, the aliens (and the flood) did not materialize, but a group of strange-looking social psychologists appeared to see how the cult would cope when their beliefs were disconfirmed. The psychologists noticed that the group initially made excuses, like, "People were wearing too much metal, which made it hard for the aliens to find them," "The aliens feared large crowds," and "The aliens did actually come, but then they left without being detected." After observing, interviewing, and trying to understand the cult members, the psychologists wrote a book called *When Prophecy Fails*. In it, they argued that when people make choices based on a particular set of beliefs, they don't simply give up those beliefs when they have a close encounter with contradictory evidence.[18]

Today, we see similarities in conspiracy theories like the idea that the COVID vaccine is laced with microchips, that the Denver airport is a secret Illuminati base, that government operatives killed Jeffrey Epstein, and that some business school professors with their passion for free trade and technology are secretly Skrull operatives from Marvel Comics. (I'm trying to start the last one, so feel free to spread it.) For believers of any conspiracies, presenting contradictory evidence just strengthens their false beliefs. But why would contradictory evidence make people's beliefs stronger rather than weaker?

If people were neutral judges of information, we would expect them to update their beliefs based on the balance of evidence. Unfortunately, classic studies on confirmation bias show that we are not always neutral judges. Instead, we prioritize, attend to, and remember information that confirms our existing beliefs. In some studies, researchers ask participants to decide on the guilt or innocence of a defendant. After the participants have made their choice, they are given more information; some of it is consistent with their verdict, and some isn't. Whether they thought the defendant was guilty or innocent, participants were more likely to look at information consistent with their choice.[19] Research shows that people similarly attend to consistent information about the quality of products they recently purchased,[20] the efficacy of their current health habits,[21] the virtue of their character,[22] and their good luck.[23] Additionally, we judge evidence consistent with our beliefs as higher quality than evidence that questions our choices.[24]

In short, by noticing information consistent with our choices, we more quickly accept proof for what we want to believe and more harshly scrutinize evidence for those we want to reject.

This large body of consistent findings shows that once we've made a choice, we attend to information and interactions that reinforce our decision and close the door to reconsidering it. As a result, we stop exploring and learning and can become further entrenched on our current path.

So why are our orientations so different before and after deciding? Why do we go from being so open to being so closed?

PRETENDING TO BE ASLEEP

The short answer is that our goals change. As we've seen, people certainly can weigh evidence in a balanced manner, particularly if we aim to "do our best" or are tasked with convincing informed and unknown others. But "doing our best" is only one of our many goals. Our reason-giving behavior is not just a simple matter of replaying the thoughts that occurred to us as we chose. We're also managing how others see us while also meeting other goals, such as making ourselves feel good about our choices. Often, we are unaware of these other social and emotional goals and might even deceive ourselves about them. These different goals act as a finger on one side of the scale, tipping things in favor of what we want to believe.

For example, people are motivated to live in a coherent and orderly world, and we bend our thinking to preserve that order and consistency,[25] denying that the world can be unfair. "No, there's no more racism!" Or the ever-popular, "Everything happens for a reason!" Second, as strange as it may sound to some, believing in conspiracy theories can be fun, and it has been shown to increase dopamine.[26] Third, we are motivated to preserve the status of our social groups.[27] For example, the more confident people are that their in-group is correct, the more confirmation bias they demonstrate.[28] If I dissect the world into oppositional groups like Somalis/Oromos, Hiloni/Masorti, Rolos/Cachacos, Assamese/Bengalis, or Republicans/Democrats, and if I'm told that I have things in common with the other side, that they aren't all bad, or that they aren't really responsible for the downfall of civilization, I start to cherry-pick beliefs to serve my goals, preserving the superior status of my group (rather than getting things right). "Of course it's their fault! What's wrong with you?"

Across a meta-analysis of eighty-one different studies and more than eight thousand participants, researchers have found that confirmation bias is best explained as a defense motivation,[29] meaning that we selectively perceive and attend to information to protect ourselves from anxiety and discomfort when essential beliefs are questioned. After making a choice, we trade our microscopes and telescopes for shields to protect ourselves from attack, both from others and from the parts of ourselves that might second-guess our decision.

Any successful attempt to change beliefs must acknowledge and address the person's *real* goals rather than naïvely assume that both parties want the same things, even if they are seemingly obvious good things like being more accurate or staying alive. When there's a mismatch in our goals, coordinating our thoughts and actions is much harder. We're playing two different games with two different sets of rules. As a proverb from the Philippines teaches, "It is difficult to wake someone who is pretending to be asleep." All this talk about confirmation bias and selectively attending to information makes it seem like this is a conscious choice, that we do this deliberately, but that's not always true. Often, we can pretend to be asleep and not know it.

IT FEELS GOOD TO BE RIGHT

Suppose that I believe the world is flat.

Please don't put the book down. Just humor me.

Believing the earth is flat or thinking it is a slightly squashed sphere—each is more or less dopaminergically costly for me to adopt. I might adopt the flat earth set of beliefs if I distrust authorities, repeatedly hear from my in-group how the earth is really a flat infinite plane, value my interactions with other people who discount the theory of gravity, get attention and social rewards by putting arrogant round-earthers in their place, and associate my identity with being skeptical of science and elites. I might make sense of the world by dividing people into those who are like me and understand that we are prey to a nefarious conspiracy and those sheep over there who are happy to be deluded into disbelieving their eyes and thinking that the world is spherical. I might use this distinction to explain everything that happens to me. "What, the store is out of milk? Damn it! Those round-earthers are at it again!" These perceptions, relationships, and interactions are the immediate drivers of my Pursue and Protect Systems, making it more likely that I will defend the flat earth beliefs when they are called into question.

In contrast, rejecting the flat earth beliefs would mean giving up things I care deeply about, losses that my brain predicts as painful. Hence, my brain picks the web of belief that will most likely continue delivering the rewards I've come to care about. For example, there is preliminary evidence that people with hyperactive Pursue Systems are more prone to conspiracy theories; specifically, they have more dopamine receptors, meaning they are more likely to choose what feels good at the moment.[30] Studying people who are prone to delusions suggests a similar conclusion—malfunctioning Pursue Systems can prevent people from updating their beliefs about the world because it's hard to give up something that feels good.[31] There is ample evidence that confirmation bias plays a protective role by dampening Protect System activity and increasing Pursue System activity for people regardless of political party, religion, or scientific faction. For example, research shows that the worse people feel, the more they engage with information that is consistent with their desired conclusions.[32] We are likely to look for information to make ourselves feel better, particularly after getting bad news.[33] "I'm not having any luck on Tinder, but look at all the matches I'm getting on OurTime!" "I didn't get the job I applied for; at least I've got it better than those guys on the Viagra commercials." Self-aggrandizement aside, scholars have concluded, "Confirmation biases exist mainly to enhance affective states or to avoid negative mood because attitude-discrepant messages may amplify cognitive dissonance and thus psychological discomfort."[34] In other words, when we encounter something that damages our self-confidence and threatens our self-composure, we shield ourselves with our favorite fantasies.

All of this research confirms (sorry) what we see daily: people are not neutral judges of facts. But it also shows us something that perhaps we don't appreciate enough. Our Pursue System steers our search, exposure, attention, and memory toward our desired conclusions to shield us from the pain of disconfirmation. When giving reasons for using addictive features in our educational apps, we can give reasons that serve our goals (to feel good about our choice) but don't serve others' goals (like keeping kids healthy). Our selective attention for reasons that make us feel good helps us protect the beliefs we desperately need, which lay the grid for the rest of our mental maps. Understanding the broader social-emotional drivers of confirmation bias is essential because when we better understand why the shields go up, we stand a chance of bringing them down.

FACTS OF LIFE

All this talk about different goals, confirmation bias, and dopamine may make us pine for a world where humans are just better at paying attention to the facts. If we could just hold up the data, point to the pie charts, statistics, and double-blind studies, and convince everyone who disagreed, we could compel people to cast down their shields. We could help so many more people and save so many more lives. It's a nice dream, but focusing on facts alone is unlikely to be helpful. But why?

A common view is that the world is neatly divided into facts and values. Facts are supposed to be observable, testable, and independent of a specific perspective. In contrast, values are supposed to be soft, squishy, and open to interpretation, and they vary from person to person because they depend on one's context, experience, and background. When we dissect the world in this way, it's only natural to believe that if we communicate our facts more clearly and consistently, we could convince those who don't get it or even those who don't want to get it.

When we talk about facts, we tend to describe them as uncontestable, irrefutable, and indisputable. But facts are a set of beliefs that have met a certain socially defined threshold of justifiability. We can be wrong about "the facts," and we have been wrong before. A majority of scientists once thought that it was a fact that the sun revolves around the earth, phlogiston made people sick, human flight was impossible, darker-skinned people were inferior, women couldn't be scientists, and atoms were the smallest building block of the universe.

If facts are indisputable and ironclad, how were people in the past so wrong yet so confident that they were right? And more important, might we be wrong today? These errors occur partly because, surprisingly, facts and values are not so easily distinguishable.

Let's zoom in to see more clearly what I mean. The basic terms, categories, and labels we use to state facts are open to interpretation and require applying values.[35] For example, is Pluto a planet, what makes a person a male, when is a fetus a person, and is a hotdog a sandwich? To apply the categories (planet, male, person, sandwich) that constitute facts about those things, we must make judgment calls and rely on social norms. For example, when does a person really become an adult? Across the globe, the legal age of adulthood varies from fifteen to twenty-one. If a community's goal is to involve more citizens or help people be responsible earlier, they may set that age lower; in contrast, if the goal is to foster more mature voters, the legal status of adulthood can be conferred later. Beyond the legal definition, communities have defined adulthood based on when people get married, character attributes like dependability, becoming a parent, and getting overly excited at the prospect of taking a nap. To decide who is an adult and who is not, we rely on social norms. Facts are expressed in a language, and any language is a set of social agreements on how to use terms. Those social agreements rely on values to decide what is in and what is out; for example, a fetus is a person at three months but not at two months, and Pluto is a dwarf planet, not a real planet (that demotion was a result of a vote by astronomers), and even though Jeff has kids, he's not really an adult because he can't take any personal responsibility. For a related point and utterly different example, the USDA considers a hotdog a sandwich, but the National Hot Dog and Sausage Council (NHDSC) thinks it's something entirely new and different. What is essential to see in these examples is the social agreement on values that is required to define terms. It takes parents, rabbis, priests, doctors, astronomers, teachers, hotdog lovers, lawyers, lobbyists, and fellow citizens who all reinforce and subscribe to the same linguistic norms to distinguish a "fact" from an artifact.

When we look at a fact more closely, we see that it is inseparable from the value judgments that help constitute it. Therefore, when we disagree on facts, we also disagree on those values, goals, and social norms. If we are blind to the values that go into defining a term or category, or if we flat-out reject them, then we underestimate the work that needs to be done to get others with different values to agree with our facts. We can argue for years about whether a fetus is a person at conception or birth or somewhere in between; if we cannot acknowledge the different goals in this debate and, more important, find some overlap in those goals, then no "fact" will magically solve it. Those who disagree will reject how that fact was defined and measured.

When we think of facts as little dollops of refined and unadulterated truth, we become more frustrated when "they" don't get it because obviously, to us, our way of seeing the world is right. We take for granted the social norms that make our worldviews coherent and consistent.

In decision-making, when we so neatly separate facts from values, we can end up doubling down on a strategy that inevitably backfires. We try to shove more facts down people's throats, causing them to raise their shields higher, which makes their concerning beliefs stronger, only reaffirming our view that they were wrong and their view that they were right. (It doesn't matter that one or both of us might be dead in the process.)

ADDICTED TO FEELING RIGHT

One summer, I was eating an overpriced ice cream bar at the zoo next to a piano, and it occurred to me that the gorilla in the enclosure could eat all day and not get love handles. Years later, I learned that it's not just because they eat fewer cookies, milkshakes, and burgers. There's emerging evidence that humans have a specific genetic adaptation that gorillas don't. According to geneticists, the human body is better able to store fat than other primates.[36] The ability to store excess energy is an amazing survival advantage when food is scarce. It allows us to rely on our energy stores while searching for something else to eat. This same survival advantage becomes a disadvantage when calorie-dense food is no longer scarce and sodas, candies, juices, and brownies are right in front of us all the time. When the restaurant serves you two portions disguised as one, storing extra calories isn't as necessary.

When calorie-dense food is plentiful, it's easier to lean toward choosing immediately pleasurable foods. For example, as countries' economies develop and people can afford more food, diabetes, obesity, and other diseases related to poor nutrition increase. As people have more resources and thus more choices about what to eat, they tend to choose the highest immediate dopaminergic payoff, which usually comes from junk food loaded with processed carbs and sugar. They also get a (un)healthy dose of encouragement from manufacturers, advertisers, and regulators, but that's another story.[37] To maintain our health and well-being, we must swim against the current.

In the same way, confirmation bias may have been an advantage in small groups where humans needed to work together and limit prolonged debate. In small tribes, people share enough experiences and backgrounds to have relatively similar goals,[38] and they don't get their news from twenty different sources. Attending to consistent information also allows us to move on and not keep relitigating our past. However, confirmation bias, like the adaptation to store energy as fat, becomes an easy tendency to exploit in the Information Age. When information is readily available, when we can google "evidence" to confirm whatever we want, search for groups online that believe whatever we do, or call that one friend from high school who always tells us we're right, we lean toward information that makes us feel good in the moment, at the expense of what might be more functional or valuable for our long-term well-being. The prevalent disease of the Information Age is the addiction to feeling right.

Can we be addicted to something like feeling right? One prominent view is that addiction causes us to seek some object, substance, or person because of an expected dopamine rise.[39] And while addiction is complex and varies considerably by substance, context, and person, despite all these important differences, all addictions involve dysregulation of our Pursue Systems. Remember, dopamine is the neuromodulator that makes anticipation feel good. We expect some reward if we engage in a particular action like walking to the vending machine, pulling the slot machine arm, or scrolling on our phones. Our brain releases some dopamine in anticipation that helps us exert effort and seek what we're after. Then, when we get what we are seeking, there is another release of dopamine, which temporarily elevates our levels above our normal baseline—and for a few seconds or minutes, the world is a perfect place.

But not long after we enjoy whatever or whoever we're pursuing, every dopamine release is accompanied by a similar drop below baseline, like a seesaw that counterbalances. We experience that drop as craving. We try to avoid (mostly subconsciously) that aversive state by seeking more of something we want until it's gone or we cannot have it. If (like me) you've ever finished an entire sleeve of saltines in one sitting, you know what I mean. Instead, if we refrain from bingeing, after some time has passed, our dopamine levels return to baseline, and our enjoyment doesn't diminish.

But if we don't wait, if we keep quickly going back for more, each time we get the thing we desire, the chocolate chip cookie, the sex, the saltine, the sangria, the ear massage, we don't get as big a spike of dopamine, resulting in needing more of the rewarding thing to get the same level of pleasure. Unfortunately, over time, this reduces our enjoyment and increases the intensity and duration of the pain from craving. When we get caught in a cycle of craving, pursuing, and gratifying, our baseline level of dopamine can reset to a lower level.

In this way, addiction demonstrates the opposite pattern to that of distraction and lack of self-control (see previous chapter). When we're addicted to something, we can't imagine anything else feeling better than what we're after right now, and we become fixated on the cues that lead us closer to what we desire. As a result, it is much harder to switch to another task. Everything else fades to the background and becomes much less important, and our mental maps become laser-focused on what we believe will alleviate our craving. While it may be tempting to think of addiction only as a severe condition impacting less fortunate others, the latest thinking is that addiction is a spectrum.[40] We are all addicted at different levels to different, often seemingly innocuous things (like those Maple Leaf cookies from Trader Joe's), and in a world with access to so much information, we all risk becoming addicted to that special, unique feeling of having our beliefs confirmed.

Just as it can be hard for a person in recovery to go from drinking martinis to drinking water, when we're addicted to feeling right, it can be harder for us to go from distorting the world to serve our social and emotional goals to a different strategy, like abandoning those goals or finding new ways to satisfy them. When others confirm our worldviews, or we hear something we already believe, it can feel good. When we've become addicted to feeling right, it's harder to endure being wrong. Again, the choice here is primarily subconscious and automatic. People are not usually calculating what to do; your Pursue System is doing it for you outside of your awareness. But the prefrontal cortex is also part of the Pursue System, and as former addicts will attest, it is possible to exert some level of control on our cravings.

Just as plentiful food can, over time, erode our health, plentiful information can erode our freedom. When we are drawn to beliefs that satisfy our immediate social and emotional needs, we are not really choosing on our own; rather, we are on the path toward becoming addicted to the reward placed in front of us. As a result, our attention is captured; we buy things we don't need, ignore important relationships, or do things that aren't in our long-term well-being. Like the gorilla who watched me add to my love handles, we too are in a cage, not one made of bars, glass, and moats, but trapped instead by our inability to turn away from the immediate reward, unable to exercise our ability to choose differently.[41]

CONFIRMATION UN-BIASED?

Thankfully, we know what can break the addiction to feeling right. Here's what can reduce confirmation bias and get people to lower their shields and entertain different perspectives while making decisions.

1. Confirmation bias can be reduced if people with different perspectives work together. For example, when a panel of judges includes both male and female judges, the male judges are twice as likely to rule for the plaintiff in sexual harassment cases and three times as likely in gender discrimination cases than if they were deliberating on their own.[42] Multiple judges can mitigate each other's biases. Similarly, working in a diverse group where different perspectives are genuinely heard and considered can help minimize confirmation bias. When people's relational goals outweigh their attachment to a specific belief, being a part of a group can improve our thinking.

2. Research has shown that the more confident we are about something, the less likely we are to revise our beliefs and the more we protect those beliefs when they are questioned. Therefore, a healthy degree of doubt and humility can keep us open to learning.[43] In a recent study, psychologists found that both liberals and conservatives who were more humble demonstrated less political bias.[44] Looking for places where our perspectives don't work or understanding the limits and boundaries of a particular view is critical to staying humble and open to learning.

3. If confirmation bias is a defense mechanism, we should see less of it when people let their defenses down because they do not feel threatened. Several studies support this effect. Participants were more likely to listen to and incorporate information they disagreed with if they first wrote about a value that was important to them or affirmed their self-worth.[45] "You're right. I *am* a good mom. What were you saying about the earth being a sphere?" Similarly, smokers are more receptive to

anti-smoking messages,[46] patients are more attentive to health information they disagree with, college students are more likely to act in line with their values,[47] underperforming workers are responsive to poor evaluations, and partisans are willing to listen to information unfavorable to their in-group when they are first self-affirmed.[48] Just as some medications need a protective coating to avoid making things worse, a spoonful of self-worth helps the inconvenient facts be heard. I know that sentence is hard to swallow, but you're smart enough to get the point.

So far, we have seen how anticipating giving reasons before making a choice can help us be more thorough, careful, and open. And after making a choice, we tend to raise our defenses, focus on feeling right, and become closed.

So, how do these patterns impact the reasons we give when we make difficult decisions?

RATIONALIZATION

Jane Toppan, known as Jolly Jane, was a nurse and serial killer who confessed to the murder of thirty-one people in 1901. When asked why, she said, "That is my ambition, to kill more people, more helpless people than any man or woman who has ever lived."[49] Similarly, Jeffrey Dahmer describes his motivation to "completely control a person; a person I found physically attractive. And keep them with me as long as possible, even if it meant just keeping a part of them."[50]

Like the weeknight lineup on Court TV, let's move from murder to fraud. One of the perpetrators of Enron's $63.4 billion scandal, Andy Fastow, said, "Never when I did these transactions did I think about the ethics. I simply said we have a rulebook, it's amoral, just a bunch of rules. . . . When you're in the business world, it's a lot harder to recognize unethical situations than you think . . . our financial statements were intentionally misleading. But did I think that was wrong? No. I was just following the rules."[51]

What do you think of these reasons? Do you approve? After reading these explanations, most people don't say, "Oh, okay—I didn't realize you were trying to set the murder record; never mind my objections, keep on serial killing!" Or "Oh, that makes sense; if you want to make even more money, you certainly can't let the accounting rules get in your way!" We see these reasons as much more than merely a personal matter. Instead, most people reject these reasons because they violate our basic moral views. Each of the lenses of moral philosophy introduced in chapter three is a source of different criteria that can lead people to accept or reject your reasons; thus, when we violate people's expectations about principles, consequences, character, and relationships, they will be less willing to accept our reasons. When they reject a set of reasons, people will justify their rejection by describing the reason-giver's behavior as unethical, immoral, or unacceptable, and do their best to try to put a stop to it.

When we make choices, ignore the risks to others, and give reasons based on a disputed set of goals or values, that is called rationalization. It might sound like a good thing, but it's not. It's a kind of self-deception where we trick ourselves into thinking we are choosing for good reasons. Still, we are not being honest with ourselves about our motives and our impact because we're not paying attention to the broader picture. Instead, we are ignorant (sometimes willfully) of others' motives and how our actions impact them. As a result, we can subconsciously twist how we see things to make our decision seem like it's the best way forward.

For example, in Enron CFO Andrew Fastow's rationalization, he admits to not seeing the importance of accounting rules and obligations to shareholders, employees, customers, the Houston community, and the citizens of California. He had a goal, increasing profits, and the rules faded to the background or became obstacles he had to maneuver around. He used his zoom lens to narrowly focus on doing whatever he needed to increase earnings, even if that meant lying to investors, hiding debt in subsidiaries, and messing with the energy markets in California to pump up revenues. Fastow (and other senior Enron executives) ultimately cost 28,500 employees their jobs, lost the company $7.2 billion in a shareholder settlement, and landed twenty-one people in jail.

We are all prone to rationalization, and thankfully, like confirmation bias, it's something that we can overcome. If you find yourself or your team relying on one of the reasons below as your primary rationale, it's a sign that you might not understand the social landscape as well as you think, that you are adding a finger to your preferred side of the scale, and that others will have a more challenging time accepting your perspective. When we rationalize a choice like using addictive features in our educational apps, we tell ourselves things like:

- Everyone is doing it. So, I should, too.
- If I don't do it, someone else will.
- It's legal, so it's okay.
- I'm not responsible; I have no choice.
- The harm is not that serious.
- It's someone else's fault; they should have known better.
- That person or group deserves what they get.
- I am helping my group (or following this rule).
- I have done other good things that make up for this action.

In contrast to rationalization, where we try to make our personal goals and reasons look good by downplaying or ignoring any inconvenient data, a "justification" takes the social ramifications of our actions more seriously. Let's look at a recent controversial justification.

JUSTIFICATION

In August 2021, United Airlines mandated a vaccine for all its sixty-two thousand employees after offering them several incentives such as paid time off and bonuses. Then, they worked closely with the pilot's union to get buy-in. United allowed people with religious or health-related concerns to file for exemptions, and two thousand employees applied. The company gave its workforce two months to comply. As a result, 92 percent of pilots favored the vaccine mandate. COVID-19 vaccines and vaccine mandates are still controversial. So naturally, the CEO, Scott Kirby, was asked why United became one of the first companies to mandate a vaccine. Here's how he explained their decision:

I first brought it up with our executive team in either October or November of last year [2020], before the first Phase III trials had even concluded because evidence was so strong on the Phase II. Safety is number one at the airline. I had been writing letters to the families of every employee that lost their lives to COVID, and I was writing a lot of letters back then. Secondly, we had been in this situation from the very beginning of crews flying to China, for example, when it very first started and a total unknown. Feeling an obligation—a humanitarian obligation—to send the crews there because they were bringing back ventilators and PPE, everything to deal with the crisis. So, feeling an obligation to keep flying, but also an obligation to those people who we were sending potentially into harm's way. So, we started talking about it in November. And then in January, it's called "Earnings Live," we do a big event after every earnings with our employees, and someone asked me about it. I said I thought it was the right thing to do. We weren't going to do it right away, not enough supply, didn't think we could be the only ones to do it, the timing wasn't there yet. But it was the right thing to do. And people shouldn't be surprised if we might be one of the first companies to do it. . . .

Then I was on vacation [in August] in Croatia, and the second death happened. I walked around by myself for about half an hour and I talked to my wife about it. Then, once the time zones were correct, I called Brett [Hart] and Kate [Gebo], our president and EVP of HR, and we talked through it. At the end of it, we said, "We're going to do it. And I'm coming back to the US on Wednesday. Let's announce this on either Thursday or Friday."

It felt like the right thing to do. But nobody else was doing it. I was worried about all the things everyone else worries about. What if we lose staff? We've got tens of thousands of people that are unvaccinated. What's the PR issue? Should United do this if no one else is doing it? What I couldn't get past was, I was doing the math in my head, I'm kind of a math geek. I knew what the case rates were. I'd been watching all the data. And my estimate was between twenty and forty United Airlines employees would lose their lives to COVID by a year from then, by the next August, if we didn't do it. They would otherwise be alive. Once I kind of had done that math in my head, had gotten to twenty to forty people, that's when I made the call. Once I got there, it was easy.

Our senior VP of tech ops, Tom Doxey, did a phenomenal job. He went into break rooms all over the country. He talked to people. He was empathetic. He listened. This wasn't an argument. There was no point in arguing with people. What we wound up saying was, "Look, I respect that there's a different viewpoint, that you have a different view. But I have a job to do what we think is the right thing for safety. This is purely a safety decision for us. And we've made the decision. And I hope you'll get vaccinated. But you now have a decision to make." But we didn't argue about different viewpoints on the science. A lot of it was because everyone believed that it was real. We weren't bluffing. That whole family relationship, those trusting relationships, people wound up talking to people they trusted. It wasn't top down from me. It was all the people that they trusted.[52]

A few things stick out when we compare Scott Kirby's reasons for mandating the COVID vaccine to the starkly different rationalizations we saw earlier. First, when they offer a justification, decision-makers demonstrate that they are aware of and have *engaged with disconfirming data*; precisely, they know what would cause their choice to be rejected by others. For example, United demonstrated that they would not outright force people to take the vaccine. Instead, they allowed time and resources for employees to get the shots, allowing for legitimate exemptions, acknowledged that they would lose some part of the workforce, and prepared for a potential PR disaster. A justification offers reasons *why* you should do something even in light of its shortcomings rather than turning a blind eye to those weaknesses.

Second, a justification demonstrates awareness and *care for others' goals*. Justifications are a social account, which means you must engage with others' reasons and goals, not just give your own. When someone asks you for your reasons, they want to know what you saw, what you were aiming for, and why you decided to navigate the situation as you did. How did you account for the decision's impact on me? United argued that "others are dying, we can do something about it, you have a choice, and we have a choice, too." Kirby and his team met with several stakeholder groups, such as the pilots' union, flight attendants, customers, and other business leaders, to understand their perspectives and concerns. A justification demonstrates that you have thought through the action from different perspectives and have taken your responsibilities to the community, employees, and other stakeholders seriously. Even if you disagree with their views, you continue to treat them with respect and dignity and take steps to minimize any real or perceived harm.

Third, a justification *shows your work*. How did you navigate the tensions and concerns in the decision? A justification opens a conversation about what you chose and why; rather than shutting down the dialogue, it opens space for working together to create and improve solutions. For example, Kirby's team worked with different groups to learn how to improve things for most employees.

Now that we've finished a deep dive into the importance and the impediments of reason-giving, let's return to the decision at the start of this chapter, where we're choosing whether to deploy features resembling gambling that might increase the risk of children's addiction. If we look at reasons for making the features the default, a rationalization would only involve saying, "It's fine to use the features because everyone is doing it," or "It's not our responsibility." Rationalizations are primarily about sharing your perspective and providing excuses, and even then, only if someone disagrees or questions you because you hope no one notices. Rationalizations, like confirmation bias, are about putting up a shield after making a decision. Here are three questions that can help give acceptable reasons to others:[53]

1. **REVERSIBILITY:** Would I be okay with this decision if I were on the other side? Why?

2. **PUBLICITY:** Would I be okay with this decision if everyone knew about it? Why?

3. **GENERALIZABILITY:** Would I be okay with this decision if everyone in a similar situation made the same choice? Why?

By changing your perspective about your choice, you can better sense whether you are "distorting the world" to achieve your social and emotional goals or have done a better job of considering the larger social context. In addition, research demonstrates that genuine curiosity and perspective-taking help people be less rigid and more open in their thinking.[54]

Regarding the choice of applying gaming features at the start of the chapter, when explaining your decision to groups, such as parents, teachers, and school administrators, providing a justification would mean demonstrating that you have considered the disconfirming data (We are aware of the potential risk and its size for different populations of students) and the weaknesses of your choices (We know that by using these features, we are slightly increasing those risks, so we made design decisions that make schools and teachers aware and allow them to choose settings by class and by student). In addition, justifications demonstrate that you understand the desires and motives of others (We have collected data about how parents and teachers think about the issue) and the process for how you navigated the decision (Here's what else we considered and why we ended up where we did). Justifications are about honestly sharing your thinking in the spirit of remaining open to working with others to improve your decisions and achieve your joint goals. (See appendix tool 4.)

Sometimes, engaging with others will change your mind about what to do, and other times, you'll learn how to sharpen the implementation of your choices. Regardless, without good justifications, fewer people will accept your ideas, and therefore you'll be backed into a corner and will need to rely on more brittle forms of power to gain their compliance.

When facing moments of doubt, like what to do when small harms can scale, if we think of decision-making as primarily a personal matter, we can downplay the importance of providing good reasons to others. That's bad. We risk adopting an overly defensive stance and confirming our beliefs, which inevitably reduces trust, makes it harder to learn and adapt, and sets us on a path toward becoming addicted to feeling right. By nimbly sidestepping common rationalizations, giving reasons sensitive to the broader social landscape, being considerate of others' goals, and being clear-eyed about weaknesses, we can better cooperate with our employees, customers, friends, and sometimes, even our three-year-olds.

6

How ≥ What

YOU ARE THE HEAD of HR for a regional airline. (Go ahead. Try out all the jobs!) You're enjoying a rare peaceful weekend in the backyard. Your partner is lounging in the hammock, surfing their social media accounts, and unexpectedly reports some sad news about one of your coworkers. A pilot, David Reiger, just learned that he has the gene for Huntington's disease. Reiger's partner (who is friends with your partner on social media) posted, "We are heartbroken. David tested positive for the HD gene. Definitely not what we were expecting when researching our ancestry." As you would expect, the comments show a heartfelt outpouring of support.

Not knowing much about HD, you do some quick searching and learn that it is a neuromuscular disease that eventually causes people to lose control of their body movements. In some rare cases, the disease can progress suddenly; in others, it progresses gradually. You feel terrible for Reiger and his family, and a part of you also feels torn. You weren't supposed to know this information, at least not yet, but his partner posted it online, and now you worry about increasing the risk to your customers' safety if Reiger has a health problem while piloting or even copiloting a flight.[1]

Of course, the HR guidebook has no existing rules about this situation. The Federal Aviation Administration (FAA) doesn't screen for HD and other genetic diseases in routine medical examinations. HIPAA protects people's health information, and the Americans with Disabilities Act (ADA) requires you to make reasonable accommodations for those with disabilities. But is having a gene for a debilitating disease the same as having the disease? While American laws like the Genetic Information Nondiscrimination Act (GINA) make it illegal for companies to collect and use genetic information in any HR decision, information shared on social media is not protected by the law. So technically, you can act on this information, but you don't know if you should. Coincidently, while you're searching, your partner reports that the original post has been removed.

You worry that passengers could get hurt if you don't say or do something. You don't want to be even partly responsible for a preventable crash that could harm hundreds of passengers and devastate your company. Also, you care about Reiger and want to support him through what you imagine must be a terrifying time, but you wonder if you might be overstepping your boundaries. He didn't disclose anything; his partner did, and then someone decided to take the post down. What if you ask him and he denies he has the gene? Reiger loves his job, so you don't see him stepping aside. You can't go back to being blissfully ignorant. *What would you do?*

Often, we encounter situations where there are information asymmetries—a wonky term for when people don't know the same things. Sometimes, you know more than others, creating tension when you wonder what you can and should say. Other times, the law prevents us from saying anything (such as when George is up for a promotion and you know he was arrested in the past—whoops, sorry, George!), or there are clear rules about what can be said to whom (think of guidelines given to juries). Still, difficult choices don't have such easy outs. The differing levels of information create ample opportunities for disrupting our expectations, causing severe harm, and raising uncomfortable questions about who knew what and when.

When we're making hard choices like those involving information we're not sure we should have, we can say something or keep quiet, and many other possibilities in between. But to act effectively, we need a plan that brings together our best thinking about what's going on, what we should do, and how to adapt and pivot as things evolve quickly. The research on implementing choices is surprisingly thin, so let's learn how to create better and more thoughtful plans that enable situational awareness and experimentation by looking at a few examples.

In my MBA courses at the University of Virginia's Darden School of Business, the final exam consists of analyzing and providing a recommendation for different moments of doubt. Let's look at two recommendations based on the types of responses I typically receive from my graduate students. For ease of comparison, I've kept both recommendations focused on the choice to let Reiger continue to fly. But this decision is usually close to fifty-fifty, and the same patterns are evident in decisions to ground him.

Recommendation 1:

- I wouldn't say anything to Reiger. I wasn't supposed to have this information, and I think it is discriminatory to use it, so I will do nothing in this case. I will let him fly and take the risk rather than break any rules.

Recommendation 2:

- First, I would call the company's legal counsel and get feedback on what to do. I would not disclose Reiger's identity but ask for help thinking about the situation. Then, assuming I have some time and am allowed to, I would give Reiger space to process the test results.

- Once I hear back from the lawyers on what the company can say and not say, assuming we could say something, I would meet with him and tell him what happened, how I learned about the situation, and how I want to help him and fulfill our obligation to protect passengers. I would ask him how he thinks we should handle the situation. I would be ready to share my perspective, which would include some time off to be with family if he would like it, a flight doctor's assessment of the risks so that we can set up a check-in system where he can continue to fly, the option of having a copilot take over during the riskiest times of flight, and adapting his testing schedule to monitor his health. Then, together with the doctors, flight safety specialists, the pilot's union, and Reiger, we would define clear criteria that would allow him to fly and define the conditions under which we would shift him to another acceptable role. He needs to know that we have his back and trust him to report any changes in his health as soon as possible. I would also work with Reiger to identify another position at the company so that when we hit the mutually agreed-upon screens to transition him out from the cockpit, he has a meaningful flight safety role at the company. I would hope that our actions help other pilots to voluntarily disclose health concerns.

- If the lawyers say that the company cannot act on a single deleted social media post, I will ask for further clarification on what can be done and follow those guidelines. We may need to review changes in the medical requirements for flying. For example, perhaps we can move Reiger to a non-flying role in the company.

- I would also work with Legal on a plan to address any concerns raised by other employees. If I learned about his results on social media, others would also know, and people would wonder about the situation. I would aim to create a message that maintains Reiger's HIPAA privacy and ensures employees that we monitor risks and have a system to address them.

- In addition, I would encourage the FAA to update their medical policies in light of genetic information. Finally, I would work with my HR team to update the rules and training at the company so that employees understand the risks of sharing genetic information online.

- I know that there is a high risk that Reiger doesn't accept this path and that he may take legal action, so I will document my actions and conversations and work with the legal team to protect ourselves and prepare for a lawsuit if and when it comes to that (hopefully not).

In which decision-maker's judgment do you have more confidence? Which one would you hire to work at your organization? (If you didn't say number two, perhaps you're trying to run your organization into the ground.) The first recommendation demonstrates what happens when students cannot effectively cope with doubt; they rationalize their first intuition, make a fast choice, and are mostly blind to the other elements of the situation. The second recommendation reflects students who can engage their Pause and Piece-Together System to make doubt a catalyst for learning. They can better identify the relevant contours of the situation, particularly the ones that don't appear in the initial framing. Let's look at the features of the second recommendation that make it stronger and suggest the decision-maker has exercised better situational awareness, judgment, and effort.

First, better recommendations exhibit *comprehensiveness*; they address the related issues that will occur but are easy to miss if we only follow our intuitive reactions. Yes, it's easy to focus only on the presenting issue of whether you should share the information about Reiger. Still, several other essential considerations don't appear in the initial framing, such as maintaining the privacy of health information at the company, anticipating future rules about genetic testing, and preventing similar situations. If you don't take the time to notice the issues, you will miss these other considerations. Each of these facets of the decision is a potential source of risk. Instead, if you can identify and shore up those facets, you increase the odds of achieving your intentions. In addition, comprehensiveness entails identifying potential downstream decisions; what are the second-order consequences and decisions we will have to make in the future? For example, once you identify this issue with Reiger, what should you do when his health changes? Comprehensiveness also requires understanding the larger system and suggesting changes that might prevent similar situations from arising again; in our example, that looks like updating employee training.

Second, better plans demonstrate *specificity*. They describe what exactly you will do. The more abstract the plan, the more likely it is that hidden assumptions lurk in those abstract ideas, increasing your risk. A better plan lays out a detailed set of activities, including the problems you want to avoid, the lines you will not cross, and the process you will use. Being specific about those actions can make testing parts of the plan more manageable, ensuring that your assumptions are reasonable. Both the devil and the angel are in the details, so specificity can help you better assess and improve your plan.

Third, because every difficult decision has strengths and weaknesses, recommendations need strategies *to mitigate* the inherent vulnerabilities in your plan. That means understanding those weaknesses and not engaging in rationalizations that ignore or minimize them. For example, suppose one disadvantage is that Reiger might sue you. In that case, a mitigation strategy is to document your actions and consult a lawyer to protect the company and yourself. The unavoidable weaknesses in your plan need to be identified, monitored, and actively mitigated so that you or your stakeholders don't bear the costs.

Fourth, plans need *flexibility* because the world will often change as you implement them. You may not know how things will turn out, so you must plan for those contingencies. Instead of saying, "I'll see what Reiger says and then react," you can better anticipate changes by saying, "I'll speak to him and convey that I'd like for him to continue to fly under very specific and monitored conditions. I think it's likely that he'll respond in one of three ways. He might be willing, unwilling, or want to negotiate the details. If he is unwilling, I will pivot to offering him another role at the company." Flexible plans and contingencies allow you to adapt more effectively as the world evolves. They also help you to become the person you aspire to be even in the face of uncertainty by thinking ahead to what could happen and being intentional about your responses. That's much better than finding yourself derailed and being forced to react in ways that don't reflect your aspirations. In addition to planning for likely scenarios, plans can be flexible by predetermining pivot points or signs that will let you know it's time to change course. For example, you may monitor regulations, Reiger's health, and his compliance with additional safety protocols to determine when to pivot your strategy. One type of pivot point is called an "unless clause." These clauses define what your plan is contingent upon. For example, "I will let him fly *unless* he is unwilling to undergo more health screenings." Pivot points demonstrate more careful thinking by specifying the relevant boundary conditions or limiting principles.

Finally, a good recommendation is *coherent*; the various facets fit together so that the whole is greater than the sum of its parts. The specific strategies and tactics reinforce each other and don't send conflicting signals. Allowing Reiger to fly without additional precautions would be inconsistent with rolling out a policy to genetically test all pilots. In one instance, the decision-maker seems to say that it's acceptable to have a gene for a disease, and in the second, it's not.

Together, all these elements help decision-makers address foreseeable risks and adapt and continue learning as they move forward in moments of doubt. When we find ourselves squinting and unable to discern a way forward because we don't have a clear mental map, we start observing, learning, and building a clearer picture of the complex social terrain. Then, we use that more detailed map to inspire and refine a hypothesis for navigating the conflicting criteria. We look for weaknesses in our choices and prepare to justify them to others. A recommendation combines all these elements into your best assessment of moving forward carefully when you find yourself stuck. It's a story of what you will do, why, and how you will adapt as things change. But while assembling good recommendations might be a temporary resting place as the final exam for my MBA students, it's only the beginning for leaders on the job.

THE BEGINNING AT THE END

Over the years, I have learned to enjoy cooking. I regret not taking an earlier interest in the culinary arts. But my mother's love language was feeding us, so growing up, I never had to learn my way around the kitchen. As I've stumbled along learning to cook dishes like ribeye steak, matar paneer, and roasted chicken, I've noticed that no recipe or video can cover all of the uncertainties in the process. How long will it take to reach a rolling boil? Is a dollop the same as a teaspoon? How nutty is it supposed to smell when browning butter? Even with a great recipe, cooking is not about robotically following those directions. The recipe guides your actions, but skilled chefs can adjust, customize, and even improve the recipe based on their specific kitchen, tools, and ingredients. Whether going from the recipe to a delicious meal, from the architectural drawings to the standing building, or from the strategy to your improved business outcomes, your effort to connect the plan with the salient contingencies is the special sauce.

THE WHAT AND THE HOW

Staying with the cooking theme for a bit. You might never have heard of him, but Frédéric Roy has become one of the world's most famous bakers of artisanal croissants. At his bakery in Nice, France, it takes him three days to make a croissant that combines a flaky, crispy exterior with a moist, buttery interior that melts when you take a bite. Roy is adamant that baking the perfect croissant requires using a precise type of flour, allowing time for the yeast to ferment, kneading the dough just so, and creating about thirty-six alternating layers of organic butter and dough.[2]

Roy has also been embroiled in controversy by trying to launch a government seal of quality for croissants, like the one that distinguishes Champagne from sparkling wine. This seal would separate his product from the mass-produced factory pastries, churned out in minutes with fewer layers, cheaper ingredients, and less attention to the art of baking. Unsurprisingly, the manufacturers of the mass-produced croissants are unwilling to be brought into the fold.

If we were to examine these two types of croissants side by side, several similarities would be evident: both are golden brown and flaky, and both are made from flour, eggs, butter, yeast, and salt. But there are differences as well. They have varying levels of buttery flavor; they crumble differently. One has more concentric layers while the other feels more like bread on the inside. Both industrial production and Roy's artisanal process result in a croissant, but does the production process matter? In other words, do the specific steps influence the final taste?

The answer is an unequivocal "oui" for Roy and millions of organic farmers, barbecue pitmasters, taishos, taqueria owners, and foodies. Despite surface similarities—having a similar name and shape—there are essential differences in taste and quality, all of which result from the process used, including the extra time, the quality ingredients, and the specific steps taken during baking. Michelin-star chefs and gourmands dedicate their lives to finding and carrying out unique processes that result in tastier outcomes. For these flavorphiles, *how* you do something is just as important as *what* you do. Whether you bake a baguette, a croissant, naan, or agege bread, there are better and worse ways of achieving your goal. There are shortcuts you can take, or you can go that extra mile to produce an outstanding product. The end results are inseparable from the process used. Sometimes, the ends might justify the means, but the means always identify the ends.

In contrast, decision-making scholars (and I include myself here) have focused primarily on *what*, not *how*. We tend to focus on the magical crossroad moment when a decision-maker chooses one path over another. Do I buy a house that is closer to work or the more affordable one? Do I pick this stock or that one? We tend to study decisions where the *how* is mostly negligible. In other words, decision-making scholars don't really talk about, study, refine, or improve the *technique* of any of the actions that come after the choice is made and prior to the results. For example, scholars studying strategic decision-making are concerned about what an executive chooses and why. They rarely study the missteps, course corrections, refining of organizational processes, iterations, motivational speeches, political negotiations, moments of panic, refining of goals, and celebrations of successes that happen after that strategy is selected and before it is brought to life.

That's because it's so much easier to study and compare the what than the how. We can more easily calculate the average and standard deviation of what people pay for an option or how many choose a specific retirement plan. Measuring how many people clicked on a particular recipe is easier, but it's not an indicator of whether they were successful, and it doesn't help us understand where they went astray in the process.

Here's an example. Imagine being fired. "Being fired" is an abstract phrase for a collection of specific actions that would be more or less terrible depending on how those specific actions made you feel. It would feel terrible if you had been fired without notice when you expected a promotion, and your boss was a jerk about it and gave little explanation. Being fired that way would feel much worse than being given ample notice, a clear explanation about your prospects at the company, six months of severance pay, access to recruiting support, and a boss who reaches out to their network to help you find a better fit. Both episodes share the same *what* but very different *hows*, and the *hows* make all the difference. The movie *Up in the Air* (conveniently about a consultant who fires people for a living) stars George Clooney, but Steve Martin was also seriously considered for the part. Think about how the two actors would have created radically different performances from the same script. Or how two musicians would create very different emotions from the same sheet music. That's the power and importance of *how* in shaping the outcomes of our choices.

Here's one more example. Today, Airbnb is a juggernaut. In 2024, it was a $73-billion company with over 8 million properties listed worldwide. Most people don't remember that in 2007, Airbnb was on the verge of bankruptcy. The business model was brilliant on paper, but customers were not booking properties in real life. In a desperate attempt to learn why, the founders sought out a few customers to understand their perspectives. They learned that the grainy cell phone photos owners posted for their steeply priced NYC apartments didn't seem worth it. (Why would I pay so much for a place that looks so fuzzy?) This insight led to an experiment where the founders had professional photographs taken of some properties, and to their relief, those properties rented quickly. The success of their idea was inextricable from *how* the properties were portrayed to customers. Today, Airbnb gives owners plenty of guidance for taking and posting photos of their rentals. Beyond the pitch decks and PDFs of their strategy, implementing their ideas was key. If errors in implementation weren't caught and corrected, we might not have the Airbnb we know today.[3] That's why military leaders have learned that "amateurs talk strategy; professionals talk logistics." Most organizational leaders need to talk about the intersection.

Notably, values we care about, like fairness, sustainability, responsibility, and equity, don't just show up in the *what* (do you fire someone or not). They also live in the process, in the specific actions, tone of voice, consideration, care, and communication that leaders take in the firing process. Indeed, the *how* is an important place to demonstrate your values and commitments. For example, if you say you care about sustainability, you don't just show it through your choices of what products to manufacture; you also demonstrate those values in how you source your materials, how you reduce your carbon footprint, and how you dispose of your waste.

Those of us who study decision-making are generally curious about which recipe you choose and why, but we are impatient and don't care to stick around for the chopping, brining, mixing, roasting, and plating despite the powerful impact those specific actions have on the meal. If *how* is just as important as *what*, that suggests that decision-making is not over once an option is selected. Maybe ironically, the essential parts of decision-making come after the magical crossroad moment, and we scholars need to stop confusing decision-making with results-achieving.

BREWING BETTER DECISIONS

"Mr. Schultz, I'm eighteen years old; and I don't know if I'll make it to nineteen." In the wake of increasing police violence against Black Americans even before George Floyd's murder, the CEO of Starbucks at the time, Howard Schultz, was visiting locations across the country to talk with employees about race in America. Based on similar moving testimonials, Schultz decided that the company had to act, and within weeks, they launched a program called #RaceTogether.[4] The company printed the campaign logo on the warmers of their coffee cups, and they encouraged their employees to discuss race with their customers. Yet despite Schultz's laudable motives to help raise awareness about racial issues, #RaceTogether ended up being weak tea. It was mocked mercilessly on *Saturday Night Live* and quickly scrapped. Starbucks customers didn't want to have conversations about a complex and divisive topic like race with their barista while they were picking up their venti goji mocha java latte with two pumps of diabetes, one pump of entitlement, and extra whipped cream (that's my go-to order).

If Starbucks had taken the time to understand how to be most effective, things might have turned out differently. For example, they could have supported racial justice by increasing investment in Black neighborhoods, training employees so that Black customers are not thrown out of the store for no reason,[5] and ensuring fair and equitable wages. To be fair, the company might also have done some of these things, but criticism of #RaceTogether drowned out any discussion of these other tactics. However laudable Starbucks' goals were in the minds of senior executives, the results they achieved aren't just based on the plan; they cannot be separated from the specific actions used to bring the recipe to life.

When your implementation is flawed, the people who disagree can use any errors or missteps as reasons why you were wrong from the start. When things don't go according to plan, unmotivated people might even capitalize on your errors and use them as reasons why others should listen to them instead. "I always knew this was a bad idea!" "If Starbucks couldn't make #RaceTogether work, then no company should ever try to support social issues." "If some companies only pretend to care about the environment, then all companies only care about profits, and concern for sustainability is fake." "If one blind date goes bad, then I'm never putting myself out there again!" Your uncharitable critics will see any errors as reasons to throw out the whole plan rather than fix the implementation. When we deeply care about a goal, we need to take the time to implement it wisely rather than rush and give the doubters, haters, and naysayers more ammunition to take the argument to extremes and throw the entire espresso out with the grounds.

ITERATION

To ensure that your *how* more accurately reflects your values and intentions, practicing and testing your ideas is essential. For example, architects create renderings and draw blueprints to see if their design is feasible, lawyers practice and iterate their arguments for mock jurors, and surgeons practice their suturing on oranges, bananas, and their annoying neighbors. In addition, prototypes like flowcharts, paper slides, and roleplays can help us test and learn to increase our confidence that our actions will produce their intended impacts.

To help our Darden MBA students refine the way they implement their choices, my colleagues and I have built a lab where students are given common leadership challenges, like choosing how to mediate a contentious meeting, giving difficult feedback to a reticent colleague, deciding who to fire and delivering that news with care, and breaking through negotiation stalemates. First, students read a short prompt and prepare their strategy. Then a group of trained actors walks into the room, and the students must implement their decision. The actors are trained to argue, cry, and push back against the students' suggestions. We record everything in the lab, and students watch their own and their peers' performances to identify strengths and areas for improvement. They also work with a coach to close the gap between their intentions and actions. While it can be hard to watch ourselves on camera, seeing the undeniable growth in students' skills and confidence after several weeks of deliberate practice is worth all the extra work.

Similarly, we all have key moments we should rehearse in every instance of doubt. Typically, these are when you've identified important assumptions about how stakeholders will interpret and value your choices, followed by assumptions about how you will implement your decision. To test these assumptions, you could practice critical conversations with stakeholders or examine how changes to a process or rule would impact past cases; you could model the financial consequences of your ideas or shadow your customers to understand their reactions more carefully. By testing and iterating your ideas, you can refine your approach and ensure your plan leads to where you want to go.

REFLECTIVE PRACTICE

"The young lieutenant of a small Hungarian detachment in the Alps sent a reconnaissance unit out into the icy wilderness. It began to snow immediately, snowed for two days, and the unit did not return. The lieutenant suffered, fearing that he had dispatched his own people to death. But the third day the unit came back. Where had they been? How had they made their way? Yes, they said, we considered ourselves lost and waited for the end. And then one of us found a map in his pocket. That calmed us down. We pitched camp, lasted out the snowstorm, and then with the map we discovered our bearings. And here we are. The lieutenant borrowed this remarkable map and had a good look at it. He discovered to his astonishment that it was not a map of the Alps but of the Pyrenees."[6]

How did these soldiers find their way back to camp using the wrong map? The legendary organizational theorist Karl Weick tells this story to suggest that sometimes when you are lost, any map will do. While finding the map catalyzed the soldiers' hope, it also triggered *reflective practice*, a process of iterating between the plan and the execution. "Hey, dumbass. I can't believe you didn't check your pocket yesterday, but anyway, it looks like maybe there's a ridge over there. Let's see if we can find it. Hmm. There's no ridge here, but we have a better view of the tree line; what if we walked to this stream to the south?" Comparing the map and the terrain helped the soldiers learn, generate different ideas, and iterate their way to familiar territory, even though their map depicted mountains two hundred and seventy miles away.

Reflective practice is critical because no planning will prepare you entirely for the world you will encounter. There comes a time when you have laid out your best plan, gotten feedback, and identified and removed the risks you can; the remaining risks can only be uncovered and addressed in implementation. It can be tempting to keep planning, but at some point, there are diminishing returns. Today, many organizations emphasize innovating by using buzzwords like agile, scrums, and waterfall development to get things done quickly. Executives are more likely to say, "I'd rather make a fast decision, fail, learn from it, and then move on than get stuck in planning." Planning has become antiquated and bureaucratic—it's what old stodgy organizations do. Young, hip organizations demonstrate their rebel cred by moving fast and breaking stuff. In contrast, in other organizations, planning is such a cultural symbol of expertise that implementation is perpetually on the horizon because the plan needs to be vetted by twenty people. Then, something changes, so the plan must be revised and re-vetted. Leaders get stuck in a frustrating cycle of planning and replanning, and nothing new gets done.

The process of learning and testing I've described in parts I and II is based on compelling evidence. But you might be thinking that it runs the risk of "analysis paralysis." So, how can we get the benefits of imagining with more detail without the dangers of being stuck ruminating on worst-case scenarios?

When the cost of making a mistake is low, learning by trial and error is valuable. For example, when you are playing *Halo* on your Xbox, and your character gets picked off in the barn by an arrogant eight-year-old assassin from Tulsa, you can press reset and start again. When playing with real money, time, effort, and lives, we don't have a reset button, so some degree of planning is helpful. In my conversations with executives, I notice that they can get stuck because they don't differentiate between the types of risks they face; either planning will help them overcome all risks, or iteration and failing fast will.

One way to think about different types of risks is to distinguish between affordable and unaffordable risks. The loss of significant money, time, reputation, and goodwill might be difficult, if not impossible, to recover from. To protect those resources and your ability to try again, some preliminary planning is helpful to figure out if you have enough supplies in your pack to make the journey, understand how far you must go, check your logic about why you should go, and what it might take to ensure you're not set up for failure. The plan lays out the general boundary conditions that help you avoid those unaffordable risks.

In contrast, there are also risks that you can recover from quickly. Having a focus group tell you they don't like the title of your movie, adjusting the way you give feedback to a colleague, or trying on different outfits until you find one that doesn't clash are all things where you can quickly iterate your way to a better outcome. In short, preliminary planning is effective in helping us gauge our unaffordable risks, the big risks we cannot recover from, and it defines the boundaries of how we'll get from point A to point B.[7] These general boundaries set the parameters for iterating and improvising the ideas we can afford to get wrong. To determine the unaffordable risks, we should ask, What is the cost of getting this wrong? Given our resources, capabilities, and preferences, we might want to plan and strategize ahead of time if the cost is unaffordable. If the cost is low and we can quickly recover from the loss, we lean more toward iteration and testing.

When we're deciding how to address a sensitive issue like Reiger's diagnosis, we need a clear plan that guides our implementation and is flexible to adapt to changing circumstances. After learning about the situation we face, generating and refining novel ideas, and gaining clarity on how we will justify our choices, we bring all of it together in a recommendation. (See appendix tool 5.) A recommendation is our best current hypothesis of what we should do, why, and how, in moments of doubt. Better recommendations demonstrate quality thinking. They are comprehensive, specific, and coherent. They contain strategies to mitigate inherent risks and adapt intentionally to uncertain conditions. Once we've defined the general boundaries of our approach, we test and iterate key actions to ensure a tighter connection between our *what* and *how*. Like the soldiers in the Hungarian army lost in the Alps, when meeting our own moments of doubt, we intentionally experiment, learn, and adapt to make our way toward who we aspire to be.

The Vista

Believe it or not, we've come halfway. In the first six chapters, we've covered a lot of ground, drawing on the latest science-based insights to help you understand the best practices and common pitfalls when facing moments of doubt. Before we move on to parts III and IV, I want to highlight a few things about this overall process:

First, the process of approaching doubt I've described is simultaneously social and personal. It's not as simple as reducing the situation only to your values and choosing quickly, nor is it just about unreflectively defaulting to the values of those around you. It's about identifying multiple criteria, finding the relevant areas of interplay, collaboration, and conflict, and having a plan that carefully considers those issues and intersections. My colleague likes to say, "Ethics is not just about whether you can live with yourself; we've got to live with you, too."

Sometimes, senior executives tell me they know they have made a good decision when they can "sleep well at night." I usually respond with, "That's great. Being able to live with ourselves is one important consideration, but is it the *only* consideration? Lots of people who've done terrible things sleep just fine, thank you very much. All you need is some Ambien and a fifth of Jack." Our own perspectives are both necessary and insufficient to judge the quality of our choices. When we only focus on our personal values and make tradeoffs, we can be willfully blind to essential parts of the social terrain that can quickly derail our efforts.

When making difficult decisions, we will stumble if we start with the zoom lens and race to reach our destination as quickly as we can, like Andrew Fastow, Walter White, and the producers of *Game of Thrones*. If we understand the social context too late, our solutions are insensitive to the pressures they will face. Additionally, how we interact with others throughout this process is an investment in our relationships and, therefore, impacts our ability to address hard choices. Without understanding both our personal aspirations and the social context, we sail into storms that we didn't have to ignore.

THE RIGHT ANSWER?

I want to highlight a question I am frequently asked. After all this learning, testing, and iterating, does this process of making difficult choices lead us to *the* right answer?

This question has several important facets, so let's look at each one. At a technical level, the idea of a single right answer is more appropriate for problems with a single criterion, where there is a large degree of social consensus, like when there is one clear law or norm. Making good choices in those situations requires remembering and aligning yourself with that clear social standard. In contrast, multi-criteria decisions have several elements that can be used to evaluate a choice. So, technically, based on the audience, we can be "right" on one dimension, be on more shaky ground on other criteria, and violate others. That's why we must be ready to justify our choices, articulate why our decisions prioritized some criteria over others, and explain how we tried to find ways of addressing multiple views of the good and minimize harm from the standards we didn't meet. When there are multiple ways of evaluating a choice, looking for a single right answer is like trying to improve someone's health and wellness by focusing only on their weight; you risk confusing the metric for the mission.

Sometimes, when leaders ask me if this process will lead them to the "right" answer, I sense they are really asking me something like, "If I follow this process, will it guarantee that others won't disagree with me?" This question seeks to know before the journey if we're headed down a path without obstacles. Unfortunately, there are no such guarantees. The strategies we've covered so far can increase your odds of success and reduce your odds of critical errors. We are perfectly willing to accept this kind of probability in other domains of life. For example, current medical science corroborates that exercising and eating healthily can add an average of seven years to your life. Of course, some people live a healthy life and tragically die young, and some flaunt all the medical advice and seem to evade illness into their nineties. Still, when we look across the population, we see exercise and nutrition are associated with longer lifespans. The research-vetted practices in this book are similarly associated with better results. If you're looking for guarantees, there are none, so I can't offer you any. No one else can either. (If they do, you should triple-check the fine print and hide your wallet.) The practices we've covered so far can improve our odds of choosing wisely, and in a complex world, that's as good as it gets.

Finally, there's a third way to interpret this question about being right. Humor me for a second. Why do we want to be "right"? I know that sounds like a nonsensical question. Some of us might believe that a "right" answer would mean that we are working with the natural order of things rather than against it—that a correct answer would mean that we're done with our part, and the world will take over the heavy lifting. Like Benoit Blanc from the murder mystery movie *Knives Out*, we would just have to identify "gravity's rainbow" by analyzing the situation and then wait for the arc of justice to bend toward our answer.

Let's look at an example to respond to this third interpretation. Imagine that Ruth believes all people deserve equal rights and dignity. She believes that men/women/non-binary people, people of different races/ethnicities, and people of different political persuasions, sexual orientations, classes, abilities, and other differences deserve dignity. Ruth believes she is "right" in the sense that she thinks this is a good idea for more humans to adopt. While this might seem obvious to some, we shouldn't forget that this is a contentious idea. Whether publicly or privately, millions of other humans don't agree; they believe their group deserves special rights, privileges, and power over others. What does it mean to say that Ruth is right and those who disagree with her are wrong? We might just mean that we agree with Ruth. But it doesn't mean that being right about this set of beliefs allows her to sit back and shift the burden of proof to others. Being right doesn't mean being done. Focusing on being right could lead Ruth to absolve herself from doing the work to help create a world with more equity and dignity.

If Ruth believes she is right, she might not listen to others who disagree with her. She might miss places where counter-intuitive strategies are needed to achieve her goals. She might think she's done once we pass laws that protect equality and dignity or remove practices that discriminate, demonize, and disparage people. Being right doesn't mean there isn't serious work to be done to refine the implementation of those laws and new practices so they don't inadvertently make things worse or create a backlash. To care about equity also means to do the work to identify gaps in pay and access to opportunities, for Ruth to examine her own biases, preferences, and actions, to listen to and amplify the voices of others, and—importantly—to be open to being wrong. Ruth may want to be right because she really wants to be free of the responsibility to keep working.

Even if we were somehow miraculously able to achieve a world where people felt equal and treated with dignity, Ruth and those who agree with her still have to work to guard against backsliding. They would need to educate younger generations who didn't understand what it took to achieve those results and who might take the current level of freedom for granted.

Great ideas can and do fail. We know that groups can lose their freedoms, democracy can devolve, and people can be less safe, so we don't have the luxury of not doing the work to continually maintain, reinforce, and improve essential values throughout the systems in which we live because we believe we are right. In moments of doubt, focusing on being right causes us to neglect the *how* in favor of the *what*. Having the "right" recipe or seeing ourselves as innately good chefs doesn't absolve us of reflective practice. *Being right is no substitute for doing good.*

TAKING STOCK

The process I described in the first six chapters aims to close the gap between our intentions and our actions, helping us choose wisely in the face of complexity and uncertainty. Here's a quick summary of what we've seen along the way:

Chapter One: Life in Between
- Moments of doubt are choices with high uncertainty, high stakes, and multiple goals.

- The brain has three interconnected systems to help you pursue the things you value (Pursue System), protect yourself from threats (Protect System), and pause and piece together clues when you don't know what to do (Pause and Piece-Together System). These systems create our experience of certainty and doubt.

- The neuroscience of uncertainty and the study of experts show that equating our initial intuition with our decision is optional; we can avoid regretful reactions and learn how to act more effectively in the face of uncertainty by treating our intuition as an initial hypothesis for learning.

Chapter Two: Update Your Mental GPS

- We reviewed the current psychological evidence for three answers to the question, Why do people do what they do? These are the Deterministic View of Character, situationism, and mental maps, or our interpretations of our self and surroundings.

- When making hard choices, we can become complacent if we assume our choices are determined predominantly by our innate, unchanging traits or the situation.

- We have more agency and control over our choices when we focus on how we think—on our mental maps. Seeing character not only as a predictor of our choices but also as an ongoing project can help us do the work to close the gap between who we want to be and who we are.

Chapter Three: No Shortcuts to Utopia

- We examined the strengths and weaknesses of the four major lenses from moral philosophy that we all use to determine what makes a good choice: principles, character, consequences, and relationships.

- Moments of doubt involve conflicts within and among these lenses.

- When we use these lenses together instead of picking just one, can help us notice our surroundings in more detail and identify tensions, gaps, and obstacles with more discipline so that we can act more deliberately.

Chapter Four: Dis-solving Problems

- We looked at the costs of thinking that good decision-making always requires making fast decisions and tradeoffs.

- We introduced practices from creativity science for generating, recombining, and refining ideas that can help dissolve tradeoffs that others find unsolvable.

- We learned how our motivation can help us persevere through uncertain and creative tasks. Current research suggests that self-control is not a battery but is potentially unlimited when paired with high motivation.

Chapter Five: Addicted to Feeling Right

- Reason-giving is essential to align our perspective with others and to promote cooperation.

- Confirmation bias is a protective measure to achieve our often subconscious and unstated social and emotional goals at the expense of learning. Unfortunately, in the Information Age, plentiful information increases our risks of becoming addicted to feeling right.

- Justifications help us remain open to working with others by honestly communicating the weaknesses of our choices, how we arrived at them, and how we incorporated others' goals. In contrast, rationalizations are about raising your shields after making a choice.

Chapter Six: How ≥ What

- Better recommendations are comprehensive, specific, flexible, and coherent; they also contain strategies to mitigate risks and adapt to uncertain conditions.

- Distinguishing between affordable and unaffordable risks can help us know when to lean toward planning and when to lean toward experimentation.

- To close the gap between the world we imagine and the world we encounter, we need to pay attention to both *what* we decide and *how* we implement our choices.

Figure 2

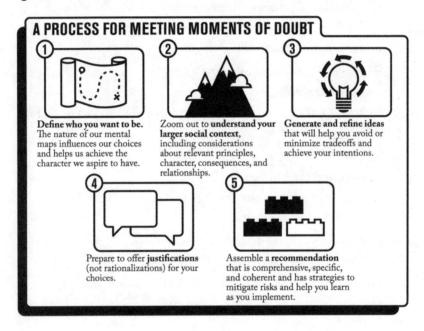

ONWARD!

Did you know that newly hatched sea turtles can't distinguish between moonlight and the artificial light of streetlamps, leading them away from the ocean toward the dangers of human cities? Similarly, bats' echolocation abilities can't differentiate between the smooth surface of water and glass, causing them to crash into the sides of skyscrapers.[1] And dogs' retinas can't distinguish between red and orange, making it hard to retrieve the correct fruit when you ask them to grab you a snack from the kitchen.

Any organism (or any system for that matter) must understand the complexity and dynamism of the environment it faces to regulate itself effectively in that environment.

Humans can be similarly out of sync with their surroundings. Investors who can't distinguish between the risks inherent in technological development and business risks can waste billions. For example, several car and tech companies have recently shuttered or sold their self-driving-car divisions because they assumed a sustainable financial model would emerge as the technology developed. Even though the technology has improved, sustainable business models have not materialized. Similarly, students can flee growth opportunities when they can't distinguish between productive and unproductive stress. And, when I swear that everything seems normal with our friends, my wife, like Sherlock Holmes, sniffs out subtle communication patterns to correctly deduce that they're getting divorced. I realize again that I'm playing checkers while she plays 3D chess. If our perceptions of the world are narrow, our actions are simplistic and less sensitive to what is required to achieve our intentions.

This observation has been named the Principle of Requisite Variety, and the simple version is, "It takes variety to respond to variety." The necessarily complex version is, "A system survives to the extent that the range of responses it is able to marshal—as it attempts to adapt to imposing tensions—successfully matches the range of situations—threats and opportunities confronting it."[2] One way to obtain this match is to simplify the incoming stimuli to economize on the resources needed to respond. For example, when I go to the modern art museum, I use broad categories to classify paintings as Cubist, Impressionist, and abstract. The docent can break these general categories into more detailed and subtle differences that go way over my head, like distinguishing between Mondrian's early Buddhist influences and his later Neo-Plasticism. Similarly, when your friends do a deep dive into the Chicago Bulls' defensive strategy, the subtle differences between an A-line and bouffant dress, or the intricate restrictions of their new fad diet, these details may not be relevant or important to you—and you can respond by saying "Interesting" as you stare blankly at the wall and prevent those details from ever getting close to your long-term memory. And as long as the details are not needed, this strategy works well enough. But when our simplifications come back to bite us (whether we're chatting about the '95–'96 Bulls' season or the finer points of Fauvism), the technicalities, details, and distinctions matter. Thus, a second strategy is to invest in creating more nuance and complexity to facilitate adjustment to our environments. The practices and ideas I introduced in the first half are ways to increase your requisite variety to meet the challenges posed by moments of doubt. Simple descriptions of where our choices come from and how we define good choices, generate alternatives, give better reasons, and act mindfully make it harder to learn and successfully achieve our intentions in a complex and dynamic world.

In part III and part IV, we'll cover five common barriers to applying this process. We'll examine prevalent assumptions that reduce our requisite variety and push us back into less sensitive and less mindful responses. By making these challenges explicit, understanding where they come from, and learning about effective strategies, the goal is to maintain our advantage in the face of likely disruptions. Unlike folks who dropped this book after reading page two and lunged for titles like *Certainty, Now!* and *Don't Think; You Already Know*, if you've made it this far, you've done a great job of practicing curiosity, patience, and a tolerance for uncertainty. So, if you're still up for the challenge, refill your coffee, adjust your earbuds, and wipe the sleep from your eyes. We're going to kick it up a notch.

III

SIDESTEPPING OBSTACLES ALONG THE WAY

7

The Limits of Cooperation

YOU WORK AS A TECHNICIAN in a surgical unit where a new brain surgeon has transferred from the East Coast. The new doctor attended one of the top medical schools and has since risen to the top of her field. However, in recent weeks, you have overheard two married male doctors in your unit make sexually suggestive comments about the new surgeon. To be clear, this isn't Seattle Grace Hospital from *Grey's Anatomy*, where doctors hook up with each other in between appendectomies and then dissect the details in front of their patients. At first, you brush it off, but the annoying behavior continues for several weeks. The doctors act normally when they're around the new surgeon, but when they know she's out of earshot, they resort to juvenile comments and innuendo. You wonder if that's why two of the nurses have suddenly requested transfers. In general, your relationship with the two male doctors is professional and courteous; you are not close to them, but you also don't avoid them. They are pretty good at their jobs but haven't gone out of their way to get to know you. The new surgeon, meanwhile, has been a great mentor to you in the few weeks she's been with the team, and she's clearly capable of handling things herself if they get out of hand.

Like most organizations' rules, the hospital's policy does not tolerate harassment of any kind. But in your experience, the hospital's practice is more lenient of explicit sexual harassment and gender-based inequities in pay, promotion, and power. There is a hotline for reporting concerns, but you're pretty sure nothing will change if you call it. You might even face risks if you report your concerns. What if the offending doctors figure out who filed a complaint? Your annual review is in the next two weeks. You really don't have the time to be interviewed for an investigation.

Would you say anything?

For some of us, it might seem like no big deal to politely and calmly let the male doctors know that their comments are unprofessional and make us uncomfortable. Others among us might worry that the doctors won't support our promotion if we say something. Research shows that most employees say they *would* speak up if needed. But if you ask them if they *did* say something when there was a chance, most report doing nothing; by some estimates, 50 percent to 80 percent of opportunities to raise issues at work are passed over.[1]

Sometimes, it can be challenging to take a personal risk to stand up for others. At other times, it can be astonishingly easy. We've all heard of heroes who run back into burning buildings to save puppies or jump into rivers to save drowning children. They don't report doing a cost-benefit analysis; they see a need and instinctively act. Helping others can be a no-brainer, mainly if we know what to do and feel strong empathy. Unfortunately, ignoring requests for help can be just as intuitive. We automatically look away, change the channel, or feel apathy.

Many of us who espouse an abstract love of humanity and a desire to help others find that our actual attention, empathy, and efforts have boundaries. We don't treat the suffering child on the other side of the world as equal to our own child. Some of us might say that we are committed to justice, dignity, and equality, yet we don't drop our jobs, stop doing things we enjoy, and funnel a large portion of our incomes and waking hours to help achieve those results. We might like the idea of loving humanity, but find the reality more challenging. Often, our helping stops at social boundaries. Republicans and Democrats might find their empathy stops at party lines. Alabama and Georgia fans, people who do Zumba, and those who want a real workout are all less willing to help those who belong to the other group. When we know that help would be appreciated but we don't feel connected to the potential beneficiaries; and we perceive social, financial, or physical risks; and/or we are just too busy; the choice becomes much more difficult.

In everyday decisions, we experience doubt about when and whom to help. In these damn confusing situations, we rely on our beliefs about human nature to find our way forward. Yet many of our default assumptions about people often point us in precisely the wrong direction.

AN ULTRASOCIAL SPECIES

Humans must be selfish to survive, right?

Why? Well, we've all heard that nature is "red in tooth and claw" (usually said to us by the people currently trying to cut us down in some way).

If that's true, we shouldn't expect help from others or feel the need to help them. Yet the evidence from evolutionary psychology suggests that humans cooperate more than other primates in volume and scale; that's why biologists and psychologists call *Homo sapiens* an ultrasocial species.[2]

In evolutionary terms, cooperation can confer a survival advantage. A group of prairie dogs is more likely to survive if a single prairie dog makes an alarm call to warn the others, even though it means calling attention to itself and increasing its own risk of being eaten. There will be other times when that prairie dog will benefit from the alarm calls of others; thus, cooperation increases the odds that the group survives. Cooperation even works across species. Birds called plovers earn a meal by cleaning the teeth of crocodiles, who accommodate them by not eating them. Bees and flowering plants work together to produce honey and spread pollen. It's not just the birds and the bees that produce benefits; we're just now learning about how plants share nutrients through their roots to promote the health of the forest.[3] I won't focus on the multitude of evolutionary strategies that demonstrate the value of cooperation. Instead, let's look at the features that helped make humans ultrasocial.

MENTALIZING

Imagine the following scene:

> A man says, "But I love you." The woman seated across from him does not answer. The man and the woman continue eating quietly.[4]

How are the people in this scene feeling? They could feel hurt, resigned, yearning, or even deeply contented and satisfied. The two people could be friends, lovers, siblings, coworkers, or two strangers on their cell phones. We don't know, but most of us cannot help but fill in the blanks. This ability to think about the mental and emotional states of others is called *mentalizing*.[5] (Every time I hear that term, I have to consciously put aside the image of David Blaine staring down the camera after freaking people out by revealing which card they're thinking about.) Its supernatural connotations notwithstanding, mentalizing allows us to more clearly imagine others' internal states.

Evidence suggests that chimpanzees can also infer others' motives; for example, they are more patient with a caretaker who cannot physically share food when compared to one who is deliberately withholding it.[6] But chimpanzees can't use a pregnant pause to communicate complex intentions to others. Also, when two chimps in an experiment cooperate to pull a piece of wood and retrieve grapes, the chimp that can grab the grapes is less likely to share the reward with its partner.[7] Even though they can infer motives, the chimps' anticipated enjoyment of the prize is more potent than their ability to mentalize about their collaborator.

In contrast, human children start to mentalize at about eighteen months.[8] Children will spontaneously comfort those who show signs of distress and will help a researcher look for something in a room by pointing to where it is. Your skeptical friend might wonder how we know it's really mentalizing and not some kind of conditioning, like how we train dogs to sit. Developmental psychologists believe that a toddler's helpfulness is motivated by concern for others because it is spontaneous;

directed at peers, not just authority figures; endures even when parents are not watching; flexibly matches the recipient's goals;[9] and continues even when there is no reward or praise.[10] Indeed, when researchers give children extrinsic rewards for helping, like candy or money, children end up helping less.[11] Finally, when two-year-olds observe a scene where a research assistant can't reach something they want or can't find the right tool to finish the job, their little pupils dilate, indicating automatic and uncontrollable arousal. Their pupils return to their normal (tiny) size when the research assistant achieves their goal.[12] By the time they reach six years of age, human children are capable of extraordinary feats of mentalizing. They can keep track of complex chains of beliefs: e.g., Chase believes that Skye believes that Paw Patrol is in danger or that Swiper the fox might be bluffing or double bluffing.[13] Unlike chimps, whose capability to imagine the internal lives of others is easily derailed, children's perspective-taking is amazingly spontaneous, resilient, and flexible.

The Whites of Our Eyes

One physical adaptation that makes mentalizing easier in humans is that the whites of our eyes, technically called *sclera*, are proportionally larger than those of other primates. When researchers show us pictures of human faces and simultaneously stare at our faces, they find we pay attention to the eyes more than other features,[14] and we tend to associate large sclera with greater health and beauty.[15] The shape of our sclera signals to others what we are looking at and what we might be thinking because visual attention and thinking are generally related. Think of all the information about your friend's mental and emotional state communicated when they give you the side-eye when talking to the recent divorcee at the bar. The British tragedy/comedy *Fleabag* used this device to great effect, building a close relationship between the audience and titular character Fleabag when she broke the fourth wall without saying a word. Similarly, in the *Planet of the Apes* movies, designers gave the advanced apes more human-looking sclera, making it easier for the audience to infer their motives. Compared to the smaller and darker sclera of other primates, the larger and brighter whites of our eyes signal what we're paying attention to and thus make it easier for others to infer what we're thinking.

Oxytocin

A second adaptation that facilitates mentalizing is the presence of a neuropeptide called oxytocin. Mammals have it, and it promotes taking care of their warm-blooded and furry young. In contrast, reptiles don't have it; and they generally don't care about what happens after the eggs hatch, sometimes even eating their own hatchlings.[16] Oxytocin has many effects that scientists are still trying to understand, and one subset is thought to encourage behavior that benefits others—called prosocial behavior. Oxytocin is a driver of mother-infant bonding, which develops our general ability to cooperate with and take the perspectives of others beyond Mom. Oxytocin increases social salience (we pay more attention to others), social motivation (we want to be with others), and social reward (we find connection intrinsically pleasurable). When we find ourselves walking back and forth to catch someone's eye, laughing a little too loudly at their jokes, feeling sad when they're sad, or happy when they're happy, that's oxytocin. When the world seems to shine like you've had too much wine, that's oxytocin. And when the moon hits your eye like a big pizza pie, that's not oxytocin; that is some kind of lunar cataclysm.

Current research suggests that oxytocin interacts with the Pursue System to make social interactions feel just as rewarding as receiving personal benefits.[17] Research has shown that people who witness others being treated fairly feel as much pleasure as when they receive personal rewards.[18] Indeed, humans have more oxytocin receptors in key brain regions than our primate cousins.[19] Oxytocin helps parents do more for their children, helps lovers be more attentive to each other's needs, and makes us all do more for "our group."

To test the effects of oxytocin on cooperation, researchers have used a laboratory game called the Trust Game, which involves two participants who are each given $10.[20] Let's play. Just get out your own money for this version. You must choose how much of your $10 to give to me. Whatever amount you choose will be tripled by the experimenters, so if you give me $1, I will actually get $3; if you give me all of your money, I will get $30. Once I receive the money, it's my turn to decide how much to return to you. I could be selfish and give you only a penny back or only your original investment back. I could be fairer and split the gains equally or be generous and give you $25. You must trust me to give me a larger portion of your money. Okay, how much are you going to Venmo me? Researchers have shown that when male participants are given a puff of oxytocin up their noses before playing the Trust Game, they cooperate more by transferring higher sums than if they are given a placebo.[21] Since that original study, scientists have amassed evidence linking oxytocin with more empathy, perspective-taking, and helping behaviors.[22] Feeling connected to others helps most people accept smaller financial rewards for themselves to help strangers.[23] Our mentalizing ability, fueled by higher levels of oxytocin and directed by the whites of our eyes, helps us imagine others' internal states with more clairvoyance than other primates (even without our own street magic TV special).

(COMPARATIVELY) LESS AGGRESSION

The second adaptation that has helped humans become an ultrasocial species is that we are less emotionally reactive than—

I know, I know, YouTube, X, TikTok, and Instagram all provide an endless stream of people having strong emotional reactions, like drunk celebrities being arrested while screaming, "Do you know who I am?" And cannibals named Charlie snacking on their brother's fingers. But I'm talking about less reactivity in comparison to our primate cousins.

For example, the fossil record indicates that male human skulls show signs of decreasing testosterone over the last hundred thousand years or so. Hominids with high testosterone levels tend to have more pronounced brow ridges and longer faces. When paleontologists carefully examine human skulls, they find that human male brow ridges have become smaller over time, and faces have become shorter. High testosterone levels can be related to increased competition, aggressive behaviors, and dominance in mammals. Together, these findings imply that modern human males have less testosterone and are, therefore, less aggressive than our distant ancestors.[24] Similar changes in the shape of skulls are also found in other domesticated species like dogs, foxes, mice, and bonobos, another primate cousin known for being more social and less aggressive than chimps. One current theory argues that humans self-domesticated. In other words, human societies selected individuals who were more cooperative and less aggressive over time. Less aggression means we stand a chance to work together because we don't lash out as much, don't kill each other over small things, or don't passive-aggressively sabotage each other's dating and career prospects.

In contrast, in a study of chimpanzee aggression, researchers observed twenty chimpanzees for over ninety hours and counted seven hundred and sixty-five instances of biting, barking, screaming, flinching, teeth-baring, and outright fighting.[25] If two young chimps started fighting, things escalated quickly; their mothers would attack each other and recruit others to join the fray. That's about one episode of aggression every fifteen minutes. Observations of chimps suggest that they are two-to-three times more aggressive than humans.[26] Additionally, the researchers found that large portions of the chimps' violence were hard to explain, seemingly spontaneous and escalating quickly, even with careful observation. "Are you looking at me? You want some of this? Hold my termite stick . . ."

In addition, lower aggression is linked to the ability to consider others' perspectives. For example, children and adults who are less upset when something goes wrong are better able to take others' perspectives[27] because their Protect Systems do not hijack their mentalizing abilities.[28] Similarly, depressed individuals have a harder time detecting other people's emotional highs and lows because they are focused inward.[29] When we are less emotionally reactive and aggressive, we open our capacity to understand others. While we have plenty of viral examples of people throwing fits and freaking out, compared to what would show up on Chimpstagram, they are the exception that proves the rule.

COGNITIVE CONTROL

The third enabler of human cooperation is our ability to inhibit and regulate our desires. Larger brains and growth in the prefrontal cortex generally indicate more self-control. As we saw earlier, when neuroscientists temporarily paralyze parts of the Pause and Piece-Together System, people make more short-term choices for immediate self-gratification,[30] like snatching the TV remote, chewing loudly, interrupting conversations, and slurping someone else's beverage—all the things my wife says I do when we binge our latest show. On the other hand, activating the Pause and Piece-Together System demonstrates the ability to inhibit some intuitive tendencies and exercise more self-control. Self-control increases our odds of choosing the most socially acceptable behaviors.

If neuroimaging studies show us that activation of specific brain regions influences self-control, then the relative size of those regions should also have an influence. And in this regard, we humans surpass our distant cousins. Brain size was a consistent proportion of our body size until about 2 million years ago, when it started to grow more rapidly. In the fossil record, brain growth coincides with evidence of stone tool use, enabling us to break open bones to eat the nutrient-rich marrow inside.[31] Over time, when compared to other hominids, humans have developed smaller jaw muscles, stomachs, and colons.[32] These changes can only support our nutritional needs if we cook our food (usually a social and cooperative task) rather than eating large quantities of less nutrient-dense plants and grasses. One fascinating theory suggests that a positive feedback loop emerged where increased self-control allowed us to work together to grow, catch, cook, and eat more nutrient-dense food, increasing brain size and self-control. Ultimately, this has led to boosting the size of our brain from one pound to almost three pounds over the last 2 million years, with much of the growth focused on the prefrontal cortex. Looking beyond humans, tests across thirty-six species, from sparrows to spider monkeys, corroborate that brain size strongly predicts self-control.[33]

So, evolution has fostered at least three changes that supercharged our cooperative ability, making it easier to help those around us. First, we better understand others' internal states thanks to adaptations like mentalizing, oxytocin, and more prominent sclera. Second, we have become less aggressive over time. And third, we exhibit greater self-control. We seem to be hardwired to help each other. Together, these adaptations make it harder to hold on to the belief that people are inherently self-interested, and they suggest that while nature can be red in tooth and claw, she is also sometimes warm in hand and embrace.

THE FERAL CHILD OF AVEYRON

In the late 1700s, a feral boy was found in the forests outside the French town of Aveyron. The boy seemed to be about nine years old, but no one could say for sure. He had been abandoned at a young age and thus never learned to speak. A local doctor named the boy Victor and cared for him with the help of a woman named Madame Guerin. The doctor worked with Victor for several years, trying to teach him how to conjugate -*ir* verbs, how to wear high socks, and perhaps how to be snobbish (I mean *discerning*) about croissants. Despite being raised without human contact, Victor showed signs of basic morality. For example, he cried when separated from Madame Guerin and would console her and the doctor when they seemed upset.

Victor also developed an irritating habit of stealing things from around the house, and the doctor would punish him by, you guessed it—locking him in a closet. One day, perhaps after having one too many cognacs, the doctor decided to run an experiment. He tried to punish Victor unjustly. He put Victor in the closet even though he hadn't stolen anything. Unlike the other times, Victor did not comply with the punishment and instead bit the doctor. After bandaging his arm, the bruised doctor consoled himself by concluding that even though Victor could not use words, he knew his punishment was unjust. Even though Victor grew up outside of human society, he had a sense of fairness and justice. The doctor eventually moved on from Aveyron and left Victor in the care of Madame Guerin. Victor died at the age of forty,[34] but his story inspired romantic philosophers to ask, Can an individual be fully human without a society? It also inspired François Truffaut to make the award-winning film *Wild Child*. And it inspires us to contend with the question, Is biological evolution enough to sustain cooperation?

While Victor demonstrated some rudiments of morality, such as kindness, consoling others, and getting angry at unfair harm, he also missed the nuance and details of human cooperation. He couldn't learn polite French society's complex etiquette, rituals, and grammar. Evolutionary theories can explain Victor's predisposition to cooperate with those he was close to. But biological evolution alone cannot explain the variety, complexity, and scale of cooperation in human societies. For example, how do we coordinate millions of pilgrims traveling safely to Mecca or Jerusalem, markets where buyers and sellers take life-altering risks, the peaceful transfer of political power, or the building of wonders like the pyramids of Giza or the Great Wall of China? Whether coordinating complex logistics, buying and selling property on the other side of the globe, or waiting in line for a cup of soup, human cooperation involves complex meanings and rituals. Evolution provides a template for cooperation but doesn't specify those complex rules. As we're about to see, nature *assumes* nurture because nurture *bestows* culture.

CULTURES OF COOPERATION

Children raised in families (not forests) demonstrate complex and novel strategies for cooperation. For example, when playing the Prisoner's Dilemma game, where partners must choose between cooperating and accepting a smaller benefit for both parties or defecting for a chance at a greater individual gain with the risk of a joint loss, chimps wait for their partner to decide and then copy their strategy. In contrast, young children do something our great ape cousins cannot do; they talk to each other—agreeing to take turns winning.[35]

The development of language and self-control makes cultural evolution possible. There are many competing definitions of culture, but we will use a sufficiently broad one for our purposes. We'll use the term to refer to the shared mental maps that people in a community use to make sense of the world, as well as the physical artifacts and social interactions that both shape and are shaped by those ways of making meaning. If evolution sets the stage for humans to become ultrasocial, then culture provides the scripts. Let's look at several ways in which culture fosters cooperation and helping.

STORIES AND EXAMPLES

Cultures pass on complicated norms about how to cooperate within and across groups; for example, according to the Islamic faith, a Muslim woman can borrow money from a non-Muslim, but she cannot marry one. In some cultures, you can help a person of a different caste build a house, but you can't eat with them. In parts of the southern US, children learn to say hello to everyone they pass on the street. This is a strange act for people from large cities and other parts of the world. When I visited Russia, I was unnerved by how no one smiled or said hello, and they were probably unnerved at my unsolicited awkward waving and grinning. (Who is this mudak, and why is he smiling so much?) Children in some parts of China grow up thinking it's perfectly normal for a husband to carry his pregnant wife across a bed of hot coals; how else would you ensure a healthy and painless pregnancy? If you are a Southern Italian, you might grow up thinking the Northern Italians are snobbish and rude, and Northern Italian children learn to see their neighbors to the south as too laid back.

These norms develop because as we grow, we observe how others walk and talk in specific situations and notice patterns in those behaviors. Watching our friends and families' choices helps shape whether we enjoy scarfing down a croque monsieur or a Reuben, our preference for jamming to Alikiba or Karamelo Santo, what features of other humans we find irresistible, whether we pray on Friday, Saturday, or Sunday, what clothes we wear, and whether we vote red, blue, green, pink, or saffron. Our ability to induce rules from observations can also lead to stereotypes such as "Black people shouldn't be CEOs," just because in the US, fewer Black people are currently in that role. Unfortunately, customs can also become cages when we mistake what is commonplace for what should be.

It takes time for children to start internalizing these cultural norms. In one experiment, researchers put young children from Boston in a virtual room with four other virtual children.[36] In this online environment, the kids were given virtual stickers to trade. In one condition, an avatar would selfishly take a sticker from the child; in that case, all the children took the sticker back, regardless of their age. "Eh, Ma! You see what this chowdahead just did to me?" In a second condition, one of the avatars would give a sticker to the child; in this case, very few four-year-olds would reciprocate and give a sticker back, but most nine-year-olds did because they had been socialized to return the favor. You don't have to teach children to take revenge (chimps do it naturally, too), but it takes culture and self-control to show positive reciprocity.

One way that culture transmits these norms is through shared stories. In the US, the story of George Washington and the cherry tree extols the virtue of honesty (and a sharp ax), and research shows that children who are told that story are subsequently more likely to be honest.[37] For

Hindus, the story of Ekalavya demonstrates the virtues of self-reliance and honoring one's teacher. Ekalavya is a low-caste boy who is a gifted archer. He is forbidden from taking archery lessons with the high-caste boys, but he stays hidden in the trees, listening to their training and diligently practicing on his own. One day, the teacher and higher-caste students come across evidence of astonishing archery skills and wonder who the gifted warrior could be. Ekalavya reveals himself and thanks the teacher for his guidance. According to custom, the teacher requests that Ekalavya give him some payment in exchange, and the boy agrees to give anything he has. The teacher asks him to cut off his right thumb to protect the status of a high-caste boy as the best archer in the kingdom. Without hesitation, Ekalavya grabs his knife, cuts off his thumb, and presents it to the teacher, demonstrating his honor and impairing his own archery abilities forever. It's a tragic and disturbing story about caste, power, privilege, and the virtues of self-sufficiency, but one that most Indian children learn to recite at an early age.

In Ghana, children are told the story of the frog and mouse. The frog is upset that his friend, the mouse, doesn't come to visit his home. So, to get revenge, he ties the mouse to his leg and jumps back into his pond. The mouse calls for help, but the obstinate frog doesn't listen, and his friend drowns. But the mouse's body also attracts a hawk who eats them both, illustrating the wise Ghanaian proverb, "Do not dig a deep pit for your enemy because you may fall into it yourself." Through stories passed on to us by our parents, teachers, and streaming services, culture promotes cooperation by reinforcing the intricate rules that define right and wrong.

SANCTIONING

Exemplars and stories are not always enough to maintain cooperation; cultural norms must also be enforced. In every group, there are ways to free-ride and benefit twice, first from others who follow a norm and second by capturing the benefits of breaking the norm yourself. For example, some people enjoy public services while avoiding taxes; they let their family do the chores while they nap or enjoy the freedom provided by democratic institutions while also profiting from keeping those institutions sick. Think of any group project; some people spend all their time online shopping and watching TikToks and then just put their names on the title slide. If these free-riding behaviors aren't called out, prevented, and even punished, it can weaken cooperation by signaling that doing your fair share is unnecessary.

Children start to care about enforcing social norms around age six. They will pay a cost to intervene against a selfish peer who refuses to share resources.[38] "Here's one Tootsie Pop so that you can punish Jimmy for taking everyone's Halloween candy." When young children are given an unfair allocation in the Dictator Game, like four candies for themselves and one for a peer,[39] they tend to eagerly accept it (More candy for me, *suckers!*). But by age seven, they would rather see no one get any candy than accept the unequal distribution.

When norms are clarified and articulated, third parties like courts, mediators, and bouncers trying to stop a fight at a bar can use them to arbitrate disputes. Society pays and authorizes people to punish norm violators. These sanctioning systems function according to cultural rules. For example, the main sanctioning entities in medieval Italy were powerful families that sought revenge for slights against their honor. As the Catholic Church rose in prominence, it weakened those kin-based institutions, making sanctioning before God a standard system across families. Thus, people came to see each other more in terms of their relationship to the church and less as belonging to the Biancis, Innocentis, or Rossis.

Sanctioning can take many different forms: revenge killing, walking the plank, having a curse placed on your home, being uninvited from a group trip, having your seat at the dinner table moved away from the guest of honor, being arrested by the criminal justice system, and having a catchy song written about you and sung at the Super Bowl halftime show—basically anything intended to publicly shame or punish individuals for violating norms. In Fijian culture, vigilante justice is allowed in particular instances. If someone repeatedly fails to share food at feasts or to follow the rules when they build their house, their family falls into bad standing. If their reputation suffers enough, fellow villagers are allowed to harass them by stealing their pots or crops. I guess it's kind of like when the power-hungry homeowners' association president tells you your lawn gnomes violate the rules and leaves severed gnome body parts in your mailbox. If the same behavior was perpetrated against a family in good standing, others would band together to stop the harassment. While most Fijians do not engage in punishment, they tolerate these behaviors to enforce norms.[40] Cultures design and implement sanctioning systems to punish the loafers, free-riders, and rule-breakers, thus maintaining cooperation.

REPUTATION

Reputation allows human groups to transition from cooperating with people they know to cooperating with strangers. Think of online transactions. In theory, exchanges between strangers should have more cheating. You could pay for something and not get anything delivered or get something very different than what you thought you were buying, like those memes of people getting ridiculously tiny versions of the cheap furniture they ordered online. Instead, reputation-based reviews can facilitate trust in large anonymous groups. People talk if you don't work well with others and follow cultural norms. They give you one-star ratings, and your opportunities for working with others evaporate. Similarly, studies of gossip show that it can serve the function of social regulation, spreading information about reputations, behaviors, norms, and values the gossipers care about.[41]

Children learn to take reputation into account as they get older. For example, two-and-a-half-year-olds cooperate the same with everyone in laboratory experiments. Yet just a year later, three-and-a-half-year-olds take reputation into account and prefer partners who are known to share.[42] While both children and chimps prefer to interact with good collaborators, there is no evidence that chimpanzees actively manage their reputations. In a study designed to understand the impact of reputation, researchers assigned five-year-olds to one of two conditions. In the first condition, they could steal a sticker from another child to complete a task (the stealing condition). In the second, they could help another child by giving them their sticker (the helping condition). Half of the children in each condition were observed by an adult. Five-year-olds stole the sticker 24 percent of the time when no one was watching and only 4 percent of the time when someone was present. Similarly, in the helping condition, children helped 11 percent of the time when they were unobserved and 28 percent of the time when someone was watching. In contrast, when chimps were given similar tasks, they did not change their behavior when observed by other chimps, stealing about 20 percent of the time and helping about 35 percent of the time, regardless.[43] Chimps don't show evidence of thinking, "Well, if I don't help Reginald now, I might develop a reputation for being selfish, and I want Patricia to think highly of me, so even though I don't really like Reginald because he's only in it for the grapes, I'll help him this time." As human societies grew, reputation facilitated cooperation between people who were not directly related to each other; therefore, most of us learn from a young age that our reputations are an essential resource we need to nurture and protect.

US AND THEM

Finally, cultures draw the boundary between who counts as "us" and who doesn't, defining what psychologists call in-group and out-group. Humans have defined groups based on every imaginable difference, from people's eye color, caste, and family reputation, to religion, socioeconomic status, race, political preferences, when they were born, where they live, what they believe in, and what sports teams they root for. These definitions can also change from situation to situation; sometimes, our group could be those that have the same training as we do. At other times, the relevant group is those sitting on the fourth floor, not those on the fifth floor.

These culturally defined groups shape how we interact with and experience others. For example, our level of trust drops as we encounter faces that look different from the ones we are used to seeing. In one study, researchers created face morphs where a stereotypical Japanese face was blended with a stereotypical Israeli face.[44] Different images had different ratios of each face; for example, one photo was a composite with 25 percent of the Japanese face and 75 percent of the Israeli face. The participants were instructed to rate the trustworthiness of morphs with different ratios. The Japanese participants reported the faces as more trustworthy the more stereotypically Japanese they were. The same was true for the Israeli participants, who also found familiar Israeli faces more trustworthy, showing that we can have a quick, intuitive repulsion to unfamiliar people.

These cultural distinctions show up as early as kindergarten. Six-year-olds are more willing to punish children from the out-group than children within their own group.[45] Children demonstrate higher moral standards for those who are similar and expect those who look different to follow different norms.[46] When adults are given a version of the trolley problem, the set of thought experiments where they must choose to push a person off a bridge to save five others, they are more likely to decide to push the person if they have a foreign-sounding name.[47] Why do you think people call me "Bobby" when my name is Bidhan? I'm not gonna get tied to another train track.

One group of researchers summarized similar findings like this: "When subjects were allowed to punish in-group and out-group members for the same norm violations, punishment of in-group members was less likely and was associated with heightened activity and connectivity [in the mentalizing regions]. Mentalizing regions become more active, suggesting that people were rationalizing their group mates' transgressions; the same regions were not as active when out-group members made the same offense."[48] In short, we use different standards when the same infractions are committed by people we are alike, rather than those that we see as unalike.

Today, in the US, Republicans and Democrats are less likely to see the other side as fully human. In a recent study, volunteers from both sides of the aisle were asked to rate how evolved and civilized they perceived members of both parties. The scale ranged from 0, meaning completely unevolved and uncivilized, to 100, meaning the group was wholly evolved and civilized. Both parties reported their in-group at around 83 and the other party at about 62. But when they were asked how the other party would rate them, Democrats assumed that Republicans saw them around an average of 35, and Republicans thought that Democrats saw them around 28. We dehumanize the political out-group and overestimate how much they dehumanize us, in turn helping us rationalize our lack of empathy toward the opposing side.[49]

Research shows that viewing pictures of someone from another group can cause a momentary blip in our amygdalae,[50] a microsecond of fear. Still, we can learn not to fear different faces when we notice similarities—for example, when they are wearing a hat from our favorite sports team, a symbol from our faith, or a shirt that we also own, or when they are smiling (or not smiling in Russia). For any two human beings, there are countless similarities and differences, which means we can choose what to pay attention to and moderate how close we feel to others. For example, writer George Orwell signed up to fight against Fascism during the Spanish Civil War. He later described how a fascist soldier came into his gunsight, half-dressed and running, holding up his trousers with both hands. Orwell recounts, "I refrained from shooting at him. . . . I did not shoot partly because of that detail about the trousers. I had come here to shoot at 'Fascists'; but a man who is holding up his trousers isn't a 'Fascist,' he is visibly a fellow creature, similar to yourself, and you don't feel like shooting at him."[51] Some of our most celebrated heroes have been able to break down cultural barriers, whether they were "insiders" who helped us see the "outsiders" as similar or outsiders who captured our attention, helping us find common humanity with those on the margins, whom we initially misunderstood and feared.

But why do we treat insiders and outsiders so differently? Surprisingly, one emerging explanation links back to the so-called love hormone, oxytocin. Scientists have discovered that it has some surprising "side effects." We saw earlier that puffs of intranasal oxytocin make men more cooperative in the Trust Game, but more recent evidence shows that it also makes them less willing to cooperate with out-group members.[52] The critical factor seems to be the perceived level of threat. Oxytocin promotes bonding and care when the perceived danger is low, but it can promote increased aggression when the threat is unknown or high.[53] Oxytocin can make people more group-focused and aggressive toward outsiders. Life Lesson: Snorting stuff never really turns out like you expect.

Scientists now call oxytocin's effect "the propensity to tend-and-defend."[54] Indeed, when groups of chimps fight each other, their bodies have higher oxytocin levels.[55] When we're under the effects of oxytocin, our attention, like a spotlight, becomes focused on those we care about to strengthen those bonds. Everything outside of that spotlight is blurred, out of focus, pixelated, or in shadow. And in those shadows, the seeds of misunderstanding find fertile ground. A simple pixelated view of others makes us more likely to miss their complexity and humanity. "Sorry, I didn't know you were interested in playing basketball after class; I thought Indians were only interested in math." When our attention is focused on our group and blurs the internal states of outsiders, the ties that bind us restrain us from helping others.

Culture directs our attentional spotlight and our choices of whom to help by picking whom we mentalize about and placing some people outside the circle where rules, values, and considerations of fairness apply. Much of the behavior that seems incomprehensibly aggressive, selfish, or antisocial at first glance can have surprising roots in protecting other groups or individuals we care deeply about. When people are less able to read and ascribe mental states to out-group members, trust dissolves, helping ceases, and we become worse versions of ourselves.[56] Therefore, the inevitable disruptions and misunderstandings that occur between groups become landmines, further entrenching the lines between us and them. Instead of giving others the benefit of the doubt, we both end up bearing the costs of our certainty. In contrast, mentalizing makes social relations easier. When we shine our attentional spotlight on people's internal states, we can better understand their intentions and motives, accommodate their behaviors, and forgive. Just because it sounds suspiciously like the bastard child of a motivational poster and fortune cookie doesn't make it any less true: the more we look for the humanity of others, the more we find our own.

CONFLICTS ABOUT COOPERATION

I once met a colleague across campus who introduced me to a faculty friend. Within two minutes of learning what I do, the faculty member tried to convince me that researching and teaching ethics is a waste of time. This faculty member believed that humans are fundamentally self-interested and that I was confusing my business students by talking about fairy tales like morality and cooperation. According to them, the sooner we prepare students to live in an unjust world, the better.

Similarly, I've met faculty at conferences who teach their students that every workplace and every industry is a fierce competition. So, they should focus on accumulating resources and influence to get ahead. The courses most of these faculty teach are packed with valuable lessons on winning friends, crushing competitors, and power-posing yourself into a greater wealth of resources. I'm not questioning the value of these skills (and by now, it's clear to everyone that I could certainly benefit from learning how to make a friend). Still, these classes rarely mention how to acquire resources ethically or use them responsibly. I worry that these courses might inadvertently encourage business students to do almost anything to get ahead, with no reservations about taking the rest of the world down in the process.

Finally, I've sat through meetings where people opine that ethics is nothing more than virtue signaling. They point out one surface-level inconsistency and then escalate to argue that ethics doesn't exist. For example, if we think lying is wrong in general, but we tell a white lie to avoid hurting someone's feelings, then we're hypocritical, which somehow shows that ethics and morality are myths. These folks think of an ethical person as someone who sacrifices everything to be consistent with a single

Figure 3

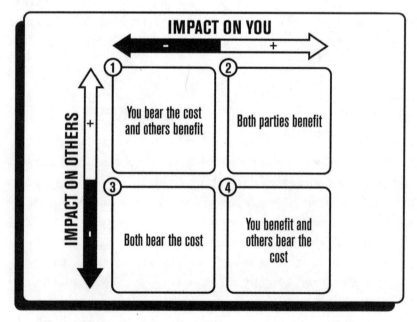

value or rule. If human beings are inconsistent in any way, then ethics must only be a way to disguise self-interest.

Despite being ripped straight from Bond-villain monologues, these perspectives are either implicitly or explicitly taught at universities and business schools around the world. Views of human nature rooted in selfishness don't reflect the latest science, and they enable oversimplified responses in moments of doubt that involve taking risks to help others. If we believe that most people won't help, then it's easier to rationalize when we don't. Each of these perspectives assumes that selfishness and selflessness sit on a single continuum, meaning that there's always an inherent tradeoff between your interests and the interests of others.

So, who's right? Should we train our students to assume that human nature is unfair, unjust, and cruel, and that they should be ready to take what they can for themselves? Should we help them see and bring about the potential, however fragile it might be, for a better world?

Let's imagine a simplified set of outcomes of a choice; for example (I don't know, just randomly), should you help someone by taking a personal risk (depicted in Figure 3 on the previous page)? Let's say you decide to help. As a result, there can be four broad categories of outcomes:

- First, you can bear a cost, and others benefit, like if you get fired for saying something to the male doctors, but the new surgeon benefits because inappropriate comments stop (Quadrant 1).

- Second, you could benefit, and the other person could bear the cost, like if you gain a positive reputation for helping, but the new surgeon must now sit through endless hours of unwelcome investigations (Quadrant 4).

- Third, there's an outcome where both parties lose, like if nothing gets better and you both are ostracized by the other doctors (Quadrant 3).

- Finally, both parties could end with a net benefit; for example, if you are recognized and thanked for speaking up, the juvenile comments stop, and you and all the surgeons have a stronger relationship (Quadrant 2).

When I show my students this figure and ask them which quadrant seems most ethical, most say Quadrant 1, where a person incurs costs to benefit someone else. But, after a few minutes, some students will argue that Quadrant 4 can also be ethical because you have obligations to yourself, like developing your skills and satisfying your values. You might not report the doctors' comments if there are high costs for the new surgeon; therefore, under some circumstances, it could be justifiable to stay silent.

The faculty who focus on teaching hard truths seem to believe that we should train and prepare students to work in Quadrant 4 because they think most people take from others to enrich themselves. They seem to believe I am interested in the opposite, pushing students into Quadrant 1, where they consistently bear costs to help others. If you think everyone else is selfish, then that would seem like an irrational strategy. However, I think that depending on specifics, Quadrants 1, 2, and 4 all involve different values and responsibilities and could be justifiable. We must be able and willing to play in all three, knowing their strengths and weaknesses and when to switch from one to another.

A weakness of playing in Quadrants 1 and 4 all the time is that they are unsustainable. We can't always sacrifice our interests to help others without any benefit (like the nurse who gives up his own health to aid others), nor can we continually impose costs on others to get what we want (like the executive who criminally raises the price of lifesaving drugs and buys a Wu-Tang Clan album). Ironically, if everyone tried to benefit themselves by externalizing costs on others, we'd inadvertently land in Quadrant 3, where we're all worse off. Quadrant 2, where both parties benefit, is the most sustainable. Some even argue that the primary function of oxytocin is to create benefits for both parties; for example, a mother feels love, and a child gets care. A problem with Quadrant 2 is that it is hard to decipher a person's motive and intention in a single snapshot, and thus, it is hard to know how much you should trust them in the future. Did you choose to help because you really care about me or because you benefit by helping? No one wants to be set up to fail or to be taken advantage of because they trusted someone they shouldn't have. But we should acknowledge that the opposite error is also costly; we can distrust people we should have trusted, leaving value on the table. Quadrants 1 and 4 seem like they offer clearer signals about a person. We feel like we have more predictive information about their future behavior. But we may be overgeneralizing from a single snapshot.

Critically, the set of outcomes in this matrix (and current scientific evidence) demonstrates that self-interest and interest in others can be *independent* rather than at the end of a single continuum. Indeed, our group psychology suggests that we are sometimes so deeply connected to others (particularly our families, friends, and favorite groups) that the very distinction between self and other becomes blurred. The role of oxytocin in modulating the Pursue System means that helping those we are connected to and seeing them benefit can feel just as good (if not better than) obtaining personal benefits.

The debate about human nature is hard to settle in the abstract because human beings are complex—we have personal interests, and our interests are connected to others, like when we feel that unique joy of seeing those we care about succeed (called *mudita* in Sanskrit). Like with all abstractions, we generalize from specific cases to meet our goals. If you want to protect your students (and yourself) against being taken advantage of, you might overgeneralize cases of selfishness. "The world is selfish and cruel—Mother knows best!" On the other hand, if you want to promote trust, you might highlight the potential for reciprocity: "People can be kind and helpful." When we can pick and choose our examples, the debate is impossible to settle. Still, it's more answerable about a specific company, group, or person, because we can collect information to triangulate their motives and better assess the benefits and risks of cooperating with them.

One strategy to consider is spending as much time in Quadrant 2 as possible, surrounding yourself with as many others who agree. Indeed, research shows that "givers" prosper when they're around other "givers" rather than when they're surrounded by "takers."[37] Despite your best efforts, you must be intentional and careful if you find yourself forced to play in Quadrant 1 or 4. In those cases, just like with all the moments of doubt in this book, you need to understand the benefits and risks in detail, be ready to justify your choices, mitigate any harm caused, and look for ways to rebalance the scales across future choices. I don't know if that's convincing to those tough-love faculty, who see the bright side as blinding, but I'm not ready to stop practicing my mentalizing powers.

I'll keep trying to understand their perspectives and find more nuanced and useful understandings of when we can and do help others.

Choosing when and how to help can be easy when we don't feel connected to the recipients, or when we do. However, when we aren't sure, or if we feel pulled in different directions, we can begin by being more intentional about our mentalizing. (See appendix tool 6.) If long-standing evidence suggests that oxytocin can increase mentalizing, then more recent evidence shows that it's a two-way street.[58] When we take the time to understand someone's perspective, our levels of oxytocin increase as a result.[59] Thus, we can use our attentional flashlight carefully, ensuring we understand our counterparts (Will this specific person appreciate and reciprocate my helping or not? How do I know?) and consider the specific potential of moving from Quadrant 3 to Quadrant 4. (Have we carefully considered all the ways we could personally benefit from helping?) For example, will speaking to the male doctors increase my ability to stand up for what I believe in? Will I feel proud of my actions? Too often, we can quickly assume that helping is costly and underestimate the benefits to ourselves.

When making choices where helping is costly, we fall back on our beliefs about human nature. Are people inherently selfish? Do people genuinely care about others? The latest research from evolutionary psychology, including how oxytocin works, suggests that the best and worst of our species' behavior hinges on our ability to attribute three-dimensional humanity to others, to see them as protagonists of their own stories rather than caricatures and two-dimensional set decoration in our own. Though there are real limits to our helping, when we find ways of connecting with the humanity of those that are different or distant, we can help enlarge the circle of who counts as "us" and shrink the circle of who counts as "them."

8

Blame Game

YOU ARE THE SENIOR VICE PRESIDENT OF SALES at a tech review website named HiveTech, where customers discuss and review the latest smart products. Your site receives more than 3 million views daily and shapes the fate of companies making everything from smartwatches to smart homes. Some of these companies also pay to advertise on your site, and you have always been careful to distinguish paid advertising from user reviews. Users appreciate that they can get honest (if not extreme) opinions on your site. You have learned that "techies" don't like censorship and have boldly gone to other sites when they feel their voice is filtered, edited, or drowned out by advertising.

Last week, you received a call from the legal counsel of MacroSung, a global tech firm with hundreds of products reviewed on your site. They also provide almost 12 percent of your ad revenue. The legal counsel presented preliminary evidence suggesting a targeted smear campaign against their products. Several negative reviews across a range of products are written in a vaguely familiar style, repeating the same points whether they are relevant to the specific product or not. In addition, despite the similarity and poor quality of the writing, hundreds of users have liked the negative reviews, amplifying their impact. Most of these users have no other activity on the website. The legal counsel suspects that one of their competitors might have coordinated the negative reviews and hired a click-farm to like the "fake" content. Click-farms are workers who are paid to like and share content across various platforms. MacroSung has recently seen a decline in sales and lost market share. Their lawyer politely requested that HiveTech remove the fake content from the site. He gently suggests that you could be sued for libel because the content is false and misleading. You responded that your team would investigate further and get back to them.

After assessing the reviews, your team agrees that something suspicious seems to be going on, but it will take months to prove definitively. You could remove the comments, risking a backlash from users who disapprove of censorship. Additionally, you could be seen as playing favorites with MacroSung, setting a precedent for other companies to request changes. It is costly and time-consuming to screen and approve all the material posted on your site, meaning you must hire additional staff. Finally, if you choose to police content, rival websites could accuse you of censorship.

HiveTech was built as a neutral platform where people could exchange honest opinions about the latest technology, thus rewarding the best products and creating a more efficient market. The founders never anticipated this kind of potential abuse of the system. You wonder if intervening on behalf of MacroSung would distort the market's perspective of their products. On the other hand, if you do nothing, MacroSung would most likely pull advertising from the site and prompt others to follow. Your next meeting with the legal counsel is scheduled for tomorrow.

What would you do?

This kind of decision is called an "unintended use case" because HiveTech was intended for honest product reviews but inadvertently provides a platform to spread misinformation. In situations like this, people experience doubt about their level of responsibility and react by fighting it, saying nothing, or doubling down and avoiding responsibility at all costs. Unfortunately, when we employ these intuitive defensive strategies, we can unintentionally cause more relational and financial damages. To prevent these errors from occurring and to bounce back more quickly (and maybe even more strongly) after they occur, let's look at how responsibility works.

WHAT IS RESPONSIBILITY?

When someone doesn't drive the posted speed limit, put away the dishes, have the correct visa information at the airport, or wear matching socks, they are held responsible—or is that just me? Being responsible to someone or some group means having to give reasons for our actions when things deviate from expectations.[1] Then, depending on our reasons and how they are interpreted, the cops, companions, customs agents, or courts assign a level of blame and punishment or praise and reward. For example, when the bartender goes above and beyond to make a great cocktail or the waiter has forgotten you're still there, we spontaneously praise and blame accordingly.

Being responsible is a social agreement to adjust our choices based on the specific individuals and groups we are responsible to. But this social arrangement is not open to just anyone. Generally, a certain level of mental capability is required to participate. That's why we don't prosecute dogs, minors, rocks, robots, and chickens in court. Even though all of these can and do cause harm—just look at the dents on my twenty-year-old Toyota as evidence. So instead, we turn to the capable humans who are supposed to mind those dogs, children, rocks, robots, and chickens and who are supposed to accept the responsibility on their behalf. In court, defenses of insanity or incapacity are meant to show that the defendant should be exempt from the responsibility arrangement.

We can interpret responsibility by focusing our positive or negative evaluations on the person or their actions. This leads to four general approaches: two kinds of positive evaluations, one of the person and one of the action, both called *praise*; negative evaluations of the person are generally called *blame*; and philosophers call negative evaluations of the action *judgments of wrongness*. These four tactics help align our actions with our social groups, encouraging us to follow norms (which can feel good), and can result in benefits such as better relationships, higher status, and more resources. Think about a time when you worked hard for someone's praise—your parents, your friends, or the sommelier when you pronounced that Basque wine correctly. In contrast, violating norms and being blamed can cause you to be ostracized and sleep somewhere else, from the doghouse to the jailhouse. Groups of all sizes, from couples to countries, regulate members' behavior by holding each other responsible.

Figure 4

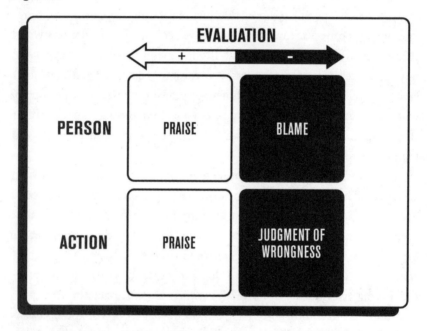

When we fire the incompetent worker, vote out the corrupt politician, and tell off the nosy neighbor, our actions are informed by our interpretations of their responsibility—in effect, we hold them accountable. Research shows that this kind of accountability is essential to sustain cooperation. In one study, researchers at Stanford University had groups of four strangers play the Public Goods game, a common protocol where participants get some money to allocate.[2] In this version, participants chose how much to keep for themselves and how much to contribute to the public fund. After everyone had decided, the researchers doubled the money in the public fund and divided it equally among the group members. Under these rules, individuals can do relatively better for themselves if they can minimize what they allocate to the public fund and maximize what they collect from others. But for the group to do well, they had to stop this free-riding. Usually, people start by contributing to the public fund, and just like rich people moving their affairs to the Cayman Islands, public investment dwindles in subsequent rounds as participants figure out that they can get away with contributing less. With strong incentives for free-riding, the Public Goods game is a helpful context for studying strategies for holding people responsible.

The researchers who conducted the study were interested in how publicly rating individual behavior (as very moral or immoral) would change contributions to the public fund. In the first condition, participants could see everyone's contributions and earnings and rated each person's actions at the end of each round. The ratings functioned like praise and blame, essentially highlighting the social consequences of their choices. Contributions to the public fund remained high across all nine rounds. "I'm sure as hell not going to be known as the free-rider in this group; I want that five-star rating. Here's my contribution, and would you like a complimentary water?" Holding people accountable for their contributions increased cooperation, even though participants were in different rooms, working on computers, and never met each other.

In a second condition of the same experiment, instead of ratings, participants were allowed to punish each other for not contributing to the public fund. Consistent with previous research, punishment (in this case, issuing fines) also improved cooperation.[3] But what happened in part two of the study was intriguing. Participants were paired with another group member and asked to complete a cooperative task. In this subsequent task, pairs that used praise and blame rather than punishment demonstrated more trust. Holding group members accountable through punishment maintained cooperation in the short term but reduced it in future interactions. Without accountability, it is much harder to sustain the mutual benefits of cooperation, and how we hold people accountable has important implications for our future relationships.

BAD > GOOD

Just because we use praise and blame to influence others' behavior doesn't mean we use them equally. Over the last several decades, psychologists have amassed considerable and consistent evidence that bad outweighs good or, more specifically, negative information outweighs positive information in our attention, memory, and thinking.[4] The first evidence of this asymmetry occurs in our language. At least in English, we have more words to describe negative experiences than positive ones. For example, we have words that describe the details and distinctions of negative states, like woe, jealousy, and indignation, helping us (and the heartbroken poets) finely differentiate between the subtleties of melancholy and misery. (The former originates from our body and mental health, and the latter results from unfortunate circumstances like poverty.) In contrast, there are fewer words to describe positive emotions. Words like adoration, admiration, pleasure, glee, and elation are less differentiated, explaining why most pop songs sound the same and that we differentiate negative emotions more precisely when compared to our differentiation of positive ones.

Our brains tip the scales in favor of negative information even more. For example, healthy volunteers in the lab were asked to write down as many words as they could in two minutes. Then, researchers categorized their words as positive, negative, and neutral. On average, about 50 percent of the words people wrote down were negative, 30 percent positive, and 20 percent neutral, demonstrating that negative things come to mind more often.[5] Other estimates suggest we recall negative events over positive ones by a four-to-one margin.[6] Similarly, research has shown that the effects of negative events last longer. For example, we feel bad longer after the divorce than we feel good after the honeymoon.[7] When workers were asked to keep diaries of what happened to them each day, including reporting their moods, analysis of their diaries showed that their boss yelling at them had a larger and longer impact on their mood than finding a primo parking spot. Similarly, we are more certain about our opinions of negative acts than our judgments about positive ones, and we rate losses as more painful than we rate equal-sized gains as pleasurable,[8] especially when the Protect System is active.[9] Finally, we are more likely to be derailed and distracted by negative than positive information.[10] Like when you spend all day in the fetal position ruminating about the one bad review on your Etsy page but ignore all the other five-star reviews.

Hundreds of similar studies suggest that in many different contexts, negative information captures our attention, impacts our choices, lingers in our thoughts, and is easier to recall. For most of us, seeing the glass half empty is much easier than seeing it half full. From an evolutionary perspective, bad might outweigh good because attention, memory, and transmission of negative information can confer a survival advantage. If we avoid bad actors, dangerous people, harmful plants, and risky situations, we stand a better chance of survival. People who are oblivious to threats may not survive them, so there are good reasons that our cautious brains tip the scale in favor of negative information. But, while there is at least one pro to this pattern, let's pay even more attention to the cons.

If bad outweighs good, then studies suggest we should improve our relationships by removing our errors first and then adding positive behaviors. Instead, most of us do the opposite; we let our errors persist and hope that adding a few niceties on top will help people forget about our fumbles. Because we minimize the impact of our harmful acts, give ourselves credit for our intentions, and overestimate our general goodness, it seems reasonable that one nice act will make up for something we messed up. But when bad outweighs good in our minds, it takes more positive interactions to compensate for negative ones. For example, research on teams and couples suggests that it takes around five positive interactions to compensate for a negative one.[11] If the scale is so imbalanced, we all have much more work to do after we mess up than we think.

When attention to bad outweighs good, we are more likely to blame than to praise (and I'm not just talking about the married folks). For example, in one study, researchers created a set of ten statements about different behaviors; five were negative and five positive.[12] One negative behavior was "smashing the rear window of a random parked car," and a positive behavior was "participating in an effort to clean up a city park." Researchers asked one group to rate how positive (on a scale of 1–5) or how negative (on a scale of 1–5) they thought each of these behaviors was. These ratings helped them find a set of statements that were rated equally good and bad. Then, the researchers had a different group of participants decide how much blame or praise was deserved for each of the actions. Despite using statements with equal levels of positivity and negativity, the average blame for the negative actions (3.71) was higher than praise for the positive actions (2.89), showing that blame is stronger than praise, even for equally extreme actions.

Let's look at one more example to understand how our natural sensitivity to negative information influences how we praise and blame. Get out your pencils. How would you rate the praiseworthiness or blame-worthiness of the following actions? 1 = extreme blame, 5 = neutral, and 9 = extreme praise.

1. _____ Jack deliberately and intentionally gave the homeless man his only jacket, even though it was freezing outside.

2. _____ Because of his overwhelming and uncontrollable sympathy, Jack impulsively gave the homeless man his only jacket even though it was freezing outside.

3. _____ Jack calmly and deliberately smashed the window of the car parked in front of him because it was parked too close to his.

4. _____ Because of his overwhelming and uncontrollable anger, Jack impulsively smashed the window of the car parked in front of him because it was parked too close to his.

Put aside your suspicion that Jack might be trippin' on hallucinogenics for a second. Here are the average responses from participants: statement 1 = 6.6, statement 2 = 6.4, statement 3 = 2.1, and statement 4 = 3.0. Notice that negative actions (statements 3 and 4) dropped ratings an average of 2.45 points from neutral. On the other hand, positive actions (statements 1 and 2) only raised ratings 1.5 from neutral, reinforcing the idea that people are generous in blame and stingy with praise. But also notice that people blame deliberate negative behavior (statement 3 = 2.1) more than impulsive negative behavior (statement 4 = 3.0). Remember, the lower the number, the more the blame. This makes sense because we are more lenient for crimes of passion than premeditated crimes. But, while we carefully differentiate bad actions, no such distinction exists for impulsive or premeditated good deeds (statements 1 and 2), which are rated virtually the same.[13]

When negative information is stickier than positive, "bad reputations are easy to acquire but hard to lose, and good reputations are difficult to acquire and easy to lose."[14] If our psychology makes blame more common than praise, then when our products and services are used in harmful and unintended ways, there's a storm of blame coming our way, and we may not understand why. To know how to prepare and respond, we must understand the process by which people come to blame others.

BLAMING

On the coast of Massachusetts, an eighteen-year-old named Conrad Roy texts his friend Michelle Carter about his desire to die by suicide. Even though they have only met three times, the pair have become close, texting daily, and Conrad, who suffers from depression and anxiety, frequently discusses ending his life. Michelle, who lives a few towns over, tries to talk him out of it.

In early July 2014, the tone of their text conversations changed. Michelle frequently asks if Conrad will kill himself, seemingly goading him on. On July 12, he starts to second-guess his plans, but that week, Michelle asks him forty times when he will kill himself. Eventually, they decide that he will get a gas-powered water pump and poison himself with carbon monoxide. He goes to a parking lot and starts the water pump that evening. At one point, Conrad gets out of the car and texts Michelle. She encourages him to get back in. He does, and tragically, the police find his body the next day.

Weeks later, when law enforcement discover their text messages, Michelle is charged with involuntary manslaughter. This tragedy broke the hearts of at least two families. It also raised several questions about technology and responsibility, such as whether someone can be liable for what happens based on their text messages. Should Michelle be blamed for Conrad's death?

Psychologists have extensively studied blame, given its importance in legal cases. The current research suggests that blame is composed of several factors. Like the defense and prosecution, we can have very different interpretations of someone's blameworthiness. Figure 5 lays out the process by which people make attributions of blame. It starts with causality (did you have a role in causing the negative event?). If yes, then people try to assess your intentions next (did you do it on purpose or not?). If yes, then why? (Did you have good reasons? and if not, did you have an obligation and the capacity to prevent the harm?) The nature of the reasons that people give, their specific obligations, and their capacity result in a particular degree of blame and consequences. Let's look at each stage more carefully.

Figure 5

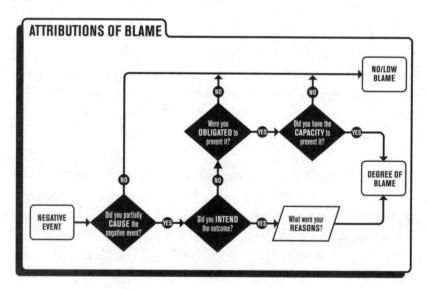

Stage 1: Causality

Were you driving the car when it hit me? Were you speaking when I was offended? Were you texting on your phone when your kid crashed their bike into my Toyota? Causality is about your actions being a part of the chain of events that led to the negative outcome. If others perceive that your actions are part of the causal chain, resulting in an adverse outcome, they are more likely to blame you. If your website caused MacroSung's sales to fall, they will see you as responsible.

While that might be intuitive, what is surprising is that people will see you as more causally related to a harmful outcome when you know ahead of time that it will occur. Here's an example. Participants read the following scenario in the lab: "Julia is mowing her lawn using an old, motorized lawnmower while listening to headphones. <u>Her lawnmower mechanic had told her weeks before to buy a new model because hers was prone to malfunction.</u> Halfway through mowing, her lawnmower malfunctions and begins to rumble back and forth wildly. When she finishes, she looks back at her lawn and realizes that her prize-winning tulips have been completely destroyed."[15]

Some participants received a version of the scenario without the underlined sentence, so in their view, Julia didn't know that her lawnmower would malfunction. Both groups were asked to identify the main cause of the tulips' being mulched. When they read the scenario where Julia knew ahead of time that the lawnmower could malfunction, she was rated as more causally connected and received more blame. Similarly, if you know the delivery on the porch will be stolen or that replying to your high school friend's hot take online is going to lead to an argument, or that the Nigerian prince isn't going to pay you back, people will say it's your fault when you're out of packages, peace of mind, or pocket money. To determine causality, people just want to know if your actions are part of a chain of events leading to the harm. If yes, even in small part, they move on to the next stage.

Stage 2: Intentionality

In the next stage, people want to know if you meant to do it. Did you intend for this to happen? If they think you did, then the amount of blame they dole out increases.

Here's another one of those devious scenarios: "An elderly woman named Gertrude gives her husband the wrong medication, which causes him to have a fatal heart attack. Gertrude has poor eyesight, and the label is hard to read. She has a rocky relationship with her husband and a sizeable life insurance policy that she could cash in upon his death."

In one condition, participants were told, "This happened last month." In a second condition, different participants were told that "this will happen in the future." Previous research demonstrates that people tend to assume that future behavior is more intentional than past behavior.[16] Both sets of participants were then asked how intentionally Gertrude acted, and participants who read about the scenario occurring in the future were more likely to think that Gertrude killed her husband intentionally and thus deserved more blame and harsher punishments. Similarly, in another experiment, shocks of equal intensity were experienced as more painful and more blameworthy if participants perceived that the shocker was doing it on purpose.[17] In short, the more people perceive a harmful act was intentional, the more blame they hand out.

Yet, despite the simplicity of this observation, it can be notoriously difficult to establish an accurate view of someone else's intentions. Each of us has more information to assess our own intentions, so we give ourselves credit that we don't give others.[18] Therefore, there's a natural gap between the amount of blame we think we deserve and the blame others assign.

In addition, our assessment of someone else's intentions is sensitive to our level of empathy. Imagine that your partner has been very busy lately. You haven't had a night out in months. On a rare occasion when they have a few hours to spare, you eagerly make a dinner reservation at their favorite trattoria, and they reluctantly agree to meet you that evening. You end up sitting alone for thirty minutes before they text you that they must cancel dinner because of a last-minute issue. You ask for the check, and the servers end their bet to see how long you would wait; and while you are sitting alone with your complimentary crab cakes and Cabernet, a researcher pops out from under the dessert cart and asks you, "How much do you blame your partner?" When researchers gave participants a similar scenario and asked them the same question, they found a strong correlation between a participant's ability to take their partner's perspective and how much blame they assigned.[19] In other words, someone who had empathy for their partner gave them credit for their intentions and attributed less blame. "It's not their fault; I know they want to come to dinner, but their damn boss is so demanding and mean!" Similar studies have shown that mentalizing changes how we interpret intentions and the amount of blame deserved.[20] In contrast, when there is little mentalizing and perspective-taking, individuals can be presumed guilty before any evidence is in. For example, when the company you don't trust says they cannot speak against an allegation, your first thought is that they are guilty. When the person from an out-group says, "I don't recall," "No comment," or "I plead the fifth," we take their silence as a sign of guilt.[21] Finally, when someone does something we find unethical, we have a more difficult time empathizing with them,[22] making it even harder to understand their intentions. Intentions are critical to our attributions of responsibility; as the famous adage illustrates, "Even a dog distinguishes between being stumbled over and being kicked."[23]

Stage 3: Because "Reasons"

Once people have established that your actions had a role in bringing about the harm (stage 1: causality) and whether you meant to do it or not (stage 2: intention), there are two paths.

First, if you didn't intend to do it, then people assess your level of obligation and capacity to prevent harm. They rely on the relevant norms, laws, and expectations about your role to determine whether you have an obligation. For example, if you are my doctor, you have different obligations to protect my health than my drug dealer (ahem . . . pharmacist), grandmothers have an obligation to keep Hallmark in business by sending greeting cards at every opportunity, and people who are in a certain club have an obligation to not talk about . . . I can't say what.

People also consider your ability or capacity to prevent harm. Most of us can't stop a runaway bus with our hands, so we don't get blamed when it crashes, but if Wonder Woman failed to stop that bus and save those people, we'd have some questions. The more capacity we have, the more we can be blamed. For example, imagine that your loved one is in the hospital for a terminal illness. After doing some online research, you learn of a risky procedure that others have tried with moderate chances of success. Still, you don't bring it up to the doctor. Tragically, your loved one dies. How much do you blame yourself? I bet you didn't guess that your answer depends partly on whether you are American or French.

Research shows that in the US, doctors are more likely to comply with requests from patients and their families about procedures and medical tests than doctors in France. Surprisingly, American patients' greater choice reduces their satisfaction with their healthcare because they feel they share responsibility if their loved ones die.[24] "I should have done more research on WebMD! I could have requested another test, or I should have stopped that second procedure." In France, patients and their families don't have the same capacity to influence medical care. Consequently, French patients report higher satisfaction partly because they don't blame themselves (and partly because a single hospital visit doesn't bankrupt them). The more capacity we think someone has, the more blame we believe they deserve, even if that person is us.[25]

Returning to the model of blame, if someone is trying to assess how much blame you deserve and thinks you intended the harm to occur, they take the second path. They ask for and take a closer look at your reasons to see if they are, well, reasonable. For example, you cracked my windshield on purpose; why did you do it? You knew using the faulty lawnmower would destroy the landscaping; why did you do it anyway? This is why your justification is so important and why I dedicated chapter five to providing good justifications. People generally give more blame when they hear antisocial, selfish, or vengeful reasons and rationalizations.[26] Saying, "Uh, I smashed your rear windshield because I thought it was parked too close to mine," doesn't engender understanding as much as it inspires spite and revenge fantasies. In contrast, justifications that appeal to the greater good or self-defense are more likely to lessen blame in court cases.

THE VERDICT

In the case of Michelle Carter, the defense built its case around minimizing Michelle's role at each stage in the model of blame. They argued that Conrad was the one who bought the water pump, set it up in his truck, and turned it on (no causality). Conrad wanted to die by suicide (no intentionality). They were just acquaintances who only met a few times (low obligation), and she was struggling with her own mental health issues and couldn't take care of him (low capacity).

In contrast, the prosecution demonstrated that Michelle's texts influenced Conrad's choices (high causality). She was talking to her other friends about Conrad's suicide and was seemingly goading him along to do it (high intentionality).[27] They also argued that Michelle had an obligation to stop Conrad; she knew what he was doing, and aiding suicide was illegal. She could have told Conrad not to do it and called others for help (high capacity).

Ultimately, the judge found Michelle Carter guilty of second-degree murder and manslaughter because she had convinced Conrad to get back in the car, knowingly putting him in a fatal situation. The judge ruled that this constituted wanton and reckless encouragement. While Conrad was contemplating suicide, and Michelle was not responsible for that, he had also gotten cold feet and exited the vehicle. The judge focused on her texts encouraging him to get back in the car. By sending those specific texts, Michelle did not fulfill her obligation to prevent harm. Also, she didn't call for help or explicitly tell him to get out of the truck, and the judge believed she had that capacity. She was sent to jail for fifteen months and given fifteen months of probation. Michelle was released early after serving eleven months in jail.

As in this tragic case, psychologists have found that causality, intentionality, capacity, obligation, and the nature of our reasons all work together for people to arrive at a specific level of blame.[28] Blame is what scholars call *multi-factorial*, meaning that it arises from the interplay of several components; thus, it's harder to get on the same page about blame when we can choose which components to focus on and which to ignore. As we've seen before, many of our most thorny disagreements arise from trying to reduce something multi-factorial to a single factor. "Ethics is only about consequences! Or it's a system problem, no, it's a personal responsibility problem!"

Coming back to responsibility, the model of blame can help us understand when and why we blame individuals and when they're likely to blame us. It can help us sort through our doubts about responsibility and find ways to reconcile our perspectives rather than entrench them. For example, in the context of medical errors, physicians (and their lawyers) used to think that the best response to a medical mistake was to say nothing or deny it to avoid a lawsuit. However, recent research shows that when doctors acknowledge what happened, take responsibility, and apologize, fewer lawsuits are actually filed.[29]

Using this nuanced model, we can identify why HiveTech and MacroSung see things differently and work to address the gaps. For example, HiveTech, in trying to save face and avoid a lawsuit, might argue that they're not to blame because they didn't write the negative reviews. MacroSung may see them as having the capacity and the obligation to remove the reviews. Once HiveTech knows about the misinformation, it's hard not to see their actions as intentional. As we've seen, we can easily convince ourselves that we don't deserve any blame by changing the weight we give to intentions and ignoring capacity, obligations, and causality. As we're about to see, all of these judgments become much more difficult to sort out when more parties are involved.

JOINT RESPONSIBILITY

In 2000, the Ford Motor Company and Firestone Tires put the brakes on their one-hundred-year relationship. Between 1996 and 2000, defects in tires manufactured in the Decatur, Illinois, factory had caused 271 deaths and 800 injuries in the US, costing Firestone over $1.67 billion and Ford $530 million. As a result, production plants were closed, employees laid off, senior executives fired, congressional hearings launched, and 14.4 million tires recalled.

Ford's position was that the treads of Firestone tires were separating from the base at high temperatures because of manufacturing problems. As a result, they argued that the Ford Explorer was no more dangerous than other SUVs and that the accident rate was lower for Explorers fitted with different tires. In contrast, Firestone's position was that the tires were not being used correctly by customers; they were not intended to be used off-road and with heavy loads. Additionally, the Explorer was too heavy, and Ford's recommended tire pressure was too low. The CEO of Firestone said at the time, "When a driver of a vehicle has something happen such as tread separation, they should be able to pull over, not roll over." Some PR executive put their kid through college by writing that line.

The Ford-Firestone case shows how difficult it can be to attribute responsibility because responsibility for harm is often shared across multiple parties. For example, Firestone tires are weaker, but when put on an SUV that is heavier, when used in specific ways by customers, the likelihood of disaster increases and leaves each party pointing the finger at the other, like a trio of Spider-Men who just happen to run into each other in an alley.

When multiple parties' actions interact to cause harm, it can be more difficult to decide who is responsible, and consequently, judgments of blame become less extreme.[30] These kinds of problems of joint responsibility are especially relevant in organizations and supply chains; that's why the joke, "being on a team means always having someone to blame," rings true. Research shows that in cases of joint responsibility, people place more blame on the most proximate actor—the company they deal with, the person who misuses the product, and the bearer of bad news.

To test the impact of proximity on blame, researchers gave participants a chain of causal events to read, like the following:

> George had been ill for a long time. His wife looked after him at home. She was tired of caring for him and gave him an overdose of his tablets. George had a heart attack. His wife phoned the ambulance. However, there was heavy traffic, and the ambulance could not get through. The ambulance did not arrive, and George died.

The chain of events described intentional, unintentional, and physical causes of George's death. Researchers mixed up the order of these causes and asked participants to rate the extent to which each event in the chain was to blame for George's death. All three types of causes were rated as deserving more blame when they showed up later in the sequence.[31]

When multiple actors are involved, doubt increases, and we need to get specific about what responsibility means for each party. When we deal with individual agents and clear harms, we can treat responsibility as a singular thing. For example, Gertrude had the means and the motive for killing her husband, so more people argue that she's responsible for his death. But under conditions of joint responsibility and in most unintended use cases, responsibility is not binary, where Firestone has it, and Ford has none, or vice versa.

Both companies failed on specific responsibilities. Ford is responsible to customers for ensuring that vehicle safety tests with the right tires are conducted. Firestone is responsible for ensuring that its tires meet safety standards even under extreme conditions. Both are responsible for reporting risks and accidents promptly when they become known.[32] One way to clarify our multiple responsibilities is to fill in the statement, "We are responsible to _____ for _____." By being more specific about who we are *responsible to* and what we are *responsible for* ahead of time, we can stand a chance to sort out joint responsibility cases and batten down the hatches before the impending storm of blame. We can be proactive and create more fine-grained understandings of our responsibilities or wait until something goes wrong and congressional commissions, lawyers, or engineers digging for root causes do it for us.

WHEN TO BLAME THE PERSON OR THE ACTION

When something goes wrong at work, like a deadline is missed, a client is dissatisfied, a project goes well over budget, or unsurprisingly, no one shows up to a 4:30 p.m. meeting on a Friday, it's astonishing how many people's first instinct is to blame others. You might have experienced the unique "joy" of working with someone whose default reaction is to blame first and try to understand later (or never). Blaming others can be a way to manage your Protect System activity, to make yourself feel superior, and to shield essential beliefs about your competence. (It's never my fault; you set me up to fail!)[33]

So far, we've been talking about blaming people as one way to hold them responsible. Recall from the start of the chapter that there are three other tactics, such as praising the person or blaming the action. When should we blame the person, and when should we blame the act? We can say that this is a "good person," a "bad person," a "good company," or a "bad company," and those heuristics may help guide our choices. But anyone who looks more closely will see that every individual and every organization is imperfect. Some companies may be applauded for reducing their carbon emissions, but they may need to work on other areas like gender equity practices, increasing employee voice, and delivering on their promises to shareholders.

Blame, when applied, is a summary judgment about an individual or organization that can activate their Protect System and cause them to put up their shields. "Hey, why are you blaming me? I didn't do it; you did it!"

Specifically, if we blame and make people feel bad about themselves, they are less willing to work to improve, whereas if they feel bad about their behavior (and not their whole self), they can be more inclined to change. In a meta-analysis of ninety studies involving more than 12,000 participants,[34] researchers found that when a mistake was seen as repairable, the people who made the mistake were more likely to try to improve. In contrast, when we blame the person, they are more likely to feel shame (I am bad), and their motivation to repair can drop.[35] Blaming the person is a more severe judgment than saying an act was wrong, suggesting that we want to be judicious in using blame.[36] Indeed, signaling that people will be blamed can be an effective deterrent. Messages that preview personal blame, like "Don't be a cheater," reduce subsequent unethical behavior more than action-focused injunctions like "Don't cheat."[37] If we can signal blame beforehand, it can forestall unethical behavior; but blaming people afterward can demotivate them from mending their ways.

If blame has pros and cons, so does praise. Most of us find praise motivating and rewarding. We repeatedly glance at kind emails, awards, and recognitions or fondly remember that one time your boss texted "thx" when you rescheduled your wedding to work on a Saturday on short notice. Research shows that praise can increase job satisfaction, retention, and creativity.[38] Praise is most effective when sincere, honest, specific, immediate, and unexpected. When praise helps motivate people to focus on the controllable aspects of their performance and reinforces high *and* attainable standards, we can reap the benefits and avoid the costs.[39] Praise perceived as controlling, unearned, dishonest, unattainable, or too general can quickly backfire as people catch a whiff of something that smells like manipulation. When your boss says things like, "Evaluating your work makes me feel good about myself," and "I just had my pupils dilated. . . . Oh, you look nice today," any positive impacts of praise are squandered.

When our Protect Systems are active, we naturally lean toward blaming the person and not praising enough, which can damage our relationships, reduce motivation, and make it much more challenging to accomplish our shared goals.

THE IMPACT OF "IMPACT NOT INTENT"

Knowing that blame is multi-factorial and results from a series of judgments helps us to be intentional about how much weight we place on each judgment. For example, imagine two people discussing the recent news about a local woman's arrest for poisoning her husband. Julia reports, "The paddywagon came by this morning to take her to jail and trampled the rest of my tulips." Her friend, Jack, is taken aback by the term "paddywagon" because he interprets it as a slur against his Irish immigrant ancestors. Historically, "Paddy" became shorthand for "Patrick," and by referring to police wagons as paddywagons, the term plays into anti-Irish stereotypes.

When Jack points out that Julia used an offensive term, it's easy for Julia to think, "Geez. Stop being so sensitive. I didn't know that and didn't mean to hurt your feelings, so I don't need to apologize or even acknowledge your reaction." Unfortunately, we can all fall into a similar pattern because we give ourselves more credit for our intentions and minimize our negative impacts. To counteract this defensive tendency, diversity trainings and orientations have introduced the phrase, "*It's about impact, not intent.*" The goal is to help more people in Julia's position recognize how their words are received. In general, that's a good thing because it makes it harder for the offender to brush off their responsibility and brings people together to talk. But given the research we just reviewed on how people attribute blame, it begs the question, Does it swing the pendulum too far? It might bring people to the table, but does it foster better conversation?

If intent doesn't matter at all, Jack might be licensed to treat the slip-up as if he had been personally attacked. When we can't distinguish between "being tripped over and when we're being kicked," we can risk treating inadvertent offenses the same way as malicious offenses and constructive feedback no differently than words unleashed with cruelty. We can overreact to mild instances or misconstrue non-violations as violations because they share some similar features. "This made me feel uncomfortable—therefore, it's wrong, and now I'm gonna slash your tires!" The relational damage from an overreaction could make Jack's efforts to address Julia's mistake ineffective or even backfire.

Both impact and intent matter (as do obligation, capacity, and our reasons). Ideally, we need to inform people about the impact of their actions and be open to adjusting the severity of our judgments based on what we know and learn about their intent. Jack should be able to share his perspective on the "paddywagon" term. If Julia says, "I don't care, that's your problem," the conversation takes a different course than if she says, "Oh, I didn't know; I'm so sorry." Carefully distinguishing between intentional and unintentional mistakes is critical to strengthening relationships, especially when addressing errors.

When confronting moments of doubt, like deciding what to do about a product or service used in unintended, harmful ways, we can struggle to make sense of our responsibility. Our motives to protect ourselves from blame can cause us to deny, ignore, or fight in ways that damage our relationships. We can rationalize our counterproductive reactions and minimize our blame by preferentially interpreting our causality, intentionality, obligations, and capacity. For example, in the case of HiveTech (where our product review site is allegedly being used to spread fake negative reviews) we might excuse our actions because we didn't intend to spread misinformation, and MacroSung might disagree because they focus on our capacity and obligation to do something about it. Once we know about the unintended use, the gap between how we see our responsibility and how others see it can widen. If responsibility is a social arrangement to take each other into account in our actions, then it relies on shared meaning about what is acceptable. This insight helps us be proactive and seek out how others think about our responsibility, thus minimizing unexpected disruptions to our relationships. (See appendix tool 7.)

The multi-factorial model of blame we introduced in this chapter can help us align our perspectives about our responsibility when errors are unavoidable or unforeseen. This model also has implications for situations of joint responsibility, helps us to be more intentional about when we use praise and blame, and reminds us of the importance of calibrating our level of blame in light of intentions, capacity, obligations, and the quality of someone's reasons. A richer way to think about responsibility is a critical resource to maintain strong relationships in the face of unpredictability. It helps us be "wise not by the recollection of our past, but by the responsibility for our future."

9

"Not in Kansas Anymore"

NEXT WEEK IS THE GRAND OPENING of your new flagship retail store in Country X, a large and lucrative global market also known for its predilection for corruption and bribery. True to form, this morning, a power company representative zips by to ask for an extra payment before connecting the electricity to your store. The rep is technically a government employee and can make your life and business operations very difficult. Additionally, the rule of law is inconsistently applied in Country X, so there is virtually no chance of dealing with this through the courts.

While you're relatively confident that no one will prosecute you here for making these questionable payments, your customers and employees back home would not be so willing to look the other way. In addition to any legal repercussions, paying these fees would threaten your hard-won reputation for corporate responsibility. Specifically, customers and suppliers worldwide would see these kinds of payments as a direct contradiction of your stated values of open and fair business practices.

Your sales could grow by as much as 30 percent once you are established in Country X, but you are concerned about sacrificing your reputation. You haven't had to pay this kind of fee in any other country, but the power company representative hints that this is how they do things here. In fact, it's so ingrained that business owners who refuse to pay often end up spending a night or two in jail. In the large scheme of things, the company has much more money on the line, and you'd be lying to yourself if you thought you'd be willing to go to jail in Country X over this.

What would you do?

―――――――

Bribery is a practice that differs across the world and even within industries in the same country, just like practices regarding women's rights, child labor, and gifting. When practices, rules, and expectations differ across geographies, we are often unsure whether we should stick to our familiar ways or adapt to local customs. We might find ourselves clinging to our familiar practices and creating harm in a new region or adapting to the new context so much that we compromise our relationships and reputation back home. It turns out that common ways of thinking about conflicting standards across boundaries ignore the benefits of doubt. So, what do we do when legal, cultural, and moral standards at home conflict with those abroad?

RELATIVISM

Moral relativism is a commonly held view that what is right or wrong depends on context.[1] Indeed, different varieties of relativism are defined by which context is assumed to be most authoritative. For example, *cultural relativism* dictates that what's right is defined by a particular culture. Americans cannot judge Malaysians, or Leblon-residing Brazilians cannot judge those who live in Vila Cruzeiro because they come from different cultures, and cultures are the final arbiter in what is considered morally correct.

Historicism is the view that we can't judge people who lived in the past by our contemporary standards. For example, what was illegal and immoral in the 1800s, like interracial marriage, is not considered wrong today, and things that were legal and considered by some to be moral then, like slavery, are regarded as clearly wrong now. Historicism argues that the time we live in determines what's right and wrong. Similarly, *role relativism* says that what's right as a business leader is different than what's right as a parent. What's right for an investor differs from what's right for a citizen. *Naïve relativism* is the view that what's right is defined by a particular person, so people cannot and should not judge each other. What does it matter if I want to show up for our meeting twenty minutes late and you would like to show up fifteen minutes early? According to a relativist, if right and wrong are the products of different frameworks of assessment (whether culture, time period, role, or individual values), then the authority of those standards for good behavior is "confined to the contexts that give rise to them." If rules only operate within their context of origin, paying the bribe in the new country would be okay because that's how things are done there. A relativist's argument starts with the observation that there are different standards. Then, the relativist claims that because of these different standards, we cannot objectively discern which is better, so we shouldn't bother. When you write about relativism, it's customary to summarize with the phrase, "When in Rome, do as the Romans do."

In contrast to moral relativism there is a view called *moral absolutism*. In this view, there is a singular universal morality by which we can say that paying bribes, child labor, or extending human rights is wrong or right everywhere and always. For example, it is wrong to put pineapple on pizza, no matter where you are from. I will deny before I try, brah. In this view, moral truths are universal and not bound by historical or social conditions. They are independent of any observer, mind, and language. Therefore, those universal moral truths are the final authority on what makes any action good or right.

Recorded discussions about relativism and absolutism have been around at least since the ancient Greeks. Throughout history, as travelers, merchants, and anthropologists returned with stories of societies fundamentally different from their own, they learned that there are other ways of organizing individual freedom, families, and federations. For example, suppose you were a priest in ancient times who enjoyed significant power and status in your community in part by convincing others that human sacrifice is necessary for a bountiful harvest. What happens when travelers encounter a civilization that doesn't sacrifice its citizens, yet has bountiful harvests? People could begin to question your power and social standing in the community. Exposure to different ways of living opens choices that were previously closed, challenges cherished stories, and questions social structures once taken for granted. Therefore, it's no surprise that relativism has been a hot-button cultural issue. Just read the following quotes:

> *"When we teach people that suspending moral judgments is a virtue, the necessary outcome is moral horror."*
>
> —PETER BOGHOSSIAN, philosopher

> *"If we wanted home truths, we should have stayed at home."*
>
> —CLIFFORD GEERTZ, anthropologist

> *"By refusing to consider as humans those who seem to us to be the most 'savage' or 'barbarous' of their representatives, we merely adopt one of their own characteristic attitudes. The barbarian is, first and foremost, the man who believes in barbarism."*
>
> —CLAUDE LÉVI-STRAUSS, philosopher

> *"If you ask me what the biggest problem in America is, I'm not going to tell you debt, deficits, statistics, economics—I'll tell you it's moral relativism."*
>
> —PAUL RYAN, former House speaker and vice presidential candidate

Given these strong views and heated debates, let's look more closely at some common arguments for and against relativism.

ARGUMENTS FOR RELATIVISM

Few people describe themselves as relativists; usually, it's an accusation hurled at them by their critics. No philosopher goes on a blind date and introduces themselves like, "Hi, I'm Merle. I like puppies, Vietnamese food, and hiking. Also, I believe anything goes, so I'm cool if you hate puppies, Vietnamese food makes you sick, and you want to kill me and sell my kidney when we go on our next hike." They usually save that for the third date. Most people reject the charge that they believe "anything goes" and nothing can distinguish between better and worse. Yet those who find themselves drawn to some of the assumptions of relativism usually defend their positions with versions of the following types of arguments:

1. **LOOK AROUND.** The first set of arguments in support of various forms of relativism highlight the observable differences in what people believe to be good. Societies, families, and individuals have different norms, beliefs, and cultural practices; some people wear their shoes inside their homes, while others walk barefoot, their bunions on full display. In some places, it's okay to burp loudly in public. In other places, that would traumatize the strangers sitting next to you at the movie theater. People engage in polygamy, cannibalism, and witchcraft; they throw penis festivals, toss and catch toddlers from high temples, and pour wine into the graves of their loved ones. When you greet someone in Switzerland, even when you first meet, it's three kisses, one on each alternating cheek starting on the right; in Spain, it's two; if you get confused, you end up accidentally French kissing a stranger. Moreover, these different practices carry the imprint of culture because they are embedded in stories, rituals, and traditions handed down from previous generations.

Even physics is forced into this debate. In the past, physicists accepted the Newtonian view that gravity is constant, that no matter where and when we found ourselves in the universe, gravity is the same. However, since Einstein, physicists say that gravity and the curvature of space-time are dependent on whatever matter, energy, and radiation are present.

Thus, what we once considered universal turned out to be confined to our neighborhood of space-time. Similarly, supporters of moral relativism argue that while our personal values and traditions might look universal at first, when we look around and see so many different practices, it's hard to conclude there is only one right way of doing things.

2. HUMILITY IS GOOD. The second set of arguments used to support forms of relativism posits that abandoning belief in a single universal truth increases virtues like tolerance, mutual accommodation, and curiosity. If we don't believe that our way of seeing the world is the only right way, we consider more possibilities, engage in better conversations with those who disagree, and stand a better chance of correcting errors in our beliefs. Humility can keep us open to learning, like when we look in the mirror and finally concede that perhaps cutting our own hair was not a good idea after all. Believing in a single universal truth can constrain our thinking. Indeed, the French philosopher Auguste Comte argued that the role of sociology as the pinnacle of education was to "render relative ideas which were first absolute." Accepting that ideas and beliefs are expressions of their time and place can offer a way to settle or explain away what appear to be profound differences. You do you. Just do it over there, please.

In contrast, when people are certain that their view is the "truth," they can justify many atrocities. The German Nazis believed that biology proved the superiority of the Aryan race and used those "truths" to justify the genocide of 20 million Jews, Poles, Slavs, Roma, Russians, gay people, people with disabilities, and others. Similarly, lying on your resume because you're sure everyone does it, treating others with contempt and disrespect because they are clearly stupid, and being violent against out-group members because they are obviously inferior are all enabled by certainty. When we are overconfident in our views, we close the door to the possibility that others living today and people living in the future can improve upon our choices and beliefs. Therefore, shades of relativism are supposed to keep us humble and tolerant.

3. NO NEUTRAL GROUND. The third set of arguments deployed in support of relativism claims that there is no neutral ground, no Archimedean point, where we can flee to adjudicate between competing views rationally. For example, if you and your friends are arguing about whose fashion choices are objectively correct, turning to Carl, who still wears flannel like it's 1992 in Seattle, is not a neutral, objective option. Carl (like all of us) has a fashion sense informed by a specific time and place—in his case, one that prioritizes comfort over cleanliness. Similarly, we cannot appeal to raceless, classless, and genderless perspectives to settle conflicts and differences of opinion. If every view is a view from somewhere, and we're only trading some blind spots and biases for others, then relativists wonder how we can objectively choose between competing versions of the good.

Even simple observations assume a perspective from somewhere. Take, for instance, the question of how many objects there are on the table. We might think this has a simple, objective answer. If we're asking from a practical human perspective, we might answer based on what we can see and count. "It's three, duh. Stop asking stupid questions." If we're talking to microbiologists, our answer might change to millions if we attend to the germs and microorganisms on the table that we can't see with our naked eye. If we're talking to chemists and physicists, what looks like three might look like trillions of atoms and molecules. Philosopher Hilary Putnam points out that the answer depends on the vocabulary and purpose of the people who ask and answer the question; there is no "perspective-independent" way to answer the question.[2]

We might hope that science can help us find a neutral, fact-based perspective, but as we have seen, there are raging debates about the role of perspective and contingency, even in science. Even views that pretend to be free of bias can't escape employing their preferred assumptions and preferences in how terms are defined, measured, and related. The same dataset can lead to different conclusions when variables and statistics are calculated based on different theories and methods. Data doesn't speak on its own, and it can't say anything, but the theories and methods researchers bring to data create a wider range of conclusions than most people assume. In short, relativists argue that every perspective is a view from somewhere that licenses some things and limits others. Therefore, we cannot escape to some imaginary perspective-independent place to figure out which standard is really the Truth.

ARGUMENTS AGAINST RELATIVISM

Absolutists on a blind date will tell you that the correct term for their views is "anti-relativist" while also letting you know you made the wrong choice of wine and cocktail attire. When people argue against relativism, they generally use a variety of different arguments like:

1. GOTCHA! The oldest and most common argument against relativism was made initially in written history by Plato. The idea that "everything is relative" is incoherent and illogical because if everything is relative, then even relativism can't be universal. Therefore, relativism must be false, and we should be able to find some universal truths. It's an *Inception*-like argument that makes undergraduates drop their bongs, sign up to be philosophy majors, and get discounts on more bongs.

2. ONLY TRUTH IS TRUTH. Related to the *Gotcha!* argument, another clash against forms of relativism is that, by definition, phrases like "true for me" or "our truth" are nonsensical. People's beliefs can vary, be inaccurate, or change over time, but truth is only one thing. If we reject the truth, we reject the natural order of the universe. In this view, moral, social, and political consequences are irrelevant to what makes something true. Conveniently, anti-relativists also tend to believe they have the truth or are closer to it than their opponents. It's rare to find someone who argues for a single universal truth and believes that some other person or group is closer to it. According to this line of argument, if we stop conflating other things with "the truth," we can focus on uncovering it.

3. DEEP DOWN. As a direct response to the *Look Around* set of arguments, opponents of relativism argue that what others see as radical differences are only superficial. There seem to be some human universals such as kinship, death, mourning, birth, empathy, sympathy, fear, hunger, laughter, thirst, and music. For example, in some places, people shake

hands; in other places, they bow, clap, sniff your face, stick out their tongue, kiss the air, or bump noses, but regardless of these superficial disparities, these are all forms of a greeting to acknowledge the presence of another human being. In this view, different moral standards are only an illusion; if we try harder, we can uncover universal moral truths.

4. RELATIVISM = COWARDICE. Finally, anti-relativists argue that relativism encourages cowardice. It makes people give up on seeking the Truth and sit down exactly when it's time to stand up for what is right. For example, we could be so focused on being "open-minded" that we tolerate evident evils; we don't stand up against Nazis or the murder of innocents. In line with this argument, Pope Benedict XVI rejected and condemned cultural relativism as "a harbinger of nihilism and 'anything goes' extreme permissiveness." Relativism can lead to hypocrisy, a willingness to forgo moral standards and rationalize whatever we want. Finally, anti-relativists argue that we don't need relativism to promote tolerance; just being aware of other standards can make us more understanding. As President John F. Kennedy said, "Tolerance implies no lack of commitment to one's own beliefs. Rather, it condemns the oppression or persecution of others." We don't need to confer "truth" or "moral correctness" on those other standards we know are wrong, but we can still be tolerant and seek the truth.

AND THE EVIDENCE SAYS?

Like most intense centuries-long debates, debates about relativism have continued because scholars trade abstract arguments back and forth without looking to see where and when their assumptions might hold. Of course, if you're arguing for a universal and unchanging truth, you might reject that very premise, but you can't deny that it's easier to maintain abstractions by making them immune to experience. Yet the importance of these issues has recently inspired psychologists and experimental philosophers to collect data about the psychological and social consequences of people's beliefs and behaviors. Admittedly, empirical work on relativism is new, but let's review what we've learned so far.

First, as you probably expect, ample evidence is consistent with the *Look Around* arguments. People act in relativist ways, changing their values and principles based on their goals and environments.[3] For example, as we saw in chapter seven, socialization into a culture matters and cultures differ on what it means to be fair.[4] We are less willing to defend the rights of those who are different from us, suggesting that we don't really believe in the universality of those rights. Additionally, there are ongoing debates about how similar these differences are "deep down." We might be able to find similarities if we abstract away all the important differences, but at some point, we risk abstracting away the very practices we're interested in comparing. For example, if you are a foodie, reducing the differences between a Wagyu Katsu Sandwich and Pollo a la Brasa to "protein" misses the whole point.

Second, there is growing evidence that supports the *Relativism = Cowardice* argument. Specifically, beliefs in relativism are associated with unethical behavior and a lack of support for group norms. For example, managers are more likely to take kickbacks and bribes if they don't believe in objective moral truths.[5] Moreover, when participants in lab studies are asked to read arguments in favor of or against relativism, those who read relativist arguments cheat more on subsequent tasks.[6] "I just learned that anything goes, so here goes!" Similarly, when companies make the "business case" for sacred values like diversity, responsibility, or sustainability and put those values on footing equal to as other considerations like profit or customer satisfaction, employees are more willing to make tradeoffs involving those sacred values. And they are also less likely to donate their time and money to enforce them.[7] When the authority or sacredness of a specific value is made relative, it doesn't exert as strong an influence on our choices. Thus, sacred values are easier to displace when executives "make the business case."

But even this effect seems to have boundaries. For example, when asked if it is permissible to "hit and shove others because you feel like it" or "consciously discriminate against someone because of their race," most people respond that they believe those actions are wrong, no matter what.[8] There is recent evidence that we might be more absolutist when it comes to identifying moral harm but more relativist when it comes to defining moral goods.[9] In addition, research shows that adults and children treat members of their in-group with more of an absolutist orientation and members of out-groups with more relativistic standards.[10] Together, these studies suggest that beliefs in relativism can make people less likely to support specific social norms and rules and that people don't treat all of their beliefs as either absolute or relative.

Third, a growing body of evidence supports the *Humility Is Good* argument. For example, when people are confident that they are correct, they tend to be impervious to compromise and resort to other means of achieving their ends, such as politics, piracy, and protests. People who are certain they are correct are less likely to appreciate a fair and transparent process and are more willing to use any means to achieve their ends.[11] It takes a high degree of moral certainty to set yourself on fire in opposition to something or to murder someone else over their beliefs. We can more easily rationalize these extreme acts by believing we are aligned with an absolute morality.[12]

When we're drop-dead certain that we're right, we prefer to surround ourselves with people who agree. In one study, adult participants living in the US were asked to identify the nation's most pressing problems.[13] Then, they reported how much they believed their view on those issues was correct. When asked how happy they would be to have someone who disagreed with their beliefs as a new neighbor, new colleague, or new son-in-law, the more confident people were about their views, the more distance they wanted to keep from those who disagreed. Ironically, the more objective and impervious to challenge we think our beliefs are, the less comfortable we are in engaging others who disagree, making it less likely that either party might revise, refine, or reject their beliefs.

In a similar study, researchers put participants with divergent views into two groups to discuss contentious social issues like abortion or gun control. The first group comprised of people who said they had strong opinions and were open to learning from others, and the second group contained individuals who believed they had the "right answer." As researchers observed both groups discussing the same contentious issues, they learned that the "right-answer" groups had the lowest reported goodwill, were less cooperative, and were seen as the most defensive by observers. In contrast, the "strong opinions loosely held" group reported greater cooperation and goodwill and were also seen as less tense and defensive.[14] Together, these studies suggest that the more people believe their view is the only right answer, the less tolerant and curious they are of divergent perspectives.

Despite being in its initial stages, research about relativism suggests that when we're choosing among conflicting cultural standards, like deciding whether to make questionable payments in another country, we should avoid the extremes; specifically believing that anything goes can weaken in-group norms, and absolutism can prevent us from having effective (or any) dialogue. So, the current evidence begs the question, Is there a Goldilocks zone, an optimal level of doubt where we have enough conviction to remain engaged and enough humility to still learn from others?

STOP MORALIZING!

Having strong opinions while also being open to learning can be a challenge. Across the country, family gatherings have become a lightning rod for divisive dinner table arguments. Whether we're debating Uncle Sheldon about global warming on Arbor Day or talking to Aunt Amy about the virtues of going dairy-free at Shavuot, often we find ourselves at a dead end when we expect dialogue. Some scholars reason that we can't have effective conversations that walk the line between tolerance and tenacity unless we stop talking about ethics. Therefore, their proposed solution is to avoid moralizing an issue. In their view, moralizing tends to excite and confuse the parties involved, further enflaming disputes and making it harder to address conflicting perspectives. For example, one modern-day philosopher writes,

> If we hope to resolve conflicts by arriving at a compromise, our task will be easier if moral disagreements are seen as partial conflicts of interest "without the embroidery of rights and moral justification." . . . [For example], [t]he controversy over abortion would not be nearly as intractable as it has become if the fiction of moral rights had not been appropriated by both sides. If the issue is not moralized, Roe v. Wade looks like a sensible compromise between two extreme positions, but when the right to life

is set against the right to choose, neither side can yield without violating morality.[15]

In other words, we can have better discussions if we drop ethics from the way we talk. Before we move on, let's take a closer look to understand the multiple functions moral judgments play in our social lives.

First, we usually talk about moral judgments as helping us *decide for ourselves* what to do. Whether in straightforward situations like avoiding cheating or in more complex multi-criteria decisions, the most common use of moral judgments is evaluating different options and alternatives to make good choices.

Second, when discussing praise and blame, as we did in chapters five and eight, we highlight another familiar role that moral judgments play in helping us *determine what is right and wrong for others* to do. We saw how judges, juries, parents, and peers help regulate behavior within their groups by using explicit moral judgments.

There are three additional uses of moral judgments that are less widely discussed but no less important. As we introduced in chapter five, moral judgments are essential to *define terms*. For example, what is a planet, and when does life begin? We need to make judgment calls about what is included and excluded in a definition. Those choices also reflect a set of values and shape our subsequent actions. Once we've defined and applied a term in a specific way, it can guide our choices even if we're unaware that it is doing so. A famous study demonstrates the power of this kind of labeling. Researchers had participants watch a baby interact with some toys in the lab. Unknown to the participants, the baby was the same nine-month-old in every case, but for some participants, the baby was called Dana, and for others, it was called David.[16] When the baby was given a male name, participants described it as more active, and when the baby cried, both male and female participants were more likely to describe David's cries as anger. In contrast, participants were more likely to interpret Dana's cries as fear. The pronouns "he" and "she," and the names David and Dana, are embedded in social narratives and associated with cultural expectations about gender that shaped how participants interpreted the baby's actions and their scripts about how they should respond. What's critical to see is that the more subtle way we employ judgments to define and label things also guides our choices, just as explicit moral judgments do.

Much of the important work in moral discourse happens even before someone makes explicit moral judgments.[17] It happens when we draw our mental maps. For example, if we describe those people over there as "uncivilized," "evil," and a "threat to our existence," then it makes more sense for us to marshal our resources to put a stop to their nefarious plans. But if they are "just different," then maybe I'm too tired to pick up my pitchfork. Similarly, if personhood begins at conception, we should do everything to protect fetuses, but other considerations can be allowed if personhood is conferred later. Moral judgments are inextricable from defining and describing the world and thus determining the paths we choose. Once you've defined the situation in a particular way, the explicit moral judgments about right and wrong naturally follow.

The fourth role that moral judgments play is to help us *draw social boundaries*. More subtle than outright evaluation, moral judgments like "I don't eat meat because it's bad for the environment" can also subtly elevate some people and denigrate others. In this case, vegetarians are elevated above meat eaters because of the assumption that meat eaters don't care about the environment. Moral judgments can shift the tone and relationship between people and groups without resorting to outright praise or blame of those individuals. Like when your passive-aggressive auntie says, "Vijay finished medical school so quickly," and you say, "Well, I didn't want to be a doctor," and she says, "Oh, I'm not saying anything about you." But everyone knows that you were taken down a peg.

You might even know someone who uses moral judgments as a social weapon, finding ways to elevate themselves above others by frequently judging while escaping judgment for their own choices. These individuals relish giving feedback about what they perceive others are doing wrong but fall apart when they are given feedback or asked to take responsibility for their actions. Additionally, their feedback isn't offered in the spirit of improving the relationship or getting along more peacefully; instead, the goal is to shift social dynamics to maintain power over others. Rules like "judge not, lest ye be judged" or "people in glass houses should not throw stones" are meant to limit the use of moral judgments in these kinds of socially toxic power plays.

Finally, moral judgments can be more intense than praise and blame or drawing subtle power differences. Generally, praising and blaming individuals assumes an ongoing relationship that can be regulated. In contrast, moral judgments can be used to outright *denounce* others when we believe they are wrong and must be put in their place. We hate the hacks, extremists, libtards, zealots, trolls, ideologues, and radicals. When we denounce them, we are not interested in changing an ongoing relationship, but rather in more drastic actions like cutting ties, obstructing their goals, or outright harming others.

When most people think about "moralizing," they are worried about moral language leading to denouncing others and the righteous anger that accompanies it. But once we see the other roles that moral judgments play in social life, getting rid of morality in our discussions seems impossible. Moral judgments are like atoms: they are what social life is made up of. Some atoms are used to make bombs and others are used to make food. Because of their additional roles in defining, deciding, and determining what we and others should do, many scholars believe it is impossible to separate moral judgments from political, financial, scientific, and social judgments.[18]

Rather than abandoning moral judgments altogether, training people to use them carefully and effectively would be more realistic and helpful. We can use them as a scalpel, not a hammer, carving out problematic practices while preserving and strengthening relationships. In short, despite the promise of an easy solution to moral disagreements, we can't escape ethics in how we talk, but we can learn to use it more responsibly.

CONVERSATION STOPPERS

Wendy is negotiating on behalf of her boating services company. She's working with a supplier on the price and quality of parts for a machine. Based on her experience and calculations, she thinks the price should fall between $130–$160 per part. Her counterpart, Omar, believes the price could be between $150–$180. They're meeting to figure out if their companies can work together.

In this negotiation example, the differences in perspectives indicate that something could be worked out, but it's not a guarantee. Maybe there is no zone of agreement on price, so Wendy and Omar shouldn't work together. Maybe Wendy has some non-negotiables, like the quality level or specific delivery dates. Whatever deal they reach will impact their organizations' profitability, the work others must do, their reputations, the capabilities of their companies, and their relationship going forward. We can't call Wendy and Omar's negotiation a failed attempt before it begins.

In contrast, in cases of moral disagreements, relativists often give up too soon by saying, "One price is just as good as any other, so what's the point of negotiating?" Or absolutists argue that "Omar has the true price. His job is to convince Wendy, with logic, arguments, threats, and maybe even force, that his way is really the right way." Both alternatives seem strange. When they avoid denouncing each other, Wendy and Omar can understand their situation and know where there is room for negotiation and where there is not based on what they value. They can explore options to reach a consensus, knowing that if there is no way to work around their non-negotiables, they will have to walk away with no deal and find another way to satisfy their goals.

Similarly, philosophers are moving past the simple dichotomy between relativism and absolutism, and some are articulating alternatives for addressing diverse values. One such view is called *pluralism*, or the idea that individuals and societies hold many moral values, and it is not always possible to equalize and rank all those goods on a single scale to arrive at a final universal standard.[19] Therefore, according to this view, there can be better and worse answers depending on context and our goals, but no answers that are true always and everywhere. Pluralism acknowledges a diversity of moral goods but rejects the complacency that comes with either relativism or absolutism. In this view, all ethical issues are not a multiple-choice test, where a person must identify the correct choice among competing incorrect interpretations. Some issues are more like a design task, where a workable solution must be fashioned out of understanding the context, the competing standards, and the strengths and weaknesses of different alternatives and choices without worrying if the current solution is also the universal solution.[20] Those solutions must be justified to and accepted by the people who are affected by them, and their views are relevant to any good design.

From a pluralist perspective, ethics is an ongoing process. We should revise and update our previous solutions in light of changing conditions and beliefs. We can always ask, "Are our current ways of describing things effective for coping? How can we do better?" By substituting our imagination for certainty and our curiosity for pride, a pluralist view of ethics asks us to understand our surroundings in more detail, recognize critical tensions and competing values, and compose a path forward in conversation with those we impact.

In the 1980s, Levi Strauss, the manufacturer of blue jeans and denim clothing, was in a tight squeeze. Their Malaysian factories were found using child labor. At the time, some children in Malaysia were more likely to take jobs and not attend school because they needed the money to support their families. In addition, working in factories kept some children from more dangerous activities like crime or prostitution. If Levi's left Malaysia and relocated its production to avoid child labor, it would have to increase the price of jeans, causing the company to lose market share to competitors such as Jordache, Guess, Wrangler, and Lee. For most of the company's American customers, child labor was a relic of the past that should be abolished. Should Levi's stop child labor in Malaysia? Should the company not worry about it because it wasn't illegal?

So, what happened? Levi's didn't exit Malaysia. Instead, they continued to pay the children who worked in their factories—not to make jeans but to go to school. They offered them full-time jobs at the factory when they were verified to be of legal working age. The company got the government to set aside money to educate 75,000 underage girls. They replicated this strategy in Bangladesh. Managers at Levi's rolled up their denim sleeves and tried to figure out how to make things work in a less-than-ideal situation. They didn't barrel forward, assuming they had the right answer or default entirely to the local rules. Instead, they had a clear sense of what they could accept and what they could not.

Of course, not every story works out so neatly. In a similar situation, when Levi's tried to work with the Uzbek government to make child labor illegal, the government refused. Subsequently, Levi's banned the use of

Uzbek cotton in all their products, choosing to exit the country when no solution that reflected their values was negotiable. Levi's didn't default to either relativism or absolutism in their approach.

The first negotiation in this chapter and the Levi's example demonstrate that relativism and absolutism prevent us from working together to figure out how to live with others with different perspectives. Said more eloquently by one of today's leading moral philosophers, Kwame Anthony Appiah,

> If relativism about ethics and morality were true, then, at the end of many discussions, we would each have to end up by saying, "From where I stand, I am right. From where you stand, you are right." And there would be nothing further to say. From our different perspectives, we would be living effectively in different worlds. And without a shared world, what is there to discuss? People often recommend relativism because they think it will lead to tolerance. But if we cannot learn from one another what it is right to think and feel and do, then conversation between us will be pointless. Relativism of that sort isn't a way to encourage conversation; it's just a reason to fall silent.[21]

When we encounter hard choices that pit different legal, cultural, and moral values against each other, we must navigate carefully between two obstacles. The first is not to be so closed-minded that we cannot learn, and the second is not to be so open-minded that our brains fall out and we fail to stand up for values that are important to us. We cannot do either without a clear sense of our non-negotiables.

Both relativism and absolutism appeal to an abstract, context-independent truth. But there's another strategy to identify our non-negotiables. Instead of looking for a single feature that puts a belief in the "true" or "false" bucket, we can move from categories to continuities and see that all our beliefs have differing levels of support from multiple sources. For example, we might see our best truth candidates as emerging from the interplay of at least three different sources of support: *coherence* with other beliefs and observations (I think it's true because it fits with the evidence), *consensus* with relevant others (I think it's true because my parents told me so), and *competence* in achieving our goals (I think it's true because I can do something that I couldn't do before). Each criterion alone does not guarantee a belief is true, but together, they help us find our firmest footing.

The push and pull among these three sources of support creates opportunities to update and revise our beliefs. For example, sometimes a belief increases our competence but doesn't cohere with our other essential beliefs, like when Copernicus devised the heliocentric model of the solar system. He drastically improved our ability to predict the position of the planets. Still, his model didn't fit well with prevailing religious beliefs, angering the Catholic Church, which banned his writings for more than two hundred years. Other beliefs have high social consensus but low competence, such as persistent health and wellness myths. Surprisingly, over the last ten years, 146 medical articles have been published demonstrating that the widely accepted medical standard of care for various conditions was not effective or actually made things worse for patients.[22] Finally, just because something increases our competence doesn't mean our views about it are coherent. For example, nitrous oxide, or laughing gas, was discovered in the 1800s, and funnily enough, people started to use it as a painkiller during surgeries. But despite increasing our competence to perform pain-free procedures (and apparently have a gas while being operated on), scientists didn't know how it worked for decades. Initially, they thought it worked by soaking up a dangerous substance; that's why laughing gas was first called "dephlogisticated air." These theories were eventually abandoned because they didn't cohere with other well-supported theories about combustion.[23] Together, the degree of competence, consensus, and coherence can help us find the firmest ground we can stand on, even if we can't know for sure whether that footing is an eternal, unmoving foundation.

For companies in Levi's position, there can be a variety of competing beliefs that are relevant to their choice, like "countries are entitled to their own rules," "children should not be allowed to work until they reach a certain age," and "children should be kept away from criminal activities." Examining each belief in terms of its coherence with other beliefs and practices, its degree of consensus with relevant others, and what it allows us to do can help us make better choices about what to prioritize and where to be more open to negotiating. More of Levi's stakeholders agreed that young children should not work; not utilizing child labor is consistent with other high-consensus principles like the UN Declaration of Human Rights. While employing child labor can allow the company to sell more jeans and immediately put money in the pockets of needy families, those outcomes can also be achieved in other ways, such as by building a reputation for responsibility and negotiating with the government.

Structural engineers don't worry if they are building on eternal unmoving foundations, nor do they throw up their hands and go home when they can't find any. Still, they are very careful to distinguish between quicksand and bedrock. Similarly, when we encounter different beliefs, examining the degree of consensus, competence, and coherence of a specific belief can help us make more informed choices about our non-negotiables.

When operating in different contexts, we experience moments of doubt about which standards are relevant. Instead of sitting on the sidelines because you think you have the correct answer and you don't need to convince others or because you think any answer is just as good as any other, we can jump into the game and ascertain where there's room for negotiation and where there's not. (See appendix tool 8.) We can avoid the pitfalls of relativism and absolutism and perform the work to create a better world, even in the face of moral disagreement. To do so, we need a sense of what we're willing to stand for, even if those values are historical, contingent, and contextual. Ideas and practices don't have to be eternal and unchanging to still be valuable, beautiful, and worth dedicating our lives to. Indeed, when people see their point of view as grounded in their social group's practices rather than in the truth, they can better strike a balance between adhering to those norms and reducing their intolerance.[24]

Whether removing child labor from the supply chain, avoiding paying bribes, or promoting more equal rights, when we avoid the extremes of relativism and absolutism, we open the potential to nudge an imperfect world toward our ideals. Said another way, if anything goes, then nothing stays.

IV

FACING THE OBSTACLES WITHIN

10

Self-Regulation

YOU ARE THE CEO of an international social media company that allows people to share pictures and short videos with others on your app. Millions worldwide share posts about their food, workouts, hobbies, hilarious moments, and that one social media face everyone makes with pouty lips and vacant eyes.

You receive an alert from your team that a popular actress, Sarah Connor, has posted something deeply offensive and controversial on your site. Typically, Connor makes hilarious observations about the headlines and her daily life. She has always prided herself on telling it like it is and shocking people with funny, hard-hitting commentary. In the offensive post, Connor went after Chinese immigrants for bringing COVID-19 to the US. When you read the post, you feel a rush of anger build up. You feel personally offended and let down by her comments, particularly in the wake of violence against Asians. People are posting enraging videos online of older immigrants being harassed and even pushed over on the street.

When the swift backlash hits, Connor doubles down, saying that people should be allowed to joke with each other and reminding her followers that freedom of speech protects her posts. Sarah accuses some fans of being "too sensitive" and acting like "snowflakes" and encourages them to just forget about it if they are offended. Several celebrities come to her defense, mentioning her charitable work, that she's a good friend, and that she makes irreverent jokes about everyone—not just Chinese people. Nevertheless, many Asian American groups are upset and call for boycotts of her movies. Employees send you emails encouraging you to drop Connor from the platform because they consider her post a form of hate speech. Others are demanding that you post an official company reply.

As to be expected, her "joke" and the reactions to it are going viral, spawning more outrageous reactions. You scroll and scroll and scroll to see the latest developments. Ironically, the controversy is also causing record usage of your app. Maybe this was just one joke that was over the line, and you should just shrug it off? If you try hard enough, you can see some reasons to give her the benefit of the doubt, but right now, it's hard to see anything through the rage.

What would you do?

Choices like these are difficult because being thoughtful and intentional is challenging when we feel strong emotions. We often find ourselves in situations where our emotions and reason are at war, creating doubt about how to move forward. Declaring a single winner in this battle can easily lead to choices that we regret. So, let's understand how we can turn the fight between emotion and reason into a rewarding partnership.

MERCHANTS OF OUTRAGE

Once upon a time, we believed that the internet would make us more effective and empowered by putting all the world's information at our fingertips. We should have known the sound of dial-up internet was an ominous forewarning because it sounded like a bluebird being transformed into a cyborg. In the last three decades, we've gone from seeing the internet as the great democratizer to being one of the greatest current threats to democracy.

Just to be clear, I'm not some anti-internet whackjob. Obviously, I know there are considerable benefits to information technology and social media. We can hail rides, get food delivered, report potholes and speed traps, learn everything about a person before we meet them, predict flu outbreaks, quickly identify who that familiar-looking actor is, report unethical behavior, stay in touch with family and friends around the world, rip off famous memes for our books, and build communities of like-minded people for anything from a retreat to a revolution.

To provide these and many other compelling conveniences, social media companies use a combination of business models like collecting a fee, taking a margin on your transactions, and gathering information about you to target advertising. The more their business model employs the last strategy, the more social media companies must maximize screen-to-eyeball contact to harvest as much information about us as possible. Since adopting an advertising-based revenue model, these companies have become uncannily good at capturing and directing our attention to keep us glued to their apps. And few things in our social environment grab our attention like anger.[1]

In our digital interactions, anger and offense are "like gravity; all it takes is a little push." (And, yes, I'm so basic that I will use every brilliant quote from the Chris Nolan *Batman* films in this book.) Research suggests that we encounter moral norm violations more online than offline.[2] Yet definitively proving the relationship between social media usage and anger is a surprisingly tricky endeavor, and the debates are far from settled. For example, there are debates about whether increased anger results from social media or cable news,[3] and whether the link is correlational or causal.[4] In addition, not all platforms enflame anger to the same degree, and the specific ways people interact and consume social media differ widely, making clear causal relationships elusive. My goal is not to prove whether social media definitively enflames anger. Instead, let's understand why it can happen so that we can appropriately respond if and when it happens to us. Social media companies have become adept at providing subtle nudges, making it more likely that we can become glued to our screens and sometimes even angry and offended. Don't get mad at me if you've heard some of these before.

First, we are anonymous in most online interactions. We can hide behind a username and feel psychological distance from the idiots who say offensive things or who take offense at things. Anonymity makes emotional outbursts more likely because it doesn't trigger any countervailing responses like concerns for personal reputation or maintaining the relationship. Researchers have shown that when players are anonymous, cooperation drops significantly in trust games.[5] A similar pattern occurs when I'm driving home and start seething at the Subaru in front of me, going ten miles below the speed limit. I raise my fists in frustration, only to see that it's Mr. Solomons, my eighty-year-old neighbor who gave us a bottle of rum last Christmas. Then I feel guilty, turning my angry fists into a sheepish wave.[6]

Second, there are few incentives to work out differences online. We don't need the trolls we disagree with to do us a favor in the future. In contrast, we will try to work out differences when relationships are valuable. Other primates also demonstrate this pattern. When relationships lead to vital resources like food, mating, protection, alliances, and season basketball tickets, over twenty different primate species display more reconciliation behaviors like grooming, sharing food, or bringing over a bottle of home brew.[7] But online, we rarely need anything from the person who insulted us, so there's little incentive to work things out. Quite the opposite, there may be incentives to fan the flames. Having a virtual audience may make it more likely that we want to win an argument, avoid looking foolish, and cyber-stalk those who insulted us to exploit their insecurities. Because negative interactions attract eyeballs, being less forgiving and angrier toward out-group members gets more people to watch, buy the product sponsoring our video, or "smash that like button and turn on notifications." And, the more people click on the anger-provoking video or story, the more the algorithm prioritizes the content, accelerating the feedback loop.

Third, curated online information can make us more confident about our beliefs and more righteous in our offense. Recommendation algorithms are designed to pull you into a rabbit hole. You watch one video on smart architecture, and then you're shown debates between atheists and other intelligent designers. Algorithms feed you whatever content they predict will keep your eyeballs on the screen. Because dozens of studies have shown that multiple exposures to the same information increase your certainty, curated content can make us all more confident that we are right and thus less tolerant of others with different views.[8] False reviews, click-farms, and bots can make our beliefs easier to manipulate. Overconfidence fuels anger and hatred. For example, researchers studied conversations on social media platforms like Gab and a Reddit forum for incels. They found that the amount of certainty in members' posts predicted their amount of hate speech. In the lab, the researchers told some participants that "most Americans agreed with their views" on contentious issues. Those participants reported being more willing to fight and die for their beliefs than those who were told: "Only a small number of Americans agree with you."[9] As we saw in chapter five, exposure to contradictory information can cause us to put up our shields and further entrench our beliefs once we're convinced we're right. In a catch-22, once people are certain in their views, increasing their exposure to different perspectives by changing the recommendation algorithm makes things worse. The information we're exposed to changes what we think, begging the same question that the main character, Winston, ponders in the novel *1984*, "If both the past and the external world exist only in the mind, and if the mind itself is controllable, what then?"

A fourth nudge to capture attention on social media is to expose people to content that features out-group animosity. When we see headlines like "Liberal Idiot Wears KN95 Burqa to Go Outside" or "Anti-Vaxxer Dies Twice from COVID," we cannot help but click on them—"Oh, what did those crazy people do now? How did they shoot themselves in the foot today?" Analyzing almost 3 million posts on Facebook and X found that content about political out-groups was shared or retweeted twice as frequently as content about the in-group.[10] Each word in a post about the political out-group increased the odds of sharing content by 67 percent. Notably, the researchers found that conservatives and liberals engage in these practices equally. The incentives for success on social media are skewed in favor of demonizing the political out-group. Apparently, "To die hating *them*, that is our freedom."

Finally, social media apps make it extremely easy to respond to infuriating content to facilitate engagement and channel our action orientation. They call it "reducing friction." You can like, comment, tag friends, or share the post with a single click or a carefully choreographed number of swipes. Research shows that just sharing something online increases our certainty about that topic.[11] And once you've liked a post, commented, or retweeted a meme, you're now much more motivated to check back in to see how others responded, perpetuating the cycle.

Unproductive conversations, hatred between groups, and toxic interactions existed well before social media and the internet. While social media companies did not invent conflict and misinformation, the carefully crafted nudges they use and the enormous scale to which they are applied (to continue paraphrasing Orwell) have the potential to tear the human mind to pieces and put it together again in new shapes that are not of our choosing.

ATTENTION FARMING

There are offline consequences of these online nudges. For example, all emotions, including anger, can bleed into other interactions because that emotion directs and filters our subsequent perceptions. The philosopher Seneca highlighted this emotional contagion when he pointed out, "Anger makes a mother a stepmother, a fellow citizen a foreign enemy, and a king a tyrant." When an X feud hijacks our attention, we're less able to empathize with our partner. A recent Gallup survey based on more than 150,000 interviews in 140 countries shows that since 2011, globally, anger has been rising.[12]

Similarly, much has also been made of social media's negative consequences on psychological well-being, including increased depression and anxiety. But the latest meta-analyses suggest just a small effect on mental health, nowhere near the alarm calls that most of us have heard about.[13] That's not to say more severe risks aren't present, just that it's less common and more complicated than the media headlines might have us think. The specific ways people use social media can lead to benefits such as social support, getting positive affirmation, finding new ideas, and connecting with like-minded others. On the other hand, we can encounter risks such as cyberbullying, FOMO, negative social comparison, and out-group hate.[14] Thus, the current research might show only a small negative relationship because social media can intensify good *and* bad interactions, and therefore, their combined effect might wash out. It's hard to nail down the overall impact on our well-being without understanding the details of how people use social media, what information they are exposed to, and how it impacts specific interactions and beliefs.

A third consequence of the design choices made by most social media companies is that they can keep us in a reactive state, making short-term choices. We see something offensive or enraging online; then randomly, we just happen to see an advertisement for a calming herbal supplement, some new and improved sleep technology, or a great deal on a timeshare in Boca. Our online interactions activate our Protect or Pursue Systems; then, to soothe ourselves or channel our agitated state, we get advertisements for things that promise relief or reward. Acute stress up-regulates our dopamine receptors, making it harder for us to turn away from the next immediate short-term fix.[15] Similarly, research has shown that people who feel more stress and anxiety make more short-term choices.[16] Meaning that when we feel upset, we're more likely to make choices we'll regret. These reactive choices might provide enough relief to enable us to jump back on social media, get angrier, and buy more crap to calm ourselves down. Me doing my best Lewis Black impersonation: "Arggh!"

Okay. Now that I've sipped my chamomile tea and calmed down, the danger of this narrowing feedback loop is that we spend an increasing amount of time bouncing back and forth between our reactive systems, either protecting ourselves or pursuing the most proximate reward. We spend less time proactively choosing how we want to live and mindfully solving problems that steadily march toward our doorstep. Just as livestock are fed to produce meat for our consumption, we are at risk of being fed content to keep us angry, horny, jealous, disgusted, or constantly saying, "Aww" at cute cat videos so that our attention can be focused, measured, and sold. Some companies are merely trying to farm our attention to sell ads, and anything that happens to our nervous systems, relationships, and democracy is just a side effect. To avoid having our attention farmed and to use social media for *our* ends, we need a way to reclaim our agency, to move from being reactive to proactive. As your calmer friend will tell you, when you're taking off your earrings and heels to fight at the club, you need to breathe and create a gap between the rage you feel bubbling up and your response.

SEEDING RAGE

To better understand how to manage anger, we need to understand what emotions are and how they work. Let's take a second to think about what happens to Bruce Banner when he becomes the Incredible Hulk. Obviously, he turns green and swells up five times his normal size, which has got to be really inconvenient when trying to sink a tricky putt on the eighteenth hole. Less obviously, he loses the ability to form full sentences and think nuanced thoughts. He becomes action-oriented and out of control, which are incredibly helpful when fighting foes. The Hulk becomes rage personified. He doesn't sit in a corner and pout; he smash.

You and I might not turn green, acquire superhuman strength, or have quick healing powers, but the Hulk is still an apt metaphor for all of us when we experience being hijacked by anger.

Psychologists describe prototypical anger as an "approach emotion." Generally, when we feel angry, we want to get up, seek out the person enraging us, and give them a piece of our minds by making "the best speech we will ever regret." In addition, anger generally involves being drop-dead sure that (1) a transgression occurred, (2) you know who exactly is responsible, and (3) you can do something about it.[17] In contrast, if we feel unsure about who caused the harm or we don't have any power to make it right, we might label our experience as fear or anxiety.

The Pursue System is essential to our experience of anger.[18] For example, patients with Parkinson's disease, whose dopamine receptors are damaged, have more difficulty feeling anger and recognizing it in others.[19] A closer look at our brains makes the link between anger and reward-seeking pop out.[20] In one study, Red Sox and Yankees fans viewed baseball plays while undergoing an MRI scan. When their team succeeded and the other team struck out, the participants' Pursue Systems became more active. So far, none of this is surprising to any sports fan, but the more the Pursue System was active, the more people were willing to be aggressive against the rival team's fans. Whether it's shaking keys, throwing trash on their field, or burning down their stadium, we've already seen why this aggression can happen. When our zoom lens is focused on winning, the humanity of our competitors (and sometimes even our own teammates) is blurry and pixelated. The more we see the other team as an obstacle, the better it feels when they are "put in their place." Indeed, as we've seen with other intuitive reactions when neuroscientists enhance the function of the Pause and Piece-Together System, people can better control their anger during reward-seeking.[21] Being angry can feel good because it helps us bring about some valuable state, like getting someone to stop doing something annoying, offensive, stupid, or unethical or interfering with our deepest desires.

In addition, we find angry people more attractive if we agree with them. Workers rate leaders who express anger at moral violations as more effective.[22] When we see our parents, best friends, and ministers turn red or clench their teeth, or we notice that vein in their forehead bulging out, their anger can become more contagious.[23] Similarly, researchers found that heterosexual women rated men who displayed moral outrage as more attractive.[24] Anger can attract others because it is a more reliable signal of what you care about than just your words. (Public Service Announcement: Please don't go around displaying anger at bars to make yourself seem more appealing.)

In addition to feeling good and attracting like-minded others, anger, like all emotions, catalyzes action. In general, our thoughts and our physiological reactions work together to provide the inputs we make sense of as anger, sadness, depression, or ennui. When we interpret our flushed face and tense leg muscles as an experience of anger, we can also feel compelled to punch, run, shout, or smash the dishes on the floor. Yet what might feel like a simple stimulus-response relationship is actually shaped much more by our cultural assumptions and beliefs than we tend to recognize.[25] A large body of research has shown that emotions are not universal triggers that elicit the same pattern of responses in all humans but vary considerably by culture, person, and context. The latest thinking is that emotions arise from a combination of factors like the characteristics of the situation, what we pay attention to, and our cultural scripts for how to make sense of our experiences.[26]

Take fairness, for example. Our cultural scripts about fairness cause us to notice things that we code as unfair (like when the entry-level job you're applying for requires five years of work experience), and we notice our physiological reaction (your heartbeat is pounding in your ears). After intuitively labeling that experience as anger, we're more likely to notice things that maintain that state (Why are they getting their food served before us? We ordered twenty minutes before them!). This tightening feedback loop between our thinking and feeling creates the necessary certainty for quick action, like throwing the remote at the TV, smacking your roommate upside the head, or leaving a passive-aggressive tip. In Western culture, we tend to be more action-oriented when angry. We are more likely to retweet something offensive, donate to political causes, or incite violence against others. Debt collectors have learned that making the person who owes money angry is an effective way to increase collections because they become motivated to prove the collector wrong.[27]

To incite action, emotions like anger can focus our attention and diminish our ability to see things differently. Research shows that experiencing anger makes clear thinking less likely,[28] and prevents people from noticing other ways of interpreting the situation.[29] When we're fuming, we are more susceptible to misinformation,[30] more likely to overestimate our intelligence[31] and our chances of success,[32] and more reliant on stereotypes that reinforce our current way of thinking.[33] The focus and action that the experience of anger incites are critical when we need to fight, stand our ground, and address clear injustices, but they are not as helpful when considering if those things are good ideas in the first place. It's also why all these insights about anger might seem obvious if you're feeling calm and relaxed while you sip your daiquiri on the beach. Still, that tranquility gets washed away the second a large family with six screaming toddlers sets up their giant canopy in front of you.

In the Marvel comics (unlike the Marvel movies), there's really no way to calm down the Hulk other than to let things pass naturally and try to contain the destruction. So to keep the plot moving and to develop the Hulk's character in the *Avengers* movies, the writers had to invent "the lullaby" when Natasha Romanoff and others say, "Hey, Big Guy. The sun's getting real low . . ." as a way to calm the Hulk and bring Bruce Banner back. Similarly, when we experience getting hijacked by anger, it can be hard to spot the runway, and we need to create a way to land safely.

FEEDING OFFENSE

Think about the last time you were offended by someone. Perhaps it was something I said in the last few pages? When someone cuts in front of you in line at the bagel shop, pushes you out of the way to grab the last seat on the airport tram, or keeps calling you the wrong name, most of us feel offended. Sometimes, someone makes derogatory remarks about your group (People who watch comic book movies are such philistines!) or mistakes you for someone of lower status, like when you are a teacher and get mistaken for a student.[34] When a man explains a book on mansplaining to the female author of the book,[35] it's natural for her to feel offended. Being offended is described as suffering "a nick to one's self-image or self-worth."[36] When our social standing is diminished or attacked, we feel estranged, and generally, when we feel offended, unlike when we're angry, we tend to withdraw rather than approach.[37] In close relationships, showing that you are offended can signal to the other person that you need to get on the same page. We can distance ourselves, give the silent treatment, walk away, and passive-aggressively comment on someone's abnormally large toes, hoping they will notice that it's a moment to try to repair what happened.[38]

Being offended is a kind of mental harm and, surprisingly, can be hard to distinguish from other evident injuries like having your legal rights violated, having your possessions stolen, and being mistreated at work. Offense diminishes our social status, which may or may not lead to further physical or legal harm.[39] For example, if someone makes fun of my comments in a meeting (Here he goes again. Tell us about another study . . . why can't he talk normally?), and I take offense, it could also harm me by reducing my promotion prospects, even though none of my rights have been violated. The nature of the harm that occurs from offense depends on what is said, who says it, how I interpret and react to it, how it impacts my future interactions, and the larger social and historical context. Just as we saw with blame in chapter eight, offense is *multi-factorial*, meaning it arises from the interplay of several things.

We don't yet have a clear, socially accepted list of which offenses are serious and should not be allowed, and which ones should be shrugged off. We have general guidelines like the tenet that we shouldn't deride things that people didn't choose. But many times, people's choices are related to factors they can't control. Did you choose the food you grew up eating, the jokes your parents found funny, the clothes you wore as a kid, and how you mispronounce "data," "pecan," and "horror"? Also, as technology develops, new potentially offensive things emerge that make a taxonomy harder to agree upon. Is it offensive if you don't comment on my post? That you keep looking at your phone when you talk to me? Did you screenshot that tweet I deleted? Without consensus, we are at liberty to interpret offenses in line with our motivations, choosing which factors to highlight and which to ignore.

Sarah Connor, from the case at the beginning of this chapter, could focus only on her comments by telling herself, "I'm treating Chinese people equally by making fun of them in the same way I make fun of everyone else; I don't believe they are lesser because they are different. If they are offended, it's their fault." In contrast, Connor's comments can be interpreted as deeply offensive because the social and historical context, like systemic power differences and the history of the Chinese Exclusion Act, prevent Chinese immigrants from being seen as and treated as equal. Sarah's comments in a specific context could lead to more violence against Asian Americans. Like a hologram that changes depending on the angle from which you view it, the severity of the offense appears and disappears depending on what else you connect it to. It's natural to interpret it as clear harm when we feel offended. We're less motivated to hold the hologram at the less flattering angle when we're the offender.

CHECK YOURSELF BEFORE YOU WRECK YOURSELF

If our emotions are a product of our expectations, socialization, and practices, they are not set in stone, even when they feel uncontrollable. We can change them (with some effort and practice) to meet our goals and achieve our intentions. Emotions are not something we should tase into submission using our rationality; that's an old, tired, and inaccurate view of human beings that misses just how important intuitions and emotions are to our lives. We shouldn't aim to subordinate our emotions to reason or vice versa, but we should aim for a careful collaboration between the two. Similarly, just because emotions are essential to making choices and may contain wisdom doesn't mean that our specific way of making sense of and acting on our emotions is always the best way (or the only way) to achieve our intentions. Sometimes, our emotional reactions can help; other times, they can hurt. If you want to regulate your emotions to be informed by their wisdom but not ruled by their grip, here are some of the most tested strategies.

1. SWITCH UP THE CIRCUMSTANCE. The easiest way to regulate an emotion like anger is to remove the cues you interpret as angering. This means avoiding situations and people you code as triggering, for example, spending less time on social media, keeping your distance from your boss toward the end of the quarter, and avoiding that one vegan who won't stop talking about doing CrossFit. Eliminating or reducing the cues that we interpret as angering diminishes the experience of unpleasant emotions. This strategy, however, does not help you directly address the beliefs and assumptions that helped manufacture the emotional response in the first place. For example, if you interpret your news feed as angering, shutting the app will reduce instances of anger, but it does nothing to help you process and change the beliefs and expectations contributing to your rage.

Nevertheless, if your reaction is too heated and you don't yet have the necessary skills to try other emotion-regulating methods, switching up the circumstance can be a good way to avoid doing more damage.

2. LOOK, OVER THERE! When you can't escape the situation, a second strategy for managing your emotions is to distract yourself from the unpleasant cues. You might tune out your annoying Uncle Charlie at Thanksgiving dinner and focus instead on the cousins you want to see. A similar strategy is to catch yourself ruminating on negative events and actively intervene, like when you notice your boss hovering for the hundredth time and turn your attention instead to helping your customers. While this strategy has been shown to reduce unpleasant emotions in the short term, it can weaken your long-term resilience, just like the circumstance-switching strategy. For example, research shows that when people trained to distract themselves from a negative interaction are re-exposed to their troublesome situations, they can actually have a stronger adverse reaction than before.[40] Similarly, suppressing emotions by pushing them down or ignoring them doesn't work; in fact, suppressing emotions can enable stronger negative reactions to things that are unrelated, like when you swallow your anger when your company fires half its employees, the CEO doubles her salary, and then you find yourself in your car screaming at the drivers going out of turn at the four-way stop.[41] So, distracting yourself and suppressing emotions are merely short-term strategies to control anger.

3. REFRAME. A third strategy for addressing negative emotions like anger is to change how you interpret the negative stimuli by reframing the situation. What might seem like an annoying act, like when your colleague rephrases every suggestion you offer in a meeting before accepting it, is less annoying when you realize there's something else going on here—it's how your colleague processes information. Reframing allows you to change the thoughts that create an emotion and thus decrease the negative emotions you feel. Indeed, reframing a situation to see yourself from an observer's perspective creates psychological distance and can help manage intense feelings.[42] For reframing to work, you must really believe the new perspective; it can't be a faint-hearted attempt to deceive yourself. "I know that bankruptcy will make me stronger!" Reframing is one of the most studied interventions for emotional regulation and is better for long-term resilience than distraction or removing the triggering stimuli. This strategy is particularly useful for uncontrollable negative stimuli. It is not as good for controllable cues because reframing can also make you complacent and reticent to make changes.[43] One risk of reframing is that you can become less motivated to act directly against the cues and situations you interpret as angering.

Also, we can reframe our emotional experiences more effectively if we have a richer emotional vocabulary. For example, when you can more carefully distinguish between feeling frustrated, insulted, or nervous, you can take targeted actions addressing your feelings. But if you can only describe your emotional states as either fine, tired, or hungry, then your strategies for intervention are similarly blunt. A richer set of emotion words can help you more carefully identify the thoughts, patterns, and situations that contribute to your experiences and thus manage them more intentionally. When you can tell the difference between feeling powerless and petrified, you stand a better chance of doing something about it. The subtle differences are essential to help yourself calm down, channel your energy positively, or cope more effectively.

4. TRY SOMETHING NEW. Finally, when you are upset and angry, a variety of behaviors can accompany your emotions. You can scream, whisper threats, cry, go silent, get curious, pound your fists, start yelling, or even start laughing or get really friendly. Modulating your responses is not about changing your emotions but about changing how you choose to express them. When we read an angering tweet, we can ignore it, joke about it, tweet something positive, change the subject, report the tweet, ask a question, reply with a counterpoint, organize a protest, and many other things. Similarly, when you feel upset, going for a walk, setting out on a run, or exercising can help you manage the physiological reactions and channel them toward a positive end. Regulating our responses is a powerful tool for being informed by our emotions and being intentional about how we express them.

RUPTURE AND REPAIR

Think of your closest relationships. Have you ever had disagreements and arguments with those that you care about? (If you said no, put this book down now and go figure out what's wrong with you. Right now. I'm done talking to you until you do.) Most of us have disagreements even with the people who share most of our genes, time, attention, and interests. The very people we would lay down our lives to protect without question also sometimes annoy the crap out of us, misinterpret our intentions, or fundamentally disagree with us about what to do. All healthy relationships have both *rupture* and *repair*. We disagree, argue, get offended, and then we also apologize, hug, and forgive. Repair is essential for healthy relationships.

To repair, we need to offer both feedback and forgiveness. Often, it's easy to emphasize one at the expense of the other. We might be too quick to forgive if we keep silent and make excuses for the person, "Oh, they didn't mean it, they won't do it again, or maybe I should just toughen up and not be so sensitive." We don't allow them to learn about the impact of their words and actions.[44] In contrast, we can focus only on feedback and give them a piece of our mind, secretly resolving to hold it against them forever, not caring if we effectively deliver our message. To maintain healthy connections, we need to give our feedback in ways that maximize the odds of it being heard and acted upon. When it is acknowledged and incorporated, we need to be willing to forgive and move forward. If we notice that our feedback is never taken or that we are doing all the forgiving and don't get any in return, then, of course, we should reevaluate and consider more drastic approaches, like calling out the pattern or reducing our interactions. Still, research confirms that when both parties with different perspectives are committed to each other's interests, they stand a better chance of working out their differences.[45]

Ruptures in relationships, particularly online relationships, are quick and easy to create. Like a car wreck, train wreck, or bawdy discotheque, we can't look away. As we saw in chapter eight, because negative information heavily outweighs positive information in our minds, it takes much more time to rebuild trust than to break it. Furthermore, repair requires that both parties come to a shared understanding of what happened, why, and what to do differently next time.[46] A meta-analysis of studies about forgiveness shows that apologies are more effective when people demonstrate that they share the same perspective about what happened.[47]

We live in a time when considerable profit can be made from rupture, and no immediate profit seems possible from repair. It's amusing to think about *Shark Tank* pitches for products that could prevent rupture or someday even repair digital relationships. Maybe there could be a timer I could set built into social media apps, forcing me to wait at least fifteen minutes before posting on a toxic or incendiary topic. Maybe there are browser plug-ins like Grammarly that can scan my content and even suggest more effective rewrites of my posts at different levels of intensity. "Warning: you are speaking on an issue that is related to historic and systemic injustices. Read this article, take this quiz, and double-check your message before posting!" We could also create app plug-ins that filter content from our social media experience based on the kind of experience we want to create. "I don't want to see any negative headlines about the other party unless three high-quality, independent sources have vetted them or at least 5,000 people have commented." "I'd like to see at least one positive story about the other party daily." We could develop toxicity scores for content, like a nutrition label for information that signals how much of our daily allowance of out-group animosity a video contains so we can choose what to consume more carefully. All these ideas have clear weaknesses, and I'm sure many better ideas are out there. But designing tools that prevent and minimize rupture is essential because one cruel fact of life is that checking ourselves is harder and much more valuable than wrecking ourselves.

Taking some personal responsibility for our choices doesn't mean social media companies, governments, or the people who say offensive things don't have responsibility. And just because other parties might have even more responsibility and power than we do doesn't mean we have none. In these complex situations, we must learn to support systemic changes *and* be more intentional about our responses where we can. Addressing complex issues like these will take governmental, corporate, and personal responsibility, just like safe driving is currently supported by laws, technology created by car manufacturers, and drivers' training and responsible use. Unfortunately, today, the design choices made by some social media companies shift the odds toward rupturing relationships; we must swim upstream to repair them if we want to. And that's the bigger, more important question. Do we want to? Why would we ever give up anger if it feels good?

FREEDOM

A few years ago, a group of students and I went backpacking in Patagonia. I noticed that we tended to get quiet when we were hiking off-trail, avoiding obstacles, bending around trees, and trying to find sure footing. We (especially me) were keenly focused on not tripping, falling, or hitting our heads on a branch. But when walking on a trail, we didn't have to think so carefully about where to place our feet, so we freed our minds to tell stories, laugh together, and figure out where to go next. Think about how differently your attention was deployed the first time you drove a car compared to the times you drive now, when driving has become a habit. Likewise, exercising our freedom and choice requires that our attention be liberated from the constant barrage of distractions both on- and offline.

If our attention is captured by fabricated fights and their mental and emotional residue, how can we really be free? Facing a constant stream of depressing news stories and online feuds, like obstacles and dangers in the wilderness, prevents us from using our attention for our own ends. If "attention is the critical resource by which we live our lives,"[48] then what happens when that resource is squandered? We are on the path to becoming weaker, more anxious, and more driven by self-protection. Attention farming risks the large-scale hijacking of our optimism, ingenuity, and freedom. Undoubtedly, these were always unequally distributed privileges, but to me, our most meaningful moments as a nation were when we worked to extend those privileges to more people.

If democracy aims to protect human flourishing and freedom, then it must also nurture the ability of its current and future citizens to think and act for themselves. In short, democracy needs a citizenry with healthy and resilient nervous systems that allow them to respond to a changing and complex world, not just to react recklessly. Organizations and systems that are well run, whether businesses, governments, courts, healthcare systems, or schools, provide us all with a baseline of predictability and security that allow us to explore and learn. Like a network of trails in the wilderness, well-run systems enable freedom by liberating more of our attention so we can choose where to place it. How can we continue to innovate, be creative, and solve necessary problems if we're constantly looking over our shoulders to survive the moment? What is freedom if we are farmed for our attention, our bodies are weakened for profits, and our nervous systems are hacked for ad revenue? Are we building our collective capacity to address the challenges of the twenty-first century? Regulating our anger can feel like bitter medicine. Many enemies of liberal democracies, both within and outside our borders, are betting big that we will refuse to take it. But without this medicine, it's getting harder to imagine a future that's not some nightmarish mashup of feudalism with smartphones.

Responding when we are angry and offended is difficult because, like all the moments of doubt in this book, you need to understand the social terrain and decide if and how you will respond. (See appendix tool 9.) It's not as simple as saying that when you're offended, you should always toughen up and take it or that you are always justified in being outraged and should burn down the system. Simple rules like these blind us to the situation's complexity; they focus us on either rupture or repair and cause more problems to address in the future. Most importantly, they strip away our agency by triggering unreflective responses. These reactions may keep us alive in some situations but harm our quality of life in others. Having agency means choosing how you respond to something annoying and offensive, not being triggered, and having a pleasurable release of anger, which may be best for social media platforms but not for our sanity, relationships, and democracy.

We've seen how our emotions and our thoughts work together to produce our behavior, yet when that delicate balance is tipped, we can quickly lose the ability to bring our actions in line with our intentions. When making choices about how to respond when we are angry, offended, and frustrated by online interactions, we need to do just that—*make* choices—create space for them when the walls of certainty are closing in. Decision-making is typically thought about as rationally choosing among the options in front of us, but sometimes the most powerful and necessary "decision" making is to generate choices and forge previously hidden paths. Indeed, if our decisions and our democracy are being eroded by imprisoning our attention and diminishing our agency, then exercising our freedom by *choosing wisely* becomes an act of revolution.

11

Confidence in the Face of Doubt

BEFORE RETIRING after a seemingly random (but surprisingly impactful) career, you take on one last role as a senior product manager at a popular professional social networking site. Your company just acquired a neuroscience startup named BrainSight, the first to make at-home electroencephalograms (EEGs) cost-effective and popular. Customers order a test kit that includes a cap with over a hundred different sensors that connect directly to their laptops. Then, while wearing the cap, they watch a few short videos, conduct about an hour of decision-making tasks, and respond to several questionnaires. As a result, customers can learn about several critical aspects of their brain, such as their attention, empathy, risk of addiction, and tolerance for uncertainty and why they keep forgetting where they put their car keys. Most people use BrainSight's personalized reports to develop more accurate self-awareness and track any cognitive decline.

After acquiring BrainSight, your company now owns the data for about 4 million brains. Your job is to program an algorithm that can predict people's career and job success by merging BrainSight's data with your data about people's education, training, previous positions, promotions, and professional networks. Then, if everything works according to plan, you can better match specific brains, jobs, and organizations. For example, your recommendations can put more analytical brains in analytical roles, more empathetic brains in customer-facing positions, and more psychopathic brains in jobs where they can tank global financial markets.

The benefits to your clients would be vast. Recruiting is always tricky, and research confirms that hiring committees can be biased and select people who are most similar to them, not necessarily the most qualified. By removing these common biases, your algorithm can help create a more equitable and meritocratic workplace. Additionally, by reducing hiring time, cost, and errors, you can save your customers millions of dollars and help them grow their organizations by finding and placing the most qualified talent.

To accomplish these ambitious goals, your team plans to use a machine learning algorithm, where the program creates new variables from the data, tries out millions of combinations, and adjusts their weight and ratio to find the best predictive fit. However, developers on your team caution that the algorithm will be a black box; you won't be able to explain exactly how it arrived at conclusions, and you must take it on faith that it's making the best decision possible.

The risks of employing this kind of algorithm are apparent. Specifically, the data used to train the algorithm could be biased or incomplete. For example, when other companies used algorithms for hiring and promotion, they found women were less likely to be recommended for jobs because the training data contained fewer observations of women in senior positions. Your data could be similarly biased; since the BrainSight at-home test kit is expensive, you might have fewer workers from lower socioeconomic statuses or fewer younger workers in your dataset. Therefore, the algorithm could further entrench existing societal privileges by making the application of historical patterns efficient and scalable. In addition, you don't know whether it is even possible to anonymize brain data; perhaps it is specific to a person, like DNA, so it may always be traceable.

Even though the team assumes that hiring managers will use the results as only one input among several in their process, to save time, you know that HR teams will make an offer to the individuals your algorithm recommends. The instruments and tests companies currently use in hiring have a high error rate, so there's a good chance your algorithm will be more accurate than current practices. Finally, you think it's only a matter of time until someone else implements a similar model; you could do it right and be ahead of the curve. This process has many uncertainties, and you don't want to get bogged down trying to sort them all out before doing anything and losing your shot to stay ahead of the competition.

What would you do?

Let's call these *Jurassic Park* problems because, like the scientists at Jurassic Park, "We get so preoccupied figuring out if we *can* do something we don't stop to ask if we *should*." For these difficult choices, our ability to do something novel (like manipulating genes, injecting micro-robots into our bodies, building general AI, and bioengineering the environment) outpaces our ability to predict and understand the future. There's just a lot we don't know, and that specific lack of knowledge could lead to significant errors and damage. When we experience uncertainty, we encounter a high-stakes inflection point. The experience of uncertainty can activate our Protect System and propel us to avoid or flee the situation. In contrast, our Pursue System could propel us to barrel ahead and ignore the risks. Under certain conditions, all three systems work together, giving us the focus and flexibility to learn when we face doubt. So, let's peer into the fog to see how exactly we can capture the promise and avoid the perils of doubt.

UNCERTAINTY IS, WELL . . .

True to form, definitions of uncertainty are ambiguous. One scholar notes, "There are almost as many definitions of uncertainty as there are treatments on the subject."[1] Great. We're screwed. Before we pack up and go home, let's at least look at a few common ways people think about uncertainty. The philosopher Charles Sanders Peirce thought about doubt and uncertainty as "a hesitancy about an imagined state of things," preventing us from knowing what to believe and how to act in specific circumstances.[2] We all hesitate and take caution in the presence of conflicting signals, like when the hot date shows signs of being a hoarder or your therapist begins each session by trauma-dumping on you. Conflicting signals make it harder for us to know if this is a situation we should approach or avoid, and as we've seen, our Pause and Piece-Together System revs up. When we can't identify the outcomes of our actions, can't discern among our alternatives, or are unsure about the credibility of the information we have, we experience uncertainty. It's important to note that uncertainty is not just the absence of knowledge but also the awareness of not knowing. When we're unaware of our ignorance but barrel ahead anyway, that's Dunning-Kruger. He's Freddy's overconfident serial killer cousin who needs his own Netflix show right now.

Some scholars prefer making increasingly fine-grained distinctions, and they have classified at least two types of uncertainty. "Risk" is technically defined as a lack of knowledge about probabilities. For example, in poker, you know the various outcomes, specifically that a straight flush beats two of a kind, and risk is the likelihood of achieving a specific known outcome (~0.00144 percent chance of a full house!). In contrast, "uncertainty" is technically defined as a lack of knowledge about the outcomes. For example, when you design a new product, you don't even imagine that some people will use it for nefarious purposes, that your campaign to end drunk driving will actually make drunk driving worse,[3] or that when you work up the courage to flirt with your crush, said crush will turn out to be your cousin. We can experience uncertainty about outcomes because our most relevant experiences and expectations are incomplete. We often have competing views of what can and will happen and don't know which outcome is most applicable.

Other scholars who prefer to highlight similarities will argue that while we often experience both risk and uncertainty as unpleasant, sometimes uncertainty can be pleasurable. When we're solving puzzles we care about, wandering to a delightful destination, imagining enjoyable things, and keeping sight of our dopamine motivators, it can be enjoyable. "I wonder who my secret admirer is? Will I get a big enough raise to buy a Porsche or a Ferrari?"[4] But all too often, we experience uncertainty as unpleasant.[5] As we saw in chapter four, when we're pausing and piecing together, our Protect Systems are on standby, making it more likely that we find uncertainty aversive. Imagine that I brought you into the lab and placed an electrode on your forearm because, apparently, that's what a psychologist's gotta do to be in the club. Then, I connected that electrode to a large, fully charged battery and said, "By the way, there's a chance you'll get a shock. How do you think you would feel?" Well, it depends on the actual probability of getting a shock. In one study, participants were hooked up to a battery and told there was either a 0 percent, 50 percent, or 100 percent chance of getting a small electric shock. Participants in the 50 percent condition reported the highest levels of stress. Apparently, uncertainty is more painful than being sure that you will get an electric jolt.[6]

When we experience uncertainty as unpleasant, we can give up, go home, jump ship, throw in the towel, and lose faith. Let's say you've spent an hour scrolling through Netflix to figure out what to watch and you give up and spend another hour scrolling through YouTube. Scientists call this phenomenon *choice overload* and have shown that we are more likely to be overwhelmed by choice when it triggers higher levels of uncertainty.[7] Similarly, powerful individuals are less decisive when they see both the pros and cons of an action,[8] and when doctors are given a choice between prescribing two similar medicines, they are more likely to prescribe nothing.[9] This common reaction to uncertainty can make us vulnerable to unscrupulous PR consultants, managers, politicians, and lawyers who muddy the waters and sow doubt to avoid blame and evade accountability. To get us to give up, people interject false alternatives like, "Smoking is good for your health! No, asbestos is a weight loss miracle!" When we face conflicting information, people often feel stuck and unsure; we can give up on figuring out what all the commotion is about and become paralyzed enough to be easily redirected by others.

Yet, while we're busy fleeing discomfort, we can fail to notice two meaningful benefits of doubt. First, the experience of uncertainty signals that our mental maps are incomplete. Thus, uncertainty can be a catalyst for learning. We can become more sensitive to our surroundings, avoid obstacles derailing our plans, and do the work to better align our actions with our intentions. Second, uncertainty allows us to do things differently and put our special mark on things. When there are clear rules, strong habits, genetic determinants, overwhelming situations, intense emotions, or single right answers that force our hand, our personal agency, creativity, and ingenuity are not needed or particularly welcome. It is precisely in moments of uncertainty that our agency matters.

We often pause, waver, and seem stuck because we have too much information, not enough information, or conflicting information about outcomes, alternatives, and risks. All of these make imagining the future more difficult and thus cause us to hesitate. These different views of uncertainty make clear (irony intended) that uncertainty is inescapable. How we think about uncertainty shapes our experience of it. If we fear it, we experience it as aversive, increasing our worry, anxiety, nervousness, and panic, and we seek to escape uncertain conditions as quickly as possible. As we've seen, if we're excited by uncertainty, we're more able to persist and learn in the face of doubt. But there's at least one more common coping strategy that we haven't met yet.

FLIGHT TO CERTAINTY

Let's take this to the lab to get a closer look at the critical moment when people experience doubt. In one study, college students were asked to write about an uncertain choice or "a personal dilemma that was not easy to solve and about which they had not already made a decision." Typically, they wrote about work or personal conflicts like choosing their major or romantic partner. Students in the second condition were asked to write about "a dilemma a friend was facing, where they knew what the friend should do." In short, participants in the first condition were asked to write about a personal uncertain choice, and those in the second condition were asked to write about the opposite: a non-personal certain choice. Then, both groups were asked to review fifteen statements about capital punishment, such as "Capital punishment is absolutely never justified," and rate how strongly they believed the statements. Students who wrote about the personal uncertain choice had more extreme attitudes (either pro or con) about capital punishment than the students who wrote about the non-personal certain choice.

In chapter five, we saw that confirmation bias shows up when our need for self-protection causes people to put up shields and bolster a set of threatened beliefs. But, in this experiment, uncertainty increased confidence in a set of entirely unrelated beliefs.[10] What gives?

This effect has been replicated dozens of times in different contexts and with very different beliefs. Take college students, for example. Those who feel uncertain about their academic performance can compensate by associating themselves with their university's winning sports team.[11] "I'm failing my computer science class, but who cares? We're going to the championship!" Similarly, when people feel uncertain about the future because they are asked to think about their own death, they compensate by seeking out high-status products,[12] choosing to be around more predictable people, aligning themselves with strong leaders,[13] and bolstering their beliefs in a just and rational world.[14] When lab participants are made to feel uncertain about their social role, they can compensate by doubling down on their in-group biases.[15] When people experience economic uncertainty, they prefer to read more absolutist moral statements,[16] and they choose more stereotypically masculine or feminine partners.[17] In all these different examples, people compensate for uncertainty in one domain by turning their attention to more certainty elsewhere. Here's how psychologists who study our need to maintain a stable, ordered, and certain worldview explain this pattern:

> People possess an associative impulse by which they seek to relate objects and events to each other and to the self. This desire to perceive relations results in people viewing their worlds and the events within them through the prism of their mental representations. These representations are constructions, and often do not accurately reflect objective relations within the world. When people become aware of events that cannot be accommodated in their relational structures, they experience a threat to their sense of meaning. These threats to meaning are dealt with in a few ways: people may reinterpret the events so that they are no longer inconsistent with their mental representations or they may revise their representations so that they are capable of incorporating the new troublesome event. . . . [P]eople might respond to meaning threats by reaffirming an alternative framework. The goal is to be attending to a viable and coherent framework of relations, and people

will be motivated to assert one even if it does not appear related to the source of threat that motivated their search in the first place.[18]

When our mental maps are unreliable, our brains look around for a more dependable map, and *any* map that promises certainty will do. Compensating by turning our attention toward solid beliefs in an unrelated domain down-regulates Protect System activity and up-regulates the Pursue System. Indeed, when a baseball player taps his shoes with the bat at home plate before stepping into the batter's box and facing god-knows-what kind of pitch, a test-taker is reminded of their own previous gold-star performance, or a worried parent rubs a rabbit's foot, they all feel better because they can reduce anxiety and increase confidence by making the unfamiliar feeling, familiar.[19] Once people feel better, they no longer need to focus on comforting certain beliefs. In the study mentioned previously, where participants had to write about a difficult decision and then rate their views on capital punishment, when some participants were given a chance to affirm their personal values before rating their views on capital punishment, their subsequent views did not become more extreme. They had already compensated for uncertainty by affirming their personal values. "I know who I am. I am a person who doesn't like having my beliefs about capital punishment manipulated by experimenters!" Whether we are scrolling through our anxiety-inducing news feed over breakfast, listening to our family members argue, or working on a challenging problem at the office, we can compensate by attending to our most certain beliefs, but we're not always aware that we're doing it.

Because we're unaware that we're compensating for the aversive feeling that results when we face the unknown, we're at risk of choosing the most straightforward or most accessible strategy rather than the most beneficial one. One example of a positive compensation strategy is seeking constructive social support. When people are primed to feel uncertain, they are more likely to sit with others than alone,[20] and they form new relationships, including romantic ones[21] (that's one reason why the number of weddings explodes during wartime). Similarly, when participants in a lab study were made to feel uncertain about themselves, their level of social support predicted how much they compensated; the more supported they felt by the group, the less they needed to compensate.[22] When we think that life is meaningless or we don't know which way is up, connecting with others can be a powerful cure.[23]

But we can also compensate in more destructive ways. For example, when people experience a lack of predictability in their close relationships, such as dealing with a difficult toddler or a contentious relationship with their spouse, they are more likely to project order and consistency on distant connections with political leaders and celebrities, becoming increasingly obsessed with what Zendaya is wearing on the red carpet.[24] The opposite also occurs when people feel they cannot trust political leaders; they impose more order and consistency on their close relationships.[25] But there are many ways of compensating beyond changing our relationships. For example, when you feel insecure and reassert your social status by yelling at others, you're anxious and order another drink, or you're overwhelmed and wrap yourself in a Snuggie, you are regulating your internal states by modifying your external environment. Surprisingly, this pattern of compensation isn't something that just affects individuals; it has fundamentally shaped the history of Western thought.

A QUEST FOR CERTAINTY

Athenians had grown pretty damn weary of pests by 399 BC. One such annoyance was a man named Socrates, an elderly teacher in the city-state who would buzz about his fellow citizens, pointing out inconsistencies in their thinking and irritating them with questions like, "What is the good life? What are justice and virtue?" His goal was to use questioning and doubt to get his fellow citizens to think critically (and probably be a general pain in the ass).

His timing wasn't great. The proud Athenians had just lost the Peloponnesian War with Sparta and were nursing their wounds. Politicians were searching for a scapegoat and believed that Socrates was sowing doubt precisely when people needed certainty.[26] So they accused Socrates of "corrupting the youth and of impiety toward the Gods." Athenians found Socrates guilty in a sham trial and forced him to choose between drinking hemlock poison or being banished. He chose the hemlock.

Plato, Socrates' most famous student, witnessed this tragedy unfold and was powerless to stop it. After his mentor died, Plato wrote down what he could remember about his teacher's views, opened his own school, and devised his own philosophy, which became a cornerstone of Western thought. In his writings, Plato famously describes the human condition as like being trapped in a cave, condemned to glimpse eternal truths as mere shadows on the wall.

Only philosophers, through diligent study, could escape the cave and know the universe's true nature. The rest of humankind, unaware that their perspectives were only shadows, could only guess at those ideal forms. The not-so-subtle implication is that the uneducated masses should respect and defer to philosophers (not make them drink poison).[27] One interpretation of Plato's views is that infallible knowledge became a way to compensate for the pain of losing a beloved mentor. To escape the unbearable uncertainty of living with the fickle Athenian mob, Plato turned knowledge into impenetrable armor, impervious even to hemlock.

In Plato's view, to obtain perfect knowledge, one had to turn away from society, from the unsophisticated, biased, and ignorant masses and their diverse opinions. This powerful idea cast the role of philosophy (and, later, of science) as discovering and sharing those foundational truths with the rest of humankind, forever removing "real" knowledge from the direct reach of the masses and subjugating the role of reflective practice in applying and refining what we know. In this view, certainty and knowledge are a kind of holy grail or a set of infinity stones that, once possessed, give the bearer powers independent of their existing human relationships. Those powers compel others to defer and provide an alluring escape from the exhausting debate, discussion, and disagreement that characterize democracies.

To a great degree, Plato's fantasy is even more compelling today, in a world where the internet and social media ensure that we are perpetually attached to our own Athenian mobs. We are always a few swipes away from people who disagree with us, make profane what we hold sacred, and make us feel like "we can't even." And like Plato, when uncertainty threatens us in one domain, we can escape and create certainty in another, from camaraderie with like-minded people, the simple three-step solution that will solve all your problems, and an unwavering and unchanging truth.

But is this what Socrates would have encouraged? From what we know, it seems that Socrates thought knowledge was partly created in conversation, as people shared their different perspectives, discussed, debated, and designed more useful explanations that better approximate the truth. Think about the Socratic Method—it is a commitment to talking when we disagree. In this view, degrees of certainty emerge from human practices of dialogue, experimentation, and shared reflection. For Socrates, knowledge sits between us (each other) just as much as it sits between us and the world. Gaining knowledge isn't just about escaping the cave to find certainty, but also about working together to create explanations that allow us to resume action when we encounter the shadows of doubt.

The Socratic ideal only works in specific conditions, and there is no guarantee that it will always work. For example, when there are so many conflicting sources of information, citizens with easily triggered nervous systems, an increasing number of distractions, and a fundamental lack of commitment and care for each other, the easiest thing to do is to stop talking, seek safety, and resort to other forms of power to force compliance. That's why it's no surprise that the Information Age has reinvigorated autocracies and dictatorships. The more we are exposed to uncertainty that disorients us, the more we crave certainty. The Socratic Method (and our democratic principles based on it) requires that we have mutual respect, self-security, skills to cope with uncertainty, and skills to talk to each other effectively to identify and practice better ways to live together. While certainly possible, these ideal conditions are fragile. The ancient story of Plato and Socrates is relevant to us today because, in the face of uncertainty and dislocation, one of our most potent coping mechanisms is to turn toward each other. But, if we seek refuge in Plato's view of perfect knowledge, we compensate by turning away.

BECOMING EDUCATED

Most of us don't explicitly learn a theory of knowledge in school, yet we subconsciously soak up a view of what knowledge is, what it's good for, and how to use it. Most of our education is about updating our mental maps based on other people's work. We learn facts like Leif Erikson was the first European to discover America, $(6 \times 9) + (6 + 9) = 69$, and that Detroit is east of Atlanta. For many of us, that's perfectly fine. We don't need to reinvent mathematics or biology to learn it. Yet there are unintended consequences of an education overly indexed on certainty, memorizing, and regurgitating ideas. Specifically, students never learn to understand and manage their experience of uncertainty. And because uncertainty is initially uncomfortable, they may even come to fear and avoid it.

In a world of instant gratification, gold stars, and parents who argue with college professors over their adult children's grades, we seem to confuse *knowing* and *learning*. Education can become about unreflectively cramming facts into students without understanding how and why those ideas are helpful and, just as importantly, understanding the assumptions and limits of those ideas. Too many students learn that being smart is what my colleague calls being a "right-answer-getter," but that's something you cannot be when you encounter moments of doubt.

I believe that the role of education is to help people be both right-answer-getters when there are right answers to get and better-answer-makers when we operate at the boundary of what we know. I know there are many great teachers out there who help learners build confidence and thrive in moments of doubt because I've been lucky to have more than my fair share of them. Today, I'm fortunate to work with several more. What these great teachers do, in addition to making their curiosity infectious, is to help students build comfort with uncertainty. They do this by inspiring everyone to co-create a learning environment for confronting optimal stress. It's too easy to get caught at one extreme—too much comfort with little stretch or too much stress with no time for recovery. In short, becoming better-answer-makers requires cultivating beliefs, skills, and a social environment where we can regulate ourselves and tolerate not having the right answer while maintaining our motivation to improve our current alternatives.

Here's one attempt I'm making with my kids. Every summer for the last twelve years, when we go to the beach, I create a puzzle hunt for my daughters, niece, and nephew. A puzzle hunt is a series of insight puzzles where you must try several things out to find the non-obvious insight and solve the puzzle. Think Escape Room meets Treasure Hunt. Each year, there's a different theme, from *The Avengers* to *Hunger Games* and *Star Wars* to *Survivor*. There are few directions, so there is a lot of uncertainty and confusion. For example, one puzzle might just be a bag of jelly beans, and the kids must figure out how that is a clue that would lead to something else. They might try counting the total number of jelly beans and notice that there are different numbers of different colors. There might be two purples, two blues, three yellows, and one green. Then they might try to take the second letter of the word "red" and the third letter of the word "green," which might uncover a string of letters to unscramble, leading them to look for the next clue near the picture of the sea "gull" on the bookshelf. When they were younger, the kids would give up quickly. They would try one thing, and if that didn't work, they would complain, "We're stuck! We give up! What's the answer?" Finally, they would just eat the bag of jelly beans.

Now, after doing this for the last decade and tolerating my annoying refrains to "Think of something else to try!" they're building a repertoire of strategies and confidence in figuring things out when they don't intuitively know what to do. More importantly, I hope they are learning that "being smart" isn't just about getting the correct answer but also includes the ability to sit with a problem, try several things, design and learn from experiments, be resilient in the face of inevitable missteps, and rely on each other throughout the process. Whether they go into engineering, biology, psychology, or sports, I hope that they become *deeply* educated, meaning that they're not just able to recite the latest knowledge that someone else spouted but also have the confidence and motivation to navigate through the fog, to solve the problems they care about.

While all of this might be well and good for the annual family beach trip, as leaders of teams that face uncertainty and as members of organizations that need to wrestle with complex challenges, what can we do to set the stage for better coping with doubt? First, we can help create social situations where our teams are less likely to tie their self-worth only to immediate outcomes and more likely to pursue the rewards of effort and perseverance when it inevitably gets complicated. Psychologist Carol Dweck has inspired a generation of leaders and educators to foster a growth mindset, and people are on it. Learning is not purely a cognitive state but also a social and emotional one. Without sources of resilience that reduce activation of our Protect System and also engage our Pursue System and Pause and Piece-Together System, we are less able to revise our beliefs, test hypotheses, and be open to being wrong. Thankfully, to lay the groundwork for learning in the face of uncertainty, we can use several general strategies beyond praising learning behaviors.

1. STRATEGY: MODEL HEALTHY COPING. Ironically, I've found that many leaders and educators love telling others that they should have a growth mindset while maintaining a fixed mindset about their own practices. As a result, we can prefer to be the "sage on the stage" rather than to model struggle and resilience. First, modeling uncertainty means admitting when we don't know what to do, detailing what we'll do to learn, why we think it's essential to keep going, showing that we can be wrong and be okay, and connecting with others. Second, we can model productive disagreement and debate, demonstrating respect for those we disagree with and highlighting what we learned from interacting with them. A third way to *model healthy coping* is setting up a conducive lifestyle, including healthy habits around food, sleep, exercise, and relationships. Each of these critical factors can limit or liberate our ability to cope with uncertainty. Yet we generally don't help people develop these habits early in life. If we believe that education is mostly a cognitive endeavor, it makes sense to try and pack more information into students' brains without paying attention to their social, physiological, and self-regulatory needs. Indeed, we celebrate cramming for tests, all-nighters to deliver a project, eating on the go, and doing whatever it takes to get an A or to memorize information. But these short-term tactics geared toward getting the right answer don't set students up for success very well when they are tackling complex challenges that require ongoing self-regulation, experimentation, and creativity. If we don't embed education in the larger context of building healthy habits, we erode people's ability to make better answers.

2. STRATEGY: ATTEND TO THE BRAIN'S TRIO. Throughout this book, we've seen how the Pursue, Protect, and Pause and Piece-Together Systems work together to help us react and respond to both predictable and unpredictable circumstances. Whether in the boardroom or the classroom, attention to how the social environment and our decision-making processes activate each system is critical. For example, in our conversations, are we pursuing rewards without caution? Are we avoiding trying new things because we are uncomfortable? When confronting uncertainty, are we keeping sight of our dopamine motivators? Leaders can optimize learning environments to facilitate productive engagement. We can avoid overly triggering the Protect System through social punishment if we want team members to take risks. This also means that there's a role for all three systems. We cannot only focus on the fun stuff and avoid challenging topics because they don't feel good or are hard to discuss. And, as we've seen in previous chapters, to extend our Pause and Piece-Together System, we need to involve our Pursue System to have a line of sight toward things we value. Carefully attending to the brain's trio can help us better create the social and emotional conditions for doing hard and important things.

3. STRATEGY: STRENGTHEN THE FILTER. Finally, our big brains allow us to insert a gap between what's inside and outside, a filter that enables us to make sense of what happens out there more productively. For example, when your boss sends you five texts in a row about tomorrow's work schedule and then ghosts you when you reply, you can respond with intention, or you can be annoyed and show it. When confronting uncertainty that is not an immediate life or death decision, strengthening our filter and building it like a muscle can help us increase our ability to respond wisely. Quick, intuitive choices can be very effective in more predictable circumstances, but as we've seen, we cannot apply that same method to difficult decisions. When we encourage our teams to follow their intuition in complex situations without taking a broader view, we're not helping others regulate their nervous systems; we're weakening the filter. Even though people might be tired of hearing it, the research is clear: practices like mindfulness and attention training effectively strengthen our filters and improve our ability to respond, not just react.[28]

Together, these general principles can help us and our teams set the stage for coping more effectively with uncertainty by allowing us to notice and rely on the necessary social and emotional resources for learning, turning a common constraint into a catalyst. So, now that we understand the broad strategies that facilitate effective coping, let's zoom in on specific tactics that can help us avoid "analysis paralysis" and move forward wisely in moments of doubt.

ANTICIPATION

To avoid being paralyzed by uncertainty, we need two kinds of tactics: tactics for anticipation and for resilience. Anticipation allows us to look ahead and identify key uncertainties before encountering them. But, noticing uncertainty is easier said than done because, as we've seen, when we're excited by our Pursue System or alarmed by our Protect System, we experience certainty and can easily overlook other perspectives. For instance, if we're so excited by the prospects of building a predictive AI based on brain-scan data, we might miss the fact that others could see the use of AI in hiring as an infringement of their rights. One practice to proactively search for uncertainty is called "anomalizing," or looking for warning signals. The more sensitive we are to subtle cues, the earlier we can intervene before some signals become full-blown dangers. For example, suppose we notice a recent dip in customer reviews; in that case, we can intervene more quickly to improve our services. Research shows that anomalizing enhances performance.[29] For example, when nursing units look for and discuss potential errors, they make fewer mistakes.[30] Sometimes, teams call this a "premortem" where they think ahead to all the things that could go wrong and then try to identify ways to prevent the most likely risks. In the BrainSight case, one way to anomalize is to identify ways the AI could backfire or cause unintended harm before we build it.

But despite its proven benefits, we tend to avoid anomalizing because if we're not motivated to catch errors, it can feel like inviting unwelcome problems. But what might seem problematic at first glance can end up being profitable. In one study, researchers examined two different models of how incubators (programs that give early-stage companies access to mentorship, investors, and other support) help entrepreneurs deal with uncertainty as they build and scale their new businesses. In the "high-certainty model," the entrepreneurs work with a single mentor who provides a clear path forward for several weeks. In the "low-certainty model," the entrepreneurs met dozens of mentors in a matter of days, each weighing in with their conflicting perspectives; thus, the entrepreneurs felt overwhelmed and confused. So, which model do you think is more likely to lead to successful entrepreneurial ventures? You guessed it—the low-certainty model. Why? Because in the first model, entrepreneurs are more likely to "zigzag," paying attention to one mentor and then altering their strategy as a new mentor encourages them to go in a different direction, squandering time and resources. While some entrepreneurs prefer this model because it feels less overwhelming, the multiple conflicting perspectives in the low-certainty model allow them to get a broader view of their business plans sooner and anomalize potential issues. "Huh. That's interesting. Several experienced founders are telling me very different things about the difficulty of sourcing my raw materials; maybe I should think more about that?" Seeking out multiple perspectives may initially increase uncertainty and discomfort, but it can allow us to get to a better initial hypothesis faster than only listening to one voice at a time.[31] That's why we practiced collecting multiple perspectives and examining a situation from several angles in chapter two.

A second popular practice for anticipation is, well . . . to wait. We may hold off on deciding if we know that more information will come to light that will help us resolve or clarify the uncertainty. For example, suppose we know that a new regulation is being passed to prevent companies from capturing and using personal brain information. In that case, we may want to wait until we know more about that law before diving into the details of this new algorithm. Similarly, we may hold off on listing our home until the market gets better, postpone a renovation until we finish saving for college, or wait to see who else asks us before saying yes to the first prom-posal. In each case, we don't know what to do now, and we anticipate new information and options that will help us address the current confusion. A risk is that it's easy to get stuck in a perpetual holding pattern and keep kicking the can down the road while conditions worsen, so this tactic works best when we can articulate what specific information or options we are waiting for, how they will impact our decision, and when we'll stop waiting, rather than just generally delaying.

The third practice for anticipation is to develop flexible plans and prepare to adapt your course of action before getting stuck. Thinking of contingency plans, pivot points, and "unless" clauses helps us know when to alter our path based on what we see in our environment. Like when you invest in banjo lessons, buy a beat-up pickup truck, and borrow your friend's bloodhound so that you can quickly pivot to a career in country music if you don't get the next promotion at work. Similarly, defining boundary conditions and guardrails ahead of time, such as identifying which errors we want to avoid or which values will inform our actions, can help us notice when we're drifting too far from our initial intentions. We might develop guidelines about how our AI should work, such as not having different outcomes based on gender, and audit the AI results to ensure it meets our values. In chapter six, we introduced one critical way to anticipate uncertainty: building flexibility into your plans and skills before you set out can enable you to adapt intentionally.

Another way of increasing our ability to adapt is to have what scholars call "a broader repertoire of actions" or what a carpenter might call "more tools in your toolkit." Research shows that leaders and organizations with more variety in their repertoires can more easily pivot as the world changes, whereas those who can only do one thing struggle when the environment changes and that one thing is no longer as valuable.[32] Think of the athlete who injures their back and must reinvent themself as a cable news host or the chef who needs to learn to use Excel after parking their food truck plans. In each case, a narrow repertoire makes adaptation more difficult.

Finally, the fourth practice for anticipation is to reduce and refine uncertainty by acting. For example, if you had to find a new supplier every time you produced a product, you would pay search costs, contracting fees, training costs, and time. But once you find a supplier you know does a good job, you can commit to that person, perhaps by a longer-term contract or by hiring them as an employee, eliminating the uncertainty of searching for a supplier at each stage. Similarly, we can preempt a response, build standard operating procedures, define a process, run an inexpensive experiment, write long-term contracts, and commit to shared values, all of which are actions that focus and remove the uncertainties you can control so that you can free up attention to focus on the uncertainties you can't. In this chapter's introductory case, we can commit ourselves to open and transparent development, saying that no matter what happens, we will not build an algorithm we cannot explain to our customers. Actions like locking in trusted actors and committing ourselves to specific values, practices, and people help us look ahead and focus our attention on the issues that need it the most.

Together, the various tactics for anticipation prepare us for uncertain situations, but we can't prepare for everything, particularly in difficult decisions. Moreover, even if we anticipate a risk, we can easily under-estimate or overestimate its impact. So, instead of just thinking ahead to prevent and minimize failures, we also need systems that allow us to bounce back quickly.

RESILIENCE

One practice that helps us avoid becoming derailed by errors is avoiding irreversible or high-cost actions unless we can afford the loss.[33] You can recover from any losses by keeping investments low when uncertainty is high and scaling up your efforts as your knowledge and confidence increase. That's why it's helpful to run clinical trials for drugs, test algo-rithms in digital sandboxes, or conduct small experiments to help you learn and contain the damage of errors. We date before getting married, interview before we sign a job contract, and read someone's dating profile carefully before swiping right (sometimes). In each case, we make small investments that we can afford to lose, helping us learn whether it's wise to make bigger ones in the future.

A second related practice for resilience is to build buffers that make our losses more affordable. Examples include building buffers of cash and goodwill, stocking extra products in the warehouse, buying insurance, building a portfolio of investments, and constructing containment tanks; all these additional resources make it more likely that when things get out of hand with one part of the plan, we will have the resources to try again. For example, FedEx does not load all of its cargo planes to full capacity, so when bad weather strikes somewhere in the US, they can reroute those planes to pick up cargo from other cities. These resources can also help you catch an error before it cascades and compounds into something unmanageable. Collecting physical, social, and informational resources can make unanticipated errors less fatal.

The third practice for resilience is to take the time to learn and improve our mental maps so that we are more capable in the future. An after-action review (AAR) is a common tool used by organizations, which has been made popular by the military and is used in various settings, from hospitals to hotels. During an AAR, people get together after a key action, such as a negotiation, a meeting, a surgery, or a product launch, and work together to answer four key questions. (1) What did we expect would happen? (2) What actually happened? (3) Why? (4) What will we do differently next time? It's critical that people can speak honestly and candidly in these conversations, and it's essential to avoid blaming specific individuals and look first for systemic and procedural sources of errors. AARs (sometimes called retrospectives or post-mortems) help teams learn about what worked and what didn't so that they can handle similar situations in the future. It's easy to go back and revise history and say, "Oh, I knew that would happen; it's all Bobby's fault," so I'm a fan of writing down your predictions before you act, sealing them in an envelope, and only examining them after. That way, you don't sacrifice your learning to be a know-it-all in front of your team.

Anticipation and resilience are helpful ways to observe, listen, and test to learn how to move forward when faced with uncertainty.[34] We use these practices when we're motivated, not willfully blind to the risks, and not paralyzed by uncertainty. Throughout this book, we've tried to walk the razor's edge of understanding what's possible while acknowledging the real pitfalls and challenges to give you the best chance of achieving those ideals. I've tried to avoid the extreme thinking that the ideal is always possible and easily achieved (if only you worked hard enough!) or that it's never possible, and we should just accept the status quo and cash out.

For hundreds of thousands of years, our senses, past experiences, and interpretations produced internal states (like anger, joy, and yearning) that help us stay alive and adjust to changing environments. But our bigger brains allowed us to flip the script more than any other species and figure out how to change our environments to sense the things that feel good. Some of us are privileged enough to adapt our surroundings to our every whim and choose networks, narratives, and necessities that make us feel better, right, or superior to others. Others are currently venturing into various metaverses to find unending gratification. When making choices about regulating our internal states, we risk only optimizing for comfort and not for challenge. We might choose to avoid rather than to cautiously approach uncertain situations. In those cases, our environments (despite being pleasurable) can also become prisons. On the other hand, some of us deal with too much stress, take abuse from too many people, run our minds and bodies ragged, and can't even find the time and space to imagine what a good life means to us. In either case, if we can't take charge of how we design our environments and interactions, others will gladly do it for us, conveniently parting us from our goals, ideas, health, and resources as we instinctively accept what they put in front of us. If we don't learn to chart our own course, we'll end up on someone else's trip.

When facing moments of doubt where we don't know how to move forward, it is helpful to understand how uncertainty can potentially derail our thinking. In general, we are more likely to give up and turn our attention to certainty than practice strategies for anticipation and resilience. Yet, as we've seen, uncertainty and doubt also open the potential for choice and impact and to do something that matters.

Uncertainty, and how we cope with it, is what gives our lives meaning. The practices we've reviewed in this chapter can help us create the resources to learn when we face doubt and confusion. (See appendix tool 10.)

When we find ourselves at a crossroads, staring at a wall, or squinting into the fog, we can twist the world so that we feel like we already have the correct answer; we can give up and walk away, or—open to learning—we can humbly walk toward the problems we are trying to solve. When we're making difficult decisions, sensing multiple interpretations of what is possible, and learning how to make them better, we're exercising our free will. Most of us think of "free will" as a noun, something that endures without our efforts. What if it's not? What if it lives in our shifting perceptions and practices, a state that comes online only when we use it, like imagination and memory? Perhaps free will is not a trait but a *skill*. Moments of doubt, with high stakes, multiple goals, and high uncertainty, provide an opportunity to practice and refine that skill to create a good life by making good choices.

The Horizon

We're approaching the end of our time together. In the book's first half, I introduced a process for making difficult choices to help you make the most of moments of doubt. We enriched our explanations of where our choices come from, what makes a choice good, and how to generate and refine novel alternatives, provide better justifications, and plan to implement your choices mindfully. In parts III and IV, we've looked at five common obstacles that push us toward reacting rather than responding. Let's quickly retrace a few of our steps as we wrap up.

Chapter Seven: When to take a detour to help others

- In choosing when and how to help others, we rely on our beliefs about human nature.

- Evolution and culture have combined their efforts to set the stage and write the scripts for human cooperation; humans are not purely selfish or selfless and generally can act with both motives.

- The potential for both one-sided and mutual benefits means we must be careful when choosing whom to cooperate with.

Chapter Eight: When you're not sure who's responsible

- We use four strategies to regulate the behavior of others—praising the individual, praising the behavior, blaming the person, or making judgments of wrongness.

- Decades of psychological research show that negative information outweighs positive in our attention, thinking, and memory, making being blamed more likely than we anticipate.

- People combine their judgments of causality, intentionality, obligation, capacity, and the quality of the reasons given to decide how much blame someone deserves.

Chapter Nine: Not in Kansas anymore

- When making decisions with conflicting standards, we must avoid two common obstacles. First, moral relativism is the idea that we cannot judge the correctness of different perspectives, so why bother? Second, moral absolutism posits that there is a single correct answer, so learning is unnecessary.

- Both relativism and absolutism are conversation-stoppers that prevent us from identifying our most defensible beliefs and being open to engaging with others when norms conflict.

- To identify our most defensible beliefs, we should pay attention to the level of support from three sources: coherence with other beliefs, consensus with relevant others, and competence in achieving goals.

Chapter Ten: When you are angry and offended

- Anger and offense are strong emotions, potentially hijacking our ability to make careful choices in favor of quick action for self-preservation.

- Some social media companies use carefully crafted nudges to capture our attention with the potential side effect of making us more reactive.

- To be informed by our emotions but not ruled by them, we can regulate our responses by removing the signals that trigger us, paying attention to something else, reframing how we think about them, and changing how we express our emotions.

Chapter Eleven: When you don't know

- Uncertainty causes us to hesitate when we become aware that we have too much, insufficient, or conflicting information, making it hard to imagine the future.

- We compensate for uncertainty by turning toward more certain beliefs. Thus, shifting from being right-answer-getters to better-answer-makers involves learning about our patterns and choosing our compensation strategies carefully.

- To avoid analysis paralysis, we need strategies for both anticipation and resilience.

Across all eleven chapters, I've tried to equip you with general insights and tools with the most robust scientific support because to engage moments of doubt effectively, you need a broad toolkit, not a perfect recipe. I didn't pitch these ideas as the "right answer," but rather as guidance to enable you to adapt and apply them to your choices with a healthy dose of reflective practice. I also tried to avoid spoon-feeding you so you could build your muscles for patience, curiosity, and coping with uncertainty—all essential skills for making the most out of moments of doubt. (Nice job, by the way.) I wanted to write a book that enhances those capabilities in the reader rather than diminishing them by providing a false sense of certainty. (Here's the magic formula for evading doubt!) I hope the tools and ideas we've covered help you learn with the right blend of focus and flexibility, and help you avoid being fixated on your goal at the expense of relevant risks or being too distracted by potential threats to make careful progress. Armed with these compelling insights, you are now ready to practice holding your intuition as a hypothesis, noticing more complexity, and generating flexible and resilient strategies. The next time you experience doubt, I hope you can turn it into your rocket fuel, not your roadblock.

MEANINGFUL CLICHÉS

When I was in middle school, a boy's most important possession was his basketball shoes. You didn't need to actually play basketball; just wear shoes that suggested you could sink a three-pointer at the buzzer if you wanted. The kids at school would constantly compare the virtues of their Nike Air Trainers, Air Jordans, Reebok Pumps, or LA Lights, all of which cost $50 or more. At the time, money was tight at home, so I wore $2 Velcro shoes from Kmart and would get teased mercilessly. "Your family's so poor you can't afford a free sample," my classmates would tease. Don't feel bad for me; I learned to give as good as I got, and there were kids who definitely had it much worse. I hated those Velcro shoes;

no matter how I tried to escape by sticking my head in the clouds, those shoes would bring me back down to earth.

Each night, I would beg, whine, get angry, and pray to win the lottery to buy just one pair of name-brand shoes. "Fifty dollars for shoes," my dad would say. "Don't be crazy!" To be fair, from his perspective, he didn't even have shoes until he was ten, so $50 would seem crazy. Little did I know that my parents were squirreling away cash, and one Saturday, we drove to an outlet mall and found a pair of brand-named shoes on sale. The shoes weren't Nikes or Pumps; they weren't even basketball shoes. My parents reasoned if they were going to spend so much money on footwear, the shoes damn well better last, so they bought me a pair of discontinued Reebok hiking boots for $19.98 after tax. Despite never going on a hike, I wore them every day until my toes tore through the caps.

This story is a meaningful cliché. It's a cliché because many of us have family and friends who saved their money, dedicated their time, and sacrificed their own interests for us. Yet this story is meaningful because this version is mine. It symbolizes everything my parents did for me, for which I'll forever be grateful. Because of my parents, I can afford to buy my daughters more expensive things, but I can only hope to give them something as valuable. A story like this can only be a cliché when you are a distant observer, and its general contours seem vaguely familiar to so many other things you have seen or heard before. When it's your heart pounding and you can still remember the feeling of being handed the shopping bag at the shoe store, or the slant of the afternoon sunlight as you lace up the shoes in the car, it's not a cliché: it's your life.

Not all of us, but many of us are blessed enough to have people in our lives who sacrificed something to give us a shot, whether they are teachers who took extra time to read philosophy with us, a coach who stayed after practice to run through additional drills, a sibling who worked a job at thirteen to make sure there was food on the table, or a grandparent who saved to pay for our college. Many of our heroes certainly faced their own challenges. In difficult moments, when they ran out of hope, perhaps they put one foot in front of the other and kept going because when they wanted to give up and didn't know what else to do, they dreamed of—*you*. Of your potential, opportunities, and happiness, even if they knew that they wouldn't be there to enjoy them with you.

Whether we are making a decision that distributes harms and benefits across different groups, trying to keep our patience with change that isn't fast enough, or choosing between two futures that are both scary and exciting, all that each of us has is the same thing that every generation before us has had—the next step. As imperfect and flawed as we all are, we are still the product of thousands of generations of human beings who crossed oceans; wandered the desert; built farms, factories, and spaceships; fought for equal rights and recognition; massacred their brothers; and made peace for their grandchildren. As tired and as confused as we can feel when we find ourselves at the edge of what we know, we cannot forget what our grandparents have gone through to give us the privilege of standing here. By taking the next step wisely, we honor those parents, friends, family members, siblings, and teachers; we amplify their kindness by passing it along to as many others as possible.

Two decades into the twenty-first century, the world is in disorder. The planet is under threat, our brothers and sisters are in pain, and at the same time, we have ways of relating that make it harder to work together to address those growing challenges. As threats loom from future pandemics, war, rising inequality, racism, sexism, technological disruption, and democratic backsliding, we will all have to make many difficult decisions. When confronting moments of doubt, like ancient navigators at the edge of the known world, we stand at the precipice of what we know, equipped with our pixelated and incomplete maps, our scars, talismans, and the memories and dreams of those who came before us. Beyond the fog lie worlds and selves we have yet to create. What happens next will be shaped by each of our choices in unfamiliar terrain. And at the same time, the next step is uniquely and irreplaceably yours.

It matters.

Choose wisely.

Tools Appendix

We've discussed several moments of doubt such as:

- Should you promote a top-performing yet troublemaking employee at your small consulting firm if your other employees want him gone?

- Should you forgo a promotion at work that requires moving to London to spend time with your dying father?

- Should your dating app sell customer data to increase profits if you don't have their informed consent?

- How should you address a situation where employees and customers disagree with a controversial law diminishing transgender rights?

- Should you use addictive gaming features in children's learning apps?

- Should you tell others that an employee at your company has been diagnosed with a rare genetic disease that could put customers in danger?

- Do you take a personal risk and speak up to stop unprofessional comments about a colleague?

- Should you remove allegedly fake reviews posted on your product review site that are damaging a major advertiser's reputation?

- Should you make questionable payments in countries where it is accepted?

- How should you respond when someone posts offensive and angering content?

- Should you use brain-scan data and machine learning techniques to predict future job success?

Now that you've read about the latest science highlighting critical missteps and promising paths forward, it's time to turn this book into a map and start finding your own way. This appendix lists several examples of each type of moment of doubt so that you can identify more relevant examples in your life and work.

The appendix also contains exercises and tools to help you apply the insights we've covered across chapters; for example, identifying the character you aspire to have, mapping multiple moral considerations, generating and refining options, giving better reasons, and pulling together a nuanced, comprehensive, and adaptable recommendation. As you practice these skills, share your thinking with close confidants, like your team at work, your partner, or a friend who is excellent at constructively pushing your logic. In addition, you can learn a lot by identifying someone you know who handles these choices well and observing their practices.

As you get reps in, remember you are building your capacity to deal with decisions that have high stakes, conflicting goals, and increased uncertainty. These are valuable skills, and you should be patient with yourself and allow time for growth; it won't happen overnight. As you practice, note your patterns and habits; for example, how are you coping with uncertainty? What might help you cope better? What are your reasons for persevering through difficult choices? When confronting uncertainty inherent in these hard choices, remember that we can all fall prey to turning away from others, exactly when we should turn toward them. Hopefully, this book has been an entertaining and informative way to inspire your practice and help you achieve your intentions as you gain more authority, influence, and responsibility at work.

Finally, any process is only as good as its application. The ideas and practices in this book are not silver bullets. They can be applied in more thoughtful and intentional ways that foster learning and help you refine and achieve your goals, or they can be used with a mindless "check-the-box" mentality that precludes the situational awareness, reflective practice, and judgment needed to tackle uncertain choices effectively. Leaning toward the former is critical to shift from being right-answer-getters to becoming better-answer-makers.

MOMENT OF DOUBT 1
WHEN YOU FEEL TORN IN TWO

Examples:

- Should you stay in a familiar job that drains you, or should you take a risk and reinvent yourself in a new career?

- Should you take the difficult feedback you receive or ignore it?

- Should you take on lucrative consulting work for a corrupt government?

- Should you accept an investment from a significant polluter to grow your sustainability consulting company?

- How should you balance your personal and professional lives and spend your time appropriately?

List a few examples of conflicting personal values that you are likely to encounter:

_____

_____

_____

_____

TOOL 1: Defining Who You Want to Become
(see page 22)

In chapter two, we saw the importance of thinking about character as a project not just a predictor. To make progress in becoming who you want to be you first need a sense of who that is. Without a clear definition, not one set in stone, but one shaped in clay, you are missing a critical guidepost for navigating difficult choices, a North Star from which you can gauge your next steps. Here are a few reflection questions to help you get started.

- Think of people you admire and want to emulate. What attributes do their behaviors exemplify?
- What attributes distinguish you from others?
- Ask a trusted friend or family member what attributes come to mind when they think of you.
- What are some attributes you want to avoid being associated with?
- Think of three moments when you have been the best version of yourself. What attributes do these moments have in common?
- Think of the values that your family and community taught you. Which of these do you want to pass on to future generations?

Reflection:

- Do you notice any patterns in your answers to the questions above? For example, do certain aspirations emerge repeatedly?
- Use the aspirational attributes you identified to write a short description. *Across different decisions in my life, I want to be the kind of person who . . .*
- How will you ensure that you will keep your aspirations on your mental map, especially when you encounter a moment of doubt?

MOMENT OF DOUBT 2
WHEN BREAKING THE RULES GETS YOU AHEAD

Examples:

- Should you disrupt an existing way of doing business to get benefits; for example, ignoring current healthcare laws to help people save money on healthcare?
- Should you break norms to win a competition? For example, disregard democratic principles to hold on to power?
- Should you pay for fake reviews to sell more products or get more views on your content?
- Should you disobey directives from a supervisor that can cause harm to others?

- Should you lie to help someone; for example, fail to disclose that a patient in need of a transplant tried to die by suicide, which would result in them being removed from the transplant list?
- Should you continue investments in diversity, equity, and inclusion programs when it's politically or financially costly?

List a few examples of choices you are likely to encounter and that have rules and outcomes in conflict:

_____

_____

_____

_____

TOOL 2: Identifying Multiple Views of Good (see page 46)

In chapter three, we saw how the four main moral traditions have strengths and weaknesses. Therefore, to see more and think ahead about our choices, we need to use the lenses together to become aware of the multiple moral considerations relevant to our decisions. We start by listing the relevant issues from each of the four lenses: principles, consequences, character, and relationships, noticing tensions within and across traditions. Start with your perspective, but also go out and ask others, discuss the pros and cons, and discover what standards are relevant for a specific audience.

The goal is to learn more about your social context and the potential impacts of your actions so that you can generate ideas about how to act more effectively, minimize disruptions, and even strengthen your relationships. By taking the time to learn from others, you are also investing in your relationships and demonstrating that you care, increasing the chances that stakeholders will be more willing to work together to solve issues that arise. In creating this list, you can't see everything, but you can see *more*, hopefully enough to help you have a general sense of where to go, what dangerous paths to avoid, and to refine your approach as new information comes to light.

Figure 6 is an example of this list from chapter three. Figure 7 gives a general template to help you think through the ten moments of doubt in this book and those you may encounter at work.

After you've written down the issues that come to mind, find a trusted friend, family member, or colleague who thinks differently from you and discuss the decisions with them. Afterward, reflect on the following questions:

Reflection questions:
- What did others see in the situation that you initially missed?
- Are there patterns to what you see first and things you forget to consider?
- How might you improve your ability to notice more?

Figure 6

WHAT ARE THE RELEVANT ISSUES?

From a PRINCIPLES lens?	From a CHARACTER lens?	From a CONSEQUENCES lens?	From a RELATIONSHIPS lens?

• Protect consumer privacy
• Do no harm
• Follow relevant laws
• Voluntary informed consent about data use
	• Employee trust
	• Be the top website for fulfilling relationships
	• Personal
	  • Be a humble leader
	  • Be someone who brings out the best in others
	  • Be creative
		• Increase in targeted relevant advertising
		• Customers asked to buy more things
		• Customers might get discounts on some items
		• $3 million in revenue
		• Ability to invest in new projects
		• Employee trust
		• Selling the data could be leaked
			• To care for employees we must grow revenues
			• To care for users we must be transparent and honest
			• To care for shareholders we must remain profitable

Figure 7

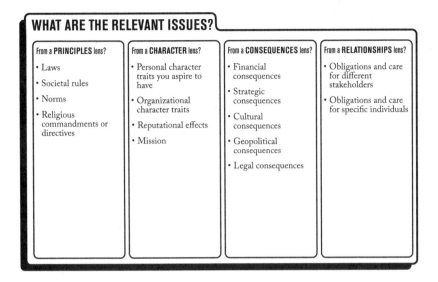

MOMENT OF DOUBT 3
WHEN YOU FEEL FORCED TO CHOOSE SIDES

Examples:

- How should you mediate between employees who don't get along?

- How can you settle differences between two groups you are a part of?

- How can you resolve tensions between long-term shareholders and shareholders who want to flip your stock?

- What do you do about the differences of opinion between your partner and your parents? Or between one set of friends and another?

List a few examples of disagreements between important stakeholders that you are likely to encounter:

_____

_____

_____

_____

TOOL 3: Generating and Refining Novel Ideas
(see page 75)

Figure 8 outlines the general process for generating and refining ideas discussed in chapter four. There are critical questions to ask along the way. Use this process to guide your thinking and improvement of ideas for addressing your moments of doubt.

Figure 8

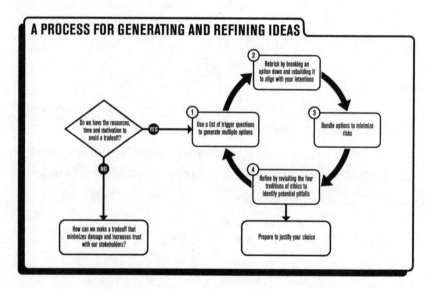

1. Sample Trigger Questions

- What could you do to benefit the least-well-off stakeholder?
- How might someone you admire address this situation?
- What could you do if you had no constraints?
- What could you do that might cause the least harm?
- What actions could preserve important relationships?
- What could you do that would satisfy the most commonly held principles or rules in a novel or unexpected way?
- What actions would you be most proud of?
- What could you never do?
- What could you do to avoid tradeoffs?

2. Rebricking

- How can we break down our best options and build them back up in ways that better reflect our intentions?
- What degrees of freedom do we have in *who, what, where, when, why,* and *how*?

3. Bundling

- Which options can be bundled together to reinforce their benefits and minimize risks?

4. Refining

- What are the weaknesses of our best options and how might we mitigate them?

MOMENT OF DOUBT 4
WHEN SMALL HARMS ADD UP

Examples:

- Should you repost a questionable news story on social media?
- Should you share your personal genetic data with companies?
- Should you design products that hijack users' attention?
- What does moderation mean when you consume addictive, unhealthy substances?
- Is it okay to deviate from a policy if the harms are small and negligible?

List a few examples of choices involving small scalable harms you are likely to encounter:

_____

_____

_____

_____

TOOL 4: A Checklist for Better Justifications
(see page 99)

In chapter five, we saw that justifying your choices is an opportunity to build a stronger relationship with key stakeholders and learn to make better choices. So, once you've settled on a course of action to try out, here are a couple of tips to help you communicate your reasons effectively. Of course, not all of these will be relevant to every conversation. Still, this checklist will give you a few strategies to consider and tailor your approach to your audience as you prepare to share your thinking and foster better coordination.

- Be clear about your goals. What are you trying to achieve with your choice?

- Support your choice by using reasons from multiple ethical lenses (principles, character, consequences, and relationships).

- Demonstrate awareness, consideration, and accommodations of stakeholders' goals, particularly those that conflict.

- Share a weakness or risk of your choice. Evidence shows that when decision-makers share a weakness of their choice, particularly one they have a plan to mitigate,[1] it builds confidence and trust in their judgment.

- Share the other alternatives you considered and why you rejected them.

- Talk about the process you used to make and share your decision.

- Demonstrate consideration of your audience's goals, values, and perspectives.

MOMENT OF DOUBT 5
WHEN YOU KNOW THINGS YOU SHOULDN'T

Examples:

- As a consultant, you learn that one of your clients, the company where your best friend works, will fire thousands of people. Should you say something to your friend?

- How clear about your product's terms should you be with customers? For example, should customers know precisely the penalties for paying a credit card late when you make most of your money from late fees?

- How honest are you about customer wait times for products? Can you collect orders for products and not tell customers that it will take months before delivery?

- Can you tell patients what their medical treatment will cost before they agree to move forward?

- Should you disclose that there are errors in the financial model that might prevent a client from investing?

- Should you tell a coworker that their partner is having an affair or mind your own business?

- As a consultant, do you share information about competitors with your clients?

List a few examples of choices where you have information you shouldn't that you are likely to encounter:

_____

_____

_____

_____

TOOL 5: A Checklist for Adaptive Plans
(see page 115)

In chapter six, we described attributes of a good recommendation that can help us implement mindfully and learn. The following checklist can help you prepare and improve the quality of your recommendations.

Comprehensiveness
- Have you identified the most likely relevant issues related to this decision?

- Have you identified the most likely downstream decisions that will result?

Specificity
- Is your recommendation specific?

- Do you know where you are making any untested assumptions?

Flexibility

- Have you identified what to look for in the environment to know if and when you should change course?

- Have you identified the boundary conditions in your plan? For example, do you have any "unless clauses"?

- Have you identified the key uncertainties in your plan?

Mitigation Strategies

- Do you know the major risks to your plan?

- Do you have strategies to minimize those risks or prepare to bear their costs?

Coherence

- Does your recommendation send consistent signals about your intentions?

- Do elements of the recommendation reinforce each other?

MOMENT OF DOUBT 6
WHEN TO TAKE A DETOUR TO HELP OTHERS

Examples:

- Do you support protests on issues that may not impact you directly, such as movements like #MeToo, BLM, or #Ukraine?

- Do you donate to charities in other parts of the world?

- Would you be willing to sign up for military service?

- Will you change your attitudes and behaviors to earn the designation of an ally for an underrepresented group?

- Would you be willing to take a pay cut so shift workers can get paid more?

- Will you pay taxes to benefit less well-off citizens?

- Do you change your habits to help the environment and benefit generations you'll never meet?

List a few examples of costly help that you are likely to encounter:

_____

_____

_____

_____

TOOL 6: Stakeholder Empathy
(see page 152)

In chapter seven, we saw the importance of oxytocin in helping us to feel empathy for others. As narrow as it may be, our spotlight of empathy can be used more effectively and intentionally. For example, when we find ourselves focused on our group or diminishing the humanity of others, instead of letting oxytocin do its work, we can exercise empathy consciously and carefully. Specifically, when we find ourselves attributing others' actions based on their personality, or their membership in a particular group ("All environmentalists are . . ."), it's a sign we might not understand that individual or group in enough detail.

Stakeholder analysis[2] is a tool that can help us empathize with the multiple individuals and groups who are impacted by our choices.

Figure 9

STAKEHOLDER ANALYSIS

- Who is potentially impacted by our decision?
- Once you have listed all the groups and indviduals you can think of, go ask others to see who you might have missed.

For each of these individuals and groups, imagine how your decision will impact them.
- What do they want?
- What do they want to avoid?
- What are they thinking and feeling in relation to your decision?
- What will they hear and see as you implement your decision?

- Collect information about key stakeholders by spending time with them, interviewing them, and collecting data about their beliefs, preferences, and behaviors.
- How might you adapt and improve your decision considering what you learn about stakeholders?

MOMENT OF DOUBT 7
WHEN YOU'RE NOT SURE WHO'S RESPONSIBLE

Examples:

- Should you use genetic information for police investigations?

- How should you respond if your inedible product (e.g., Tide Pods) is used as a snack by some children (and adults)?

- Should you use geolocation data to track customers?

- How should social media platforms respond to disinformation?

- Is it okay if your company uses lobbying to subvert democracy?

List a few examples of unintended use cases that you are likely to encounter:

_____

_____

_____

_____

TOOL 7: Minding the Responsibility Gap
(see page 173)

In chapter eight, we saw that our responsibility can be hard to decipher in unintended-use cases. Therefore, it helps to look for alternate ways of interpreting our responsibility rather than just going with our first and most likely defensive instinct. We can use the model of blame described in chapter eight to clarify our perspective about our level of responsibility and understand how others interpret it. For example, you might see yourself acting unintentionally, while others might see you as a direct causal link to negative outcomes. Once we know where the largest differences occur, we can find ways to fill those gaps.

Figure 10

MINDING THE RESPONSIBILITY GAP

Use the elements from the model of blame to identify where there are gaps in how you and your stakeholder think about your responsibility. In each box, write your interpretation of each stage and why. Then fill out a second version from the perspective of a stakeholder who was harmed.

WHERE ARE THE KEY DIFFERENCES?

ELEMENT	YOUR PERSPECTIVE	A HARMED STAKEHOLDER'S PERSPECTIVE
CAUSALITY What was your role in causing the harm?		
INTENTIONALITY What were your intentions related to the harm?		
OBLIGATION What was your obligation in preventing the harm?		
CAPACITY What was your capacity to prevent the harm?		
REASONS What were your reasons for acting/not acting as you did?		
LEVEL OF BLAME How much blame do you believe is deserved?		

- What can you do to align your interpretations of responsibility with the other parties?
- What can you communicate more effectively or learn about from their perspective?

MOMENT OF DOUBT 8
"NOT IN KANSAS ANYMORE"

Examples:

- Do you support women's rights (and other human rights) in regions where it is less common?
- Do you accept government intervention and surveillance in other countries?
- Do you take advantage of different countries' lower wages, salaries, and standards?
- Do you accept higher standards in other countries? For example, should you use each country's most stringent emission standards or the lowest standard?

- Should you move your headquarters to pay lower taxes in another country than in your home country?

List a few examples of conflicting global and local norms that you are likely to encounter:

_____

_____

_____

_____

TOOL 8: Determining What Stays (see page 193)

In chapter nine, we saw the importance of avoiding the traps of relativism and absolutism. By sidestepping these obstacles, we can do the work to create better outcomes in the face of moral plurality. To do this, we need a clear sense of where we can and cannot negotiate and the risks of a successful and unsuccessful deal. Here is a list of questions to help assess the likelihood of negotiating favorable outcomes when standards conflict.

Figure 11

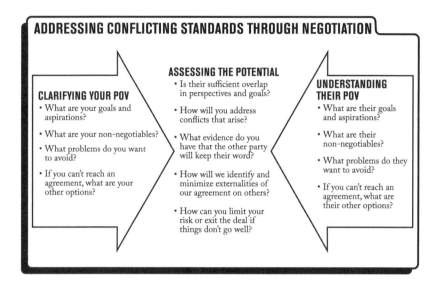

ADDRESSING CONFLICTING STANDARDS THROUGH NEGOTIATION

CLARIFYING YOUR POV
- What are your goals and aspirations?
- What are your non-negotiables?
- What problems do you want to avoid?
- If you can't reach an agreement, what are your other options?

ASSESSING THE POTENTIAL
- Is their sufficient overlap in perspectives and goals?
- How will you address conflicts that arise?
- What evidence do you have that the other party will keep their word?
- How will we identify and minimize externalities of our agreement on others?
- How can you limit your risk or exit the deal if things don't go well?

UNDERSTANDING THEIR POV
- What are their goals and aspirations?
- What are their non-negotiables?
- What problems do they want to avoid?
- If you can't reach an agreement, what are their other options?

MOMENT OF DOUBT 9
WHEN YOU ARE ANGRY AND OFFENDED

Examples:

- How should you respond when a soap company's advertising implies that having dark skin is dirty?

- How should you respond when a famous athlete speaks on a divisive political issue, and you deeply disagree with them?

- How should you respond when a social media personality posts misinformation about another group?

- How should you respond when an employee posts an offensive tweet, and the company faces pressure to fire that individual?

List a few examples of angering or offensive situations that you are likely to encounter:

_____

_____

_____

_____

TOOL 9: From Reacting to Responding
(see page 214)

In chapter ten, we learned that it is possible to clearly and calmly share our perspective while minimizing relational damage if we can effectively regulate ourselves. The following questions can help us determine if we should contribute to a topic and what we should say when we do.

Figure 12

FROM REACTING TO RESPONDING

When others say things that are angering and offensive:

Should I say something?
- Why do I want to say something? What are my goals?
- What are others saying?
- Do I understand the other perspective and can I describe it in a way that the other party will agree?
- Is my perspective necessary and helpful in this situation?

What should I say?
- How can I be most constructive and least critical?
- If I think that I need to be confrontational in this situation, why? What could convince me that I'm wrong?
- What will help me achieve my intended impact, even if it might not feel the best in the moment?

MOMENT OF DOUBT 10
WHEN YOU DON'T KNOW

Examples:

- How can you develop genetic engineering and cloning responsibly?

- How can bioengineering, such as increasing oxygen in the atmosphere by creating algae blooms, be used responsibly?

- How can we learn about the impacts of new medical procedures or drugs?

- Can AI be developed and deployed responsibly?

- How can we gain the benefits and reduce the harms of adopting self-driving cars?

List a few examples of decisions where you are doing something new so it might be hard to predict the consequences of your choices:

_____

_____

_____

_____

TOOL 10: Good Life Audit (see page 236)

In chapter eleven, we learned that we create our vision of a good life by effectively making hard choices, but the opposite is also true. Our ability to make hard choices is also shaped by how we live. Use the following audit to identify the areas where your current practices enable or impede your achievement of a good life. Then, highlight one or two places you want to focus on more deeply. You may seek further help from experts, friends, and colleagues on how to alter your practices to help grow your capacity to achieve your intentions.

In each of the domains of life listed below, (1) list the things that come to mind about what you currently do (your practices) as well as (2) things that happen to you (like events or interactions). While each domain will have practices, not all will have events or interactions.

DOMAINS: Sleep, Nutrition and Food, Impactful Relationships, Physical Health, Mental Health, Work, Financial Health, Sex, Recreational Substances, Physical Space and Material Possessions, Your Aspirational Character, Digital Interactions, Hobbies/Interests.

Then, (3) think about how those practices and interactions help or prevent you from achieving your view of the good life. Remember, the same practice or interaction might help you in some ways and hinder you in others.

Figure 13

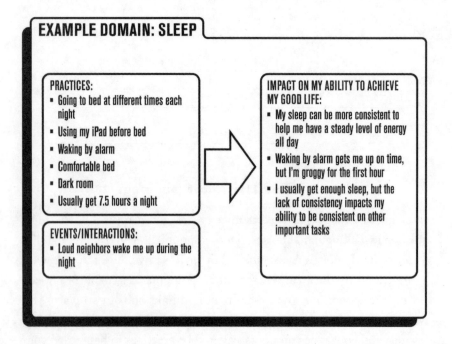

Once you've worked through all the domains (and feel free to add others that are important to you), use your list to reflect on the following questions:

Reflection Questions:
- What is going well? What are a few of your strengths?
- Across all the domains, what are your most significant opportunities to change your practices or alter the events and interactions you encounter to get closer to your view of the good life?
- Where might you find guidance, support, and help to make these critical changes?

Acknowledgments

Writing a book involves making thousands, if not millions, of choices. Some are seemingly small, like where to place a comma, and others are more consequential, like choosing a title. I've been incredibly lucky to have so many outstanding colleagues, students, and thought partners who influenced the choices that resulted in the final published version of *Radical Doubt*.

There are several people without whom I would have never thought to write a book, let alone this one. I owe a very special debt of gratitude to my colleagues and mentors who welcomed me into the field of business ethics and, more importantly, inspired me to strive to live a good life: R. Edward Freeman, Patricia Werhane, and Andrew C. Wicks. My conversations with my amazing colleagues at the Darden Business School at the University of Virginia echo in these pages, particularly Jim Detert, Jeanne Liedtka, Saras Sarasvathy, and Sankaran Venkataraman. I am grateful to my outstanding students over the last eighteen years who have pushed my thinking, asked terrific questions, and reported back to me live from the trenches as they put these ideas into practice. I am also indebted to the hundreds of scholars whose research I've cited in these pages. I hope this book shines a light on your painstaking efforts. Thank you.

There are several people whose counsel helped bring this manuscript to completion. First, Marty Asher was kind enough to read an unreadable draft and encouraged me to continue writing this book when I was about to give up. Special thanks to Jenny Mead and Susie Langenkamp for their perseverance through early rough drafts, and their constructive and kind guidance. Because of their wise and necessary editorial suggestions, I can now write a whole other book titled *Cut Distracting Jokes: You're Not as Funny as You Think*. Several trusted friends, colleagues, and students generously donated their time to read some or all of the manuscript, and gave me invaluable feedback: Helet Botha, Rachel Brozenske,

Skyler Clark-Hamel, Pranav Dalmia, Maggie Dykstra, Eric Fletcher, Lauren Kaufmann, Abhishek Kulkarni, Isabella Lamacchia, Ben Leiner, Steve Momper, Dr. Terry Petrella, Robert Phillips, Anusha Ramesh, Adarsh Rupen, and Riley Steiner. Thank you all; this book is better because of you.

I am grateful to my agent, Christopher Combemale, for his sage advice and unwavering enthusiasm about this book (and me). I am grateful to my editors, Keith Wallman and Clara Linhoff, for their careful reading, and for making suggestions that strengthened my voice while also greatly improving the experience for the readers. Special thanks to the entire team at Diversion Books and Simon & Schuster Distribution for their efforts to make this book as good as it can be.

Finally, to my family, the Parmars and the Mannings. Because of you, I have the strength to do hard things, and because of you, I will never give up. To Susan, Asha, Aya, and Sophie for letting me sneak away to write and supporting me unconditionally. I love you to the moon and back.

Notes

CHAPTER ONE

1. Zhang, T., Gino, F., & Margolis, J. D. (2018). Does "could" lead to good? On the road to moral insight. *Academy of Management Journal*, *61*(3), 857–895; **2.** Dane, E., & Pratt, M. G. (2007). Exploring intuition and its role in managerial decision making. *Academy of Management Review*, *32*(1), 33–54; **3.** Haidt, J. (2001). The emotional dog and its rational tail: A social intuitionist approach to moral judgment. *Psychological Review*, *108*(4), 814; Guglielmo, S. (2018). Unfounded dumbfounding: How harm and purity undermine evidence for moral dumbfounding. *Cognition*, *170*, 334–337; **4.** Kandel, E. R., Schwartz, J. H., Jessell, T. M., Siegelbaum, S., Hudspeth, A. J., & Mack, S. (Eds.). (2000). *Principles of neural science* (Vol. 4, pp. 1227–1246). New York: McGraw-Hill; Gable, P. A., Neal, L. B., & Threadgill, A. H. (2018). Regulatory behavior and frontal activity: Considering the role of revised-BIS in relative right frontal asymmetry. *Psychophysiology*, *55*(1), e12910; Carver, C. S., & Connor-Smith, J. (2010). Personality and coping. *Annual Review of Psychology*, *61*, 679–704; **5.** Coan, J. A., & Allen, J. J. (2003). Frontal EEG asymmetry and the behavioral activation and inhibition systems. *Psychophysiology*, *40*(1), 106–114; Kalivas, P. W., & Nakamura, M. (1999). Neural systems for behavioral activation and reward. *Current Opinion in Neurobiology*, *9*(2), 223–227; **6.** Kalivas & Nakamura, "Neural systems," 223–227; **7.** Roelofs, K. (2017). Freeze for action: Neurobiological mechanisms in animal and human freezing. *Philosophical Transactions of the Royal Society of London. Series B, Biological Sciences*, *372*(1718), 20160206. https://doi.org/10.1098/rstb.2016.0206; **8.** Gable et al., "Regulatory behavior and frontal activity"; **9.** Sonenshein, S. (2007). The role of construction, intuition, and justification in responding to ethical issues at work: The sensemaking-intuition model. *Academy of Management Review*, *32*(4), 1022–1040; Ahmadi, S., Khanagha, S., Berchicci, L., & Jansen, J. J. (2017). Are managers motivated to explore in the face of a new technological change? The role of regulatory focus, fit, and complexity of decision-making. *Journal of Management Studies*, *54*(2), 209–237; **10.** Gray, J., & McNaughton, N. (2000). *The neuropsychology of anxiety* (2nd ed.). Oxford Medical Publications; **11.** Kool, W., Shenhav, A., & Botvinick, M. M. (2017). Cognitive control as cost-benefit decision making. In *The Wiley handbook of cognitive control* (pp. 167–189). John Wiley & Sons Ltd. https://doi.org/10.1002/9781118920497; **12.** Clark, L., Manes, F., Antoun, N., Sahakian, B. J., & Robbins, T. W. (2003). The contributions of lesion laterality and lesion volume to decision-making impairment following frontal lobe damage. *Neuropsychologia*, *41*(11), 1474–1483; Mukherjee, A., Lam, N. H., Wimmer, R. D., & Halassa, M. M. (2021). Thalamic circuits for independent control of prefrontal signal and noise. *Nature*, *600*(7887), 100–104; **13.** Hecht, D., Walsh, V., & Lavidor, M. (2010).

Transcranial direct current stimulation facilitates decision making in a probabilistic guessing task. *Journal of Neuroscience, 30*(12), 4241–4245; **14.** Heym, N., Ferguson, E., & Lawrence, C. (2008). An evaluation of the relationship between Gray's revised RST and Eysenck's PEN: Distinguishing BIS and FFFS in Carver and White's BIS/BAS scales. *Personality and Individual Differences, 45*(8), 709–715; **15.** Hecht, D., Walsh, V., & Lavidor, M. (2013). Bi-frontal direct current stimulation affects delay discounting choices. *Cognitive Neuroscience, 4*(1), 7–11; **16.** Lembke, A. (2021). *Dopamine nation: Finding balance in the age of indulgence.* Penguin; **17.** Enticott, P. G., Ogloff, J. R., & Bradshaw, J. L. (2006). Associations between laboratory measures of executive inhibitory control and self-reported impulsivity. *Personality and Individual Differences, 41*(2), 285–294; **18.** Goel, V., Tierney, M., Sheesley, L., Bartolo, A., Vartanian, O., & Grafman, J. (2007). Hemispheric specialization in human prefrontal cortex for resolving certain and uncertain inferences. *Cerebral Cortex, 17*(10), 2245–2250; **19.** Gable et al., "Regulatory behavior and frontal activity"; **20.** Shallice, T., & Cipolotti, L. (2018). The prefrontal cortex and neurological impairments of active thought. *Annual Review of Psychology, 69,* 157–180; **21.** Serfaty, D., MacMillan, J., Entin, E. E., & Entin, E. B. (2014). The decision-making expertise of battle commanders. In *Naturalistic decision making* (pp. 253–266). Psychology Press; **22.** McVea, J. F. (2009). A field study of entrepreneurial decision-making and moral imagination. *Journal of Business Venturing, 24*(5), 491–504; **23.** Hoffman, K. A., Aitken, L. M., & Duffield, C. (2009). A comparison of novice and expert nurses' cue collection during clinical decision-making: Verbal protocol analysis. *International Journal of Nursing Studies, 46*(10), 1335–1344; **24.** Dane, E. (2013). Things seen and unseen: Investigating experience-based qualities of attention in a dynamic work setting. *Organization Studies, 34*(1), 45–78; **25.** Hayes, J. R., & Flower, L. S. (1986). Writing research and the writer. *American Psychologist, 41*(10), 1106; **26.** Westerman, D. A. (1991). Expert and novice teacher decision making. *Journal of Teacher Education, 42*(4), 292–305; **27.** van den Eeden, C. A., de Poot, C. J., & van Koppen, P. J. (2019). The forensic confirmation bias: A comparison between experts and novices. *Journal of Forensic Sciences, 64*(1), 120–126; **28.** Weick, K. E., & Sutcliffe, K. M. (2001). *Managing the unexpected* (Vol. 9). Jossey-Bass; **29.** Salas, E., Rosen, M. A., & DiazGranados, D. (2010). Expertise-based intuition and decision making in organizations. *Journal of Management, 36*(4), 941–973; **30.** Quote attributed to Nicholas Chrisman.

CHAPTER TWO

1. Thielmann, I., Spadaro, G., & Balliet, D. (2020). Personality and prosocial behavior: A theoretical framework and meta-analysis. *Psychological Bulletin, 146*(1), 30; **2.** Thielmann et al., "Personality and prosocial behavior," 30; **3.** Fleeson, W. (2004). Moving personality beyond the person-situation debate: The challenge and the opportunity of within-person variability. *Current Directions in Psychological Science, 13*(2), 83–87; **4.** Roberts, B. W., & Yoon, H. J. (2022). Personality psychology. *Annual Review of Psychology, 73,* 489–516; **5.** Sanderson, C. A. (2010) *Social psychology.* John Wiley and Sons; **6.** Gross, T. (2019, October 11). "Breaking Bad" creator Vince Gilligan reflects on meth and morals. *NPR.*

https://www.npr.org/2019/10/11/769312766/breaking-bad-creator-vince-gilligan -reflects-on-meth-and-morals; **7.** Marsh, A. (2017). *The fear factor: How one emotion connects altruists, psychopaths, and everyone in-between.* Basic Books; **8.** Ross, L. (1977). The intuitive psychologist and his shortcomings: Distortions in the attribution process. In Leonard Berkowitz (ed.), *Advances in experimental social psychology* (Vol. J), (pp. 173–220). Academic Press; **9.** Rosenthal, R., & Jacobson, L. (1968). Pygmalion in the classroom. *The Urban Review, 3*(1), 16–20; **10.** Kierein, N. M., & Gold, M. A. (2000). Pygmalion in work organizations: A meta-analysis. *Journal of Organizational Behavior, 21*(8), 913–928; **11.** Reggev, N., Chowdhary, A., & Mitchell, J. P. (2021, December). Confirmation of interpersonal expectations is intrinsically rewarding. *Social Cognitive and Affective Neuroscience, 16*(12), 1276–1287; Turpin, M. H., Walker, A. C., Fugelsang, J. A., Sorokowski, P., Grossmann, I., & Białek, M. (2021). The search for predictable moral partners: Predictability and moral (character) preferences. *Journal of Experimental Social Psychology, 97,* 104196; **12.** Cox, D. (2021, March 26). Support for political violence among Americans is on the rise. It's a grim warning about America's political future. *Insider.* https://www.businessinsider.com/poll-shows-third-of-americans-support-use-of-political-violence-2021-3; **13.** Theriault, S. M. (2006). Party polarization in the US Congress: Member replacement and member adaptation. *Party Politics, 12*(4), 483–503; **14.** Wang, W. (2020, November 3). Marriages between Democrats and Republicans are extremely rare. *Institute for Family Studies.* https://ifstudies.org/blog /marriages-between-democrats-and-republicans-are-extremely-rare; **15.** Brown, J. R., & Enos, R. D. (2021). The measurement of partisan sorting for 180 million voters. *Nature Human Behavior, 5,* 998–1008. https://doi.org/10.1038/s41562-021-01066-z; **16.** Graham, J., Haidt, J., & Nosek, B. A. (2009). Liberals and conservatives rely on different sets of moral foundations. *Journal of Personality and Social Psychology, 96*(5), 1029; **17.** Hurst, K., & Stern, M. J. (2020). Messaging for environmental action: The role of moral framing and message source. *Journal of Environmental Psychology, 68,* 101394; **18.** Kivikangas, J. M., Fernández-Castilla, B., Järvelä, S., Ravaja, N., & Lönnqvist, J. E. (2021). Moral foundations and political orientation: Systematic review and meta-analysis. *Psychological Bulletin, 147*(1), 55; Atari, M., Haidt, J., Graham, J., Koleva, S., Stevens, S. T., & Dehghani, M. (2023). Morality beyond the WEIRD: How the nomological network of morality varies across cultures. *Journal of Personality and Social Psychology;* **19.** Dang, J., King, K. M., & Inzlicht, M. (2020). Why are self-report and behavioral measures weakly correlated? *Trends in Cognitive Sciences, 24*(4), 267–269; **20.** Kivikangas, J. M., Lönnqvist, J. E., & Ravaja, N. (2017). Relationship of moral foundations to political liberalism-conservatism and left-right orientation in a Finnish representative sample. *Social Psychology, 48*(4), 246–251. https://psycnet.apa.org/doi/10.1027/1864-9335 /a000297; **21.** Smith, K. B., Alford, J. R., Hibbing, J. R., Martin, N. G., & Hatemi, P. K. (2017). Intuitive ethics and political orientations: Testing moral foundations as a theory of political ideology. *American Journal of Political Science, 61*(2), 424–437; **22.** Smith et al., "Intuitive ethics and political orientations," 424–437; **23.** Doris, J. M. (2002). *Lack of character: Personality and moral behavior.* Cambridge University Press; **24.** Milgram, S. (1974). *Obedience to authority.* Harper Perennial; **25.** Blass, T. (1999). The Milgram paradigm after 35 years: Some things we now know about obedience to authority. *Journal of*

Applied Social Psychology, 29(5), 955–978; **26.** Doliński, D., Grzyb, T., Folwarczny, M., Grzybała, P., Krzyszycha, K., Martynowska, K., & Trojanowski, J. (2017). Would you deliver an electric shock in 2015? Obedience in the experimental paradigm developed by Stanley Milgram in the 50 years following the original studies. *Social Psychological and Personality Science*, 8(8), 927–933; **27.** Darley, J. M., & Batson, C. D. (1973). "From Jerusalem to Jericho": A study of situational and dispositional variables in helping behavior. *Journal of Personality and Social Psychology*, 27(1), 100; **28.** Greenwald, A. G. (1975). Does the Good Samaritan parable increase helping? A comment on Darley and Batson's no-effect conclusion. *Journal of Personality and Social Psychology*, 32(4), 578–583; **29.** Zhong, C. B., Bohns, V. K., & Gino, F. (2010). Good lamps are the best police: Darkness increases dishonesty and self-interested behavior. *Psychological Science*, 21(3), 311–314; **30.** Zhong, C. B., Strejcek, B., & Sivanathan, N. (2010). A clean self can render harsh moral judgment. *Journal of Experimental Social Psychology*, 46(5), 859–862; **31.** Dear, K., Dutton, K., & Fox, E. (2019). Do "watching eyes" influence antisocial behavior? A systematic review & meta-analysis. *Evolution and Human Behavior*, 40(3), 269–280; **32.** Gerlach, P., Teodorescu, K., & Hertwig, R. (2019). The truth about lies: A meta-analysis on dishonest behavior. *Psychological Bulletin*, 145(1), 1; **33.** Funder, D. C., & Ozer, D. J. (2019). Evaluating effect size in psychological research: Sense and nonsense. *Advances in Methods and Practices in Psychological Science*, 2(2), 156–168; **34.** Kish-Gephart, J. J., Harrison, D. A., & Treviño, L. K. (2010). Bad apples, bad cases, and bad barrels: Meta-analytic evidence about sources of unethical decisions at work. *Journal of Applied Psychology*, 95(1), 1; **35.** Yeager, D. S., Hanselman, P., Walton, G. M., Murray, J. S., Crosnoe, R., Muller, C., Tipton, E., Schnieder, B., Hulleman, C. S., Hinojosa, C. P., Paunesku, D., Romero, C., Flint, K., Roberts, A., Trott, J., Iachan, R., Buontempo, J., Yang, S. M., Carvalho, C. M., . . . & Dweck, C. S. (2019). A national experiment reveals where a growth mindset improves achievement. *Nature*, 573(7774), 364–369; **36.** Yeager, D. S., & Dweck, C. S. (2020). What can be learned from growth mindset controversies? *American Psychologist*, 75(9), 1269; **37.** Balliet, D., & Van Lange, P. A. (2013). Trust, punishment, and cooperation across 18 societies: A meta-analysis. *Perspectives on Psychological Science*, 8(4), 363–379; **38.** Trope, Y., & Liberman, N. (2003). Temporal construal. *Psychological Review*, 110(3), 403; **39.** Cojuharenco, I., Shteynberg, G., Gelfand, M., & Schminke, M. (2012). Self-construal and unethical behavior. *Journal of Business Ethics*, 109(4), 447–461; **40.** Parmar, B. L. (2017). Disobedience of immoral orders from authorities: An issue construction perspective. *Organization Studies*, 38(10), 1373–1396. **41.** Yeager et al., "A national experiment reveals," 364–369; **42.** Dubljević, V., Sattler, S., & Racine, E. (2018). Deciphering moral intuition: How agents, deeds, and consequences influence moral judgment. *PloS One*, 13(10), e0204631; **43.** Bruner, J. S. (1973). *Beyond the information given: Studies in the psychology of knowing*. W. W. Norton; **44.** Blanken, I., van De Ven, N., & Zeelenberg, M. (2015). A meta-analytic review of moral licensing. *Personality and Social Psychology Bulletin*, 41(4), 540–558; **45.** Furr, R. M., & Funder, D. C. (2004). Situational similarity and behavioral consistency: Subjective, objective, variable-centered, and person-centered approaches. *Journal of Research in Personality*, 38(5), 421–447; **46.** Walton, G. M., & Wilson, T. D. (2018). Wise interventions: Psychological remedies for social and personal problems. *Psychological*

Review, 125(5), 617; **47.** Pennebaker, J. W. (2000). The effects of traumatic disclosure on physical and mental health: The values of writing and talking about upsetting events. In J. M. Violanti, D. Paton, & C. Dunning (Eds.), *Posttraumatic stress intervention: Challenges, issues, and perspectives* (pp. 97–114). Charles C. Thomas Publisher, Ltd; **48.** Brown, J. D. (1986). Evaluations of self and others: Self-enhancement biases in social judgments. *Social Cognition, 4*(4), 353–376.

CHAPTER THREE

1. Alexander, L., & Moore, M. Deontological ethics. In E. N. Zalta (Ed.), *The Stanford encyclopedia of philosophy* (Winter 2021 ed.). https://plato.stanford.edu/archives/win2021/entries/ethics-deontological/; **2.** Uhlmann, E. L., Zu, L., & Tannenbaum, D. (2013). When it takes a bad person to do the right thing. *Cognition 126*, 326–334. https://doi.org/10.1016/j.cognition.2012.10.005; **3.** Turpin et al., "The search for predictable moral partners"; **4.** Moore, M. S. (2010). *Placing blame: A theory of the criminal law.* Oxford University Press; **5.** Liu, B. S., & Ditto, P. H. (2013). What dilemma? Moral evaluation shapes factual belief. *Social Psychological and Personality Science, 4*(3), 316–323; **6.** Martin, G. R. R. (1999). *A clash of kings.* Bantam Books; **7.** Mill, J. S. (1998). *Utilitarianism.* Oxford University Press. (Original work published 1861); **8.** Bentham, J. (1843). *The works of Jeremy Bentham*, vol 1. William Tait; **9.** Thomson, J. J. (1976). Killing, letting die, and the trolley problem. *The Monist, 59*(2), 204–217; **10.** Ng, N. L., Luke, D. M., & Gawronski, B. (2023). Moral judgment under uncertainty: A CNI model analysis. *European Journal of Social Psychology*, 1–23; **11.** Gilbert, D. (2009). *Stumbling on happiness.* Vintage Canada; **12.** Mill, "*Utilitarianism*"; **13.** Alicke, M. D. (2000). Culpable control and the psychology of blame. *Psychological Bulletin, 126*(4), 556; **14.** Hartman, E. (2013). *Virtue in business: Conversations with Aristotle.* Cambridge University Press; **15.** Hursthouse, R., & Pettigrove, G. Virtue ethics. In E. N. Zalta (Ed.), *The Stanford encyclopedia of philosophy* (Winter 2018 ed.). https://plato.stanford.edu/archives/win2018/entries/ethics-virtue/; **16.** Goodwin, G. P. (2015). Moral character in person perception. *Current Directions in Psychological Science, 24*(1), 38–44; **17.** Hursthouse & Pettigrove, G. "Virtue ethics"; **18.** Kohlberg, L., & Hersh, R. H. (1977). Moral development: A review of the theory. *Theory Into Practice, 16*(2), 53–59; **19.** Gilligan, C. (1982). *In a different voice: Psychological theory and women's development.* Harvard University Press; **20.** Beauvoir, S. (1976). *The ethics of ambiguity* (B. Frechtman, Trans.). Citadel Press; **21.** Engster, D. (2011). Care ethics and stakeholder theory. In M. Hamington and M. Sander-Staudt (Eds). *Applying care ethics to business* (pp. 93–110). Oxford; **22.** Earp, B. D., McLoughlin, K. L., Monrad, J. T., Clark, M. S., & Crockett, M. J. (2021). How social relationships shape moral wrongness judgments. *Nature Communications, 12*, 5776. https://doi.org/10.1038/s41467-021-26067-4; **23.** Norlock, K. Feminist ethics. In E. N. Zalta (Ed.), *The Stanford encyclopedia of philosophy* (Summer 2019 ed.). https://plato.stanford.edu/archives/sum2019/entries/feminism-ethics/; **24.** Groenhout, R. (1998). The virtue of care: Aristotelian ethics and contemporary ethics of care. In C. A. Freeland (Ed.), *Feminist interpretations of Aristotle* (pp. 171–200). Pennsylvania State University Press; **25.** Dewey, J. (1930). The quest for certainty: A study of the relation of knowledge and action. *The Journal of Philosophy, 27*(1), 14–25; **26.** Bourget, D., & Chalmers, D. J. (2023). Philosophers on philosophy: The 2020 PhilPapers Survey. *Philosophers' Imprint, 23*(11); **27.** Hennig, M., & Hütter, M. (2020). Revisiting the divide between deontology and utilitarianism in moral dilemma judgment: A multinomial modeling approach. *Journal of Personality and Social Psychology, 118*(1), 22–56. https://doi.org/10.1037/pspa0000173; **28.** Foot, P. (1967). The problem of abortion and the doctrine of the double effect. *Oxford Review, 5;* **29.** Greene, J. D., Cushman, F. A., Stewart, L. E., Lowenberg, K., Nystrom, L. E., & Cohen, J. D. (2009). Pushing moral buttons: The interaction between personal force and intention in moral judgment. *Cognition, 111*(3), 364–371; **30.** Malle, B. F., Guglielmo, S., & Monroe, A. E. (2012). Moral, cognitive, and social: The nature of blame. In *Social thinking and interpersonal behavior* (pp. 313–331). Psychology Press; Siegel, J. Z., Crockett, M. J., & Dolan, R. J. (2017). Inferences about moral character moderate the impact of consequences on blame and praise. *Cognition, 167,* 201–211; **31.** Ghosh, S. K. (2015). Human cadaveric dissection: A historical account from ancient Greece to the modern era. *Anatomy & Cell Biology, 48*(3), 153–169; **32.** Weick & Sutcliffe, *Managing the unexpected.*

CHAPTER FOUR

1. Amiri, S. (2020). Prevalence of suicide in immigrants/refugees: A systematic review and meta-analysis. *Archives of Suicide Research,* 1–36; Fisher, S., Reynolds, J. L., Hsu, W. W., Barnes, J., & Tyler, K. (2014). Examining multiracial youth in context: Ethnic identity development and mental health outcomes. *Journal of Youth and Adolescence, 43*(10), 1688–1699; Siegel, J. M., Aneshensel, C. S., Taub, B., Cantwell, D. P., & Driscoll, A. K. (1998, August). Adolescent depressed mood in a multiethnic sample. *Journal of Youth and Adolescence, 27,* 413–427. https://doi.org/10.1023/A:1022873601030; Phinney, J., Horenczyk, G., Liebkind, K., & Vedder, P. H. (2001). Ethnic identity, immigration, and well-being: An interactional perspective. *Journal of Social Issues, 57*(3), 493–510; **2.** Harker, K. (2001). Immigrant generation, assimilation, and adolescent psychological well-being. *Social Forces, 79*(3), 969–1004; **3.** George, J. (2014, May 15). Forget right or wrong: Decision-making is about trade-offs. *Forbes.* https://www.forbes.com/sites/sungardas/2014/05/15/forget-right-or-wrong-decision-making-is-about-trade-offs/?sh=52400641cf2c; **4.** Mullainathan, S., & Shafir, E. (2013). *Scarcity: Why having too little means so much.* Macmillan; **5.** Bishop, S., Duncan, J., Brett, M., & Lawrence, A. D. (2004). Prefrontal cortical function and anxiety: Controlling attention to threat-related stimuli. *Nature Neuroscience, 7*(2), 184–188; **6.** Saxena, J. (2020, December 22). Menu prices will go up with a higher minimum wage. But you've been underpaying for years. *Eater.* https://www.eater.com/22189054/how-a-15-dollar-minimum-wage-will-effect-restaurants; **7.** Mast Reforestation. (n.d.) *About.* Retrieved on May 1, 2022, at https://droneseed.com/#about-us; **8.** Freeman, R. E., & Evan, W. M. (1990). Corporate governance: A stakeholder interpretation. *Journal of Behavioral Economics, 19*(4), 337–359; **9.** Sinaceur, M., Maddux, W. W., Vasiljevic, D., Nückel, R. P., & Galinsky, A. D. (2013). Good things come to those who wait: Late first offers facilitate creative agreements in negotiation. *Personality and Social Psychology Bulletin, 39*(6), 814–825. https://doi

.org/10.1177/0146167213483319; **10.** Zhang et al., "Does 'could' lead to good?" 857–895; **11.** Liedtka, J., & Ogilvie, T. (2011). *Designing for growth: A design thinking tool kit for managers.* Columbia University Press; **12.** Hargadon, A. (2003). *How break-throughs happen: The surprising truth about how companies innovate.* Harvard Business Press; **13.** Bakalar, N. (2011, September 26). Self-adjustable eyeglass lenses. *New York Times.* https://www.nytimes.com/2011/09/27/health/27glasses.html; **14.** Muraven, M., Gagné, M., & Rosman, H. (2008). Helpful self-control: Autonomy support, vitality, and depletion. *Journal of Experimental Social Psychology, 44*(3), 573–585; **15.** Muraven, M., Tice, D. M., & Baumeister, R. F. (1998). Self-control as a limited resource: Regulatory depletion patterns. *Journal of Personality and Social Psychology, 74*(3), 774; **16.** Baumeister, R. F., Bratslavsky, E., Muraven, M., & Tice, D. M. (1998). Ego deple-tion: Is the active self a limited resource? *Journal of Personality and Social Psychology, 74*(5), 1252–1265; **17.** Schmeichel, B. J. (2007). Attention control, memory updating, and emotion regulation temporarily reduce the capacity for executive control. *Journal of Experimental Psychology: General, 136*(2), 241; **18.** Kurzban, R. (2010). Does the brain consume additional glucose during self-control tasks? *Evolutionary Psychology, 8*(2), 147470491000800208; Hockey, R. (2013). *The psychology of fatigue: Work, effort and control.* Cambridge University Press; **19.** Draganich, C., & Erdal, K. (2014). Placebo sleep affects cognitive functioning. *Journal of Experimental Psychology: Learning, Memory, and Cognition, 40*(3), 857; **20.** Inzlicht, M., Berkman, E., & Elkins-Brown, N. (2016). The neuroscience of "ego depletion": How the brain can help us understand why self-control seems limited. In *Social neuroscience* (pp. 101–123). Routledge; **21.** Inzlicht, M., Schmeichel, B. J., & Macrae, C. N. (2014). Why self-control seems (but may not be) limited. *Trends in Cognitive Sciences, 18*(3), 127–133; **22.** Gray & McNaughton, "The neuropsychology of anxiety," 61–134; **23.** Berger, A., Mitschke, V., Dignath, D., Eder, A., & van Steenbergen, H. (2020). The face of control: Corrugator supercilii tracks aver-sive conflict signals in the service of adaptive cognitive control. *Psychophysiology, 57*(4), e13524; **24.** Inzlicht et al., "The neuroscience of 'ego depletion,'" 101–123; **25.** Ng, B. (2018). The neuroscience of growth mindset and intrinsic motivation. *Brain Sciences, 8*(2), 20; **26.** Inzlicht, M., & Schmeichel, B. J. (2012). What is ego depletion? Toward a mechanistic revision of the resource model of self-control. *Perspectives on Psychological Science, 7*(5), 450–463; **27.** Isen, A. M., Johnson, M., Mertz, E., & Robinson, G. F. (1985). The influence of positive affect on the unusualness of word associations. *Journal of Personality and Social Psychology, 48*(6), 1413; Isen, A. M. (1999). On the relationship between affect and creative problem solving. *Affect, Creative Experience, and Psychological Adjustment, 3*(17), 3–17; **28.** Amabile, T. M., Barsade, S. G., Mueller, J. S., & Staw, B. M. (2005). Affect and creativity at work. *Administrative Science Quarterly, 50*(3), 367–403; **29.** Abele-Brehm, A. (1992). "Positive and negative mood influences on creativ-ity: Evidence for asymmetrical effects." *Polish Psychological Bulletin*; **30.** Amabile et al., "Affect and creativity at work," 367–403; **31.** Baas, M., De Dreu, C. K., & Nijstad, B. A. (2008). A meta-analysis of 25 years of mood-creativity research: Hedonic tone, activa-tion, or regulatory focus? *Psychological Bulletin, 134*(6), 779; **32.** Kessel, M., Kratzer, J., & Schultz, C. (2012). Psychological safety, knowledge sharing, and creative performance in healthcare teams. *Creativity and Innovation Management, 21*(2), 147–157; Carmeli, A.,

Reiter-Palmon, R., & Ziv, E. (2010). Inclusive leadership and employee involvement in creative tasks in the workplace: The mediating role of psychological safety. *Creativity Research Journal*, *22*(3), 250–260; Palanski, M. E., & Vogelgesang, G. R. (2011). Virtuous creativity: The effects of leader behavioural integrity on follower creative thinking and risk taking. *Canadian Journal of Administrative Sciences/Revue Canadienne des Sciences de l'Administration*, *28*(3), 259–269; Gu, Q., Wang, G. G., & Wang, L. (2013). Social capital and innovation in R&D teams: The mediating roles of psychological safety and learning from mistakes. *R&D Management*, *43*(2), 89–102; **33.** Botha, H., & Parmar, B. (n.d.). The psychology of integrating stakeholder interests [Unpublished manuscript]. Retrieved on April 1, 2023; **34.** Brooks, A. W. (2014). Get excited: Reappraising pre-performance anxiety as excitement. *Journal of Experimental Psychology: General*, *143*(3), 1144; **35.** Liberman, N., Sagristano, M. D., & Trope, Y. (2002). The effect of temporal distance on level of mental construal. *Journal of Experimental Social Psychology*, *38*(6), 523–534; **36.** Fishbach, A., & Woolley, K. (2022). The structure of intrinsic motivation. *Annual Review of Organizational Psychology and Organizational Behavior, 9*, 339–363.

CHAPTER FIVE

1. Birn, R. M., Roeber, B. J., & Pollak, S. D. (2017). Early childhood stress exposure, reward pathways, and adult decision making. *Proceedings of the National Academy of Sciences, 114*(51), 13549–13554; **2.** Köymen, B., Rosenbaum, L., & Tomasello, M. (2014). Reasoning during joint decision-making by preschool peers. *Cognitive Development, 32*, 74–85; **3.** Rubin, K. H., Lynch, D., Coplan, R., Rose-Krasnor, L., & Booth, C. L. (1994). "Birds of a feather . . .": Behavioral concordances and preferential personal attraction in children. *Child Development*, *65*(6), 1778–1785; **4.** Köymen, B., & Tomasello, M. (2020). The early ontogeny of reason giving. *Child Development Perspectives*, *14*(4), 215–220; Köymen, B., Mammen, M., & Tomasello, M. (2016). Preschoolers use common ground in their justificatory reasoning with peers. *Developmental Psychology*, *52*(3), 423; **5.** Domberg, A., Köymen, B., & Tomasello, M. (2018). Children's reasoning with peers in cooperative and competitive contexts. *British Journal of Developmental Psychology*, *36*(1), 64–77; **6.** Lerner, J. S., & Tetlock, P. E. (1999). Accounting for the effects of accountability. *Psychological Bulletin*, *125*(2), 255; Pennington, J., & Schlenker, B. R. (1999). Accountability for consequential decisions: Justifying ethical judgments to audiences. *Personality and Social Psychology Bulletin*, *25*(9), 1067–1081; **7.** Brief, A. P., Dukerich, J. M., & Doran, L. I. (1991). Resolving ethical dilemmas in management: Experimental investigations of values, accountability, and choice. *Journal of Applied Social Psychology, 21*(5), 380–396; **8.** Antonioni, D. (1994). The effects of feedback accountability on upward appraisal ratings. *Personnel Psychology*, *47*(2), 349–356; **9.** Fandt, P. M., & Ferris, G. R. (1990). The management of information and impressions: When employees behave opportunistically. *Organizational Behavior and Human Decision Processes*, *45*(1), 140–158; **10.** Buchman, T. A., Tetlock, P. E., & Reed, R. O. (1996). Accountability and auditors' judgments about contingent events. *Journal of Business Finance & Accounting*, *23*(3), 379–398; **11.** Tetlock, P. E., Skitka, L., & Boettger, R. (1989). Social and cognitive strategies for coping with accountability: Conformity, complexity, and bolstering. *Journal of Personality and Social Psychology, 57*(4), 632; Cialdini, R. B., Levy, A., Herman, C. P., Kozlowski, L. T., & Petty, R. E. (1976). Elastic shifts of opinion: Determinants of direction and durability. *Journal of Personality and Social Psychology, 34*(4), 663; Klimoski, R., & Inks, L. (1990). Accountability forces in performance appraisal. *Organizational Behavior and Human Decision Processes, 45*(2), 194–208; **12.** Lerner, J. S., & Tetlock, P. E. (1999). Accounting for the effects of accountability. *Psychological Bulletin, 125*(2), 255; **13.** Lord, A. T. (1992). Pressure: A methodological consideration for behavioral research in auditing. *Auditing, 11*(2), 90; **14.** Doney, P. M., & Armstrong, G. M. (1995). Effects of accountability on symbolic information search and information analysis by organizational buyers. *Journal of the Academy of Marketing Science, 24*(1), 57–65; **15.** Thompson, L. (1995). "They saw a negotiation": Partisanship and involvement. *Journal of Personality and Social Psychology, 68*(5), 839; **16.** Pitesa, M., & Thau, S. (2013). Masters of the universe: How power and accountability influence self-serving decisions under moral hazard. *Journal of Applied Psychology, 98*(3), 550; **17.** Simonson, I., & Staw, B. M. (1992). Deescalation strategies: A comparison of techniques for reducing commitment to losing courses of action. *Journal of Applied Psychology, 77*(4), 419; **18.** Festinger, L., Riecken, H., & Schachter, S. (2017). *When prophecy fails: A social and psychological study of a modern group that predicted the destruction of the world.* Lulu Press, Inc.; **19.** Ask, K., & Granhag, P. A. (2005). Motivational sources of confirmation bias in criminal investigations: The need for cognitive closure. *Journal of Investigative Psychology and Offender Profiling, 2*(1), 43–63; **20.** Jarcho, J. M., Berkman, E. T., & Lieberman, M. D. (2011). The neural basis of rationalization: Cognitive dissonance reduction during decision-making. *Social Cognitive and Affective Neuroscience, 6*(4), 460–467; Yin, D., Mitra, S., & Zhang, H. (2016). Research note—When do consumers value positive vs. negative reviews? An empirical investigation of confirmation bias in online word of mouth. *Information Systems Research, 27*(1), 131–144; **21.** Ditto, P. H., & Lopez, D. F. (1992). Motivated skepticism: Use of differential decision criteria for preferred and non-preferred conclusions. *Journal of Personality and Social Psychology, 63*(4), 568; **22.** Beer, J. S., & Hughes, B. L. (2010). Neural systems of social comparison and the "above-average" effect. *Neuroimage, 49*(3), 2671–2679; **23.** Sharot, T., Korn, C. W., & Dolan, R. J. (2011). How unrealistic optimism is maintained in the face of reality. *Nature Neuroscience, 14*(11), 1475–1479; **24.** Lord, C. G., Ross, L., & Lepper, M. R. (1979). Biased assimilation and attitude polarization: The effects of prior theories on subsequently considered evidence. *Journal of Personality and Social Psychology, 37*(11), 2098; **25.** Kunda, Z. (1990). The case for motivated reasoning. *Psychological Bulletin, 108*(3), 480; **26.** van Prooijen, J. W., Ligthart, J., Rosema, S., & Xu, Y. (2022). The entertainment value of conspiracy theories. *British Journal of Psychology, 113*(1), 25–48; **27.** Cikara, M., & Van Bavel, J. J. (2014). The neuroscience of intergroup relations: An integrative review. *Perspectives on Psychological Science, 9*(3), 245–274; **28.** Knobloch-Westerwick, S., & Meng, J. (2011). Reinforcement of the political self through selective exposure to political messages. *Journal of Communication, 61*(2), 349–368; Stroud, N. J., Muddiman, A., & Lee, J. K. (2014). Seeing media as group members: An evaluation of partisan bias perceptions. *Journal of Communication, 64*(5), 874–894; **29.** Hart, W., Albarracín, D., Eagly, A. H., Brechan, I., Lindberg, M. J., & Merrill, L. (2009). Feeling validated versus being correct: A meta-analysis of selective exposure to information. *Psychological Bulletin*, *135*(4), 555; **30.** Doll, B. B., Hutchison, K. E., & Frank, M. J. (2011). Dopaminergic genes predict individual differences in susceptibility to confirmation bias. *Journal of Neuroscience*, *31*(16), 6188–6198; **31.** Broyd, A., Balzan, R. P., Woodward, T. S., & Allen, P. (2017). Dopamine, cognitive biases and assessment of certainty: A neurocognitive model of delusions. *Clinical Psychology Review*, *54*, 96–106; **32.** Taylor, S. E., & Brown, J. D. (1988). Illusion and well-being: A social psychological perspective on mental health. *Psychological Bulletin*, *103*(2), 193; Jonas, E., Graupmann, V., & Frey, D. (2006). The influence of mood on the search for supporting versus conflicting information: Dissonance reduction as a means of mood regulation? *Personality and Social Psychology Bulletin*, *32*(1), 3–15; **33.** Kunda, "The case for motivated reasoning," 480; **34.** Knobloch-Westerwick, S., Mothes, C., & Polavin, N. (2020). Confirmation bias, ingroup bias, and negativity bias in selective exposure to political information. *Communication Research*, *47*(1), 104–124; **35.** Putnam, H. (2016). *The fact/value dichotomy and the future of philosophy*. Routledge; **36.** Swain-Lenz, D., Berrio, A., Safi, A., Crawford, G. E., & Wray, G. A. (2019, July). Comparative analyses of chromatin landscape in white adipose tissue suggest humans may have less beigeing potential than other primates. *Genome Biology and Evolution*, *11*(7), 1997–2008, https://doi.org/10.1093/gbe/evz134; Pontzer, H., Brown, M. H., Raichlen, D. A., Dunsworth, H., Hare, B., Walker, K., Luke, A., Dugas, L. R., Durazo-Arvizu, R., Schoeller, D., Plange-Rhule, J., Bovet, P., Forrester, T. E., Lambert, E. V., Thompson, M. E., Shumaker, R. W., & Ross, S. R. (2016). Metabolic acceleration and the evolution of human brain size and life history. *Nature*, *533*(7603), 390–392; **37.** Bohara, S. S., Thapa, K., Bhatt, L. D., Dhami, S. S., & Wagle, S. (2021). Determinants of junk food consumption among adolescents in Pokhara Valley, Nepal. *Frontiers in Nutrition*, *8*, 644–650; **38.** Nickerson, R. S. (1998). Confirmation bias: A ubiquitous phenomenon in many guises. *Review of General Psychology*, *2*(2), 175–220; **39.** Lembke, *Dopamine nation*; **40.** Angres, D. H., & Bettinardi–Angres, K. (2008). The disease of addiction: Origins, treatment, and recovery. *Disease-a-Month*, *54*(10), 696–721; **41.** Kobayashi, K., & Hsu, M. (2019). Common neural code for reward and information value. *Proceedings of the National Academy of Sciences*, 201820145; **42.** Peresie, J. L. (2004). Female judges matter: Gender and collegial decisionmaking in the federal appellate courts. *Yale Law Journal*, *114*, 1759; **43.** Somerville, K. (2020, October 15). The hidden power of intellectual humility. *The Decision Lab*. https://thedecisionlab.com/insights /society/the-hidden-power-of-intellectual-humility/; **44.** Bowes, S. M., Costello, T. H., Lee, C., McElroy-Heltzel, S., Davis, D. E., & Lilienfeld, S. O. (2022). Stepping outside the echo chamber: Is intellectual humility associated with less political myside bias? *Personality and Social Psychology Bulletin*, *48*(1), 150–164; **45.** Cohen, G. L., & Sherman, D. K. (2014). The psychology of change: Self-affirmation and social psychological intervention. *Annual Review of Psychology*, *65*, 333–371; Harris, P. R., & Epton, T. (2009). The impact of self-affirmation on health cognition, health behaviour and other health-related responses: A narrative review. *Social and Personality Psychology Compass*, *3*(6), 962–978; **46.** Seaman, E. L., Robinson, C. D., Crane, D., Taber, J. M., Ferrer, R. A., Harris, P. R., & Klein, W. M. (2021). Association of spontaneous and induced self-affirmation with smoking cessation in users of a mobile app: Randomized controlled trial. *Journal of Medical Internet Research*, *23*(3), e18433-e18433; **47.** Chugh, D., Kern, M. C., Zhu, Z., & Lee, S. (2014). Withstanding moral disengagement: Attachment security as an ethical intervention. *Journal of Experimental Social Psychology*, *51*, 88–93; **48.** Seaman et al., "Association of spontaneous and induced self-affirmation"; **49.** Murderpedia. (n.d.). *Jane Toppan*. Retrieved on May 1, 2022, from https://murderpedia.org/female.T/ t/toppan-jane.htm; **50.** Wynne, K. (2019, July 22). Today in history: Jeffery Dahmer, infamous Milwaukee cannibal, was arrested 28 years ago. *Newsweek*. Retrieved on May 1, 2022, from https://www.newsweek.com/today-history -jeffrey-dahmer-infamous-milwaukee-cannibal-was-arrested-28-years-ago-1450563; **51.** Coonan, C. (2016, January 6). Former Enron CFO Andrew Fastow: "You can follow all the rules and still commit fraud," *Irish Times*; **52.** O'Brien, T. L. (2021, November 22). How United Airlines decided to lead on vaccine mandates. *Bloomberg*. https://www .bloomberg.com/opinion/articles/2021-11-22/how-united-airlines-decided-to-lead -on-vaccine-mandates; **53.** Freeman, R. E., Wicks, A. C., Harris, J. D., Parmar, B. L., & Mead, J. (2017, May 30). Bad arguments and rationalization in business. *Darden Case No. UVA-E-0406*. http://dx.doi.org/10.2139/ssrn.2974202; **54.** Todd, A. R., Galinsky, A. D., & Bodenhausen, G. V. (2012). Perspective taking undermines stereotype mainte-nance processes: Evidence from social memory, behavior explanation, and information solicitation. *Social Cognition*, *30*(1), 94–108.

CHAPTER SIX

1. Mead, J., & Wicks, A. C. (2004). Danville Airlines. *Darden Business Publishing Cases*; **2.** Nice-Matin. (2020, February 15). *La confédération des boulangers désavoue le Niçois Frédéric Roy, pourfendeur du croissant industriel*. https://www.nicematin.com/ vie-locale/la-confederation-des-boulangers-desavoue-le-nicois-frederic-roy-pourfend-eur-du-croissant-industriel-464371; **3.** Rana, P., & Farrell, M. (2020, October 12). How Airbnb pulled back from the brink. *Wall Street Journal*. https://www.wsj.com/articles/ how-airbnb-pulled-back-from-the-brink-11602520846; **4.** UniBocconi. (2017, March 14). *Howard Schultz speech—A coffee with Howard Schultz* [Video]. YouTube. https:// www.youtube.com/watch?v=QL9mr8Y2pt4; **5.** Stevens, M. (2018, April 15). Starbucks C.E.O. apologizes after arrests of 2 Black men. *New York Times*. https://www.nytimes. com/2018/04/15/us/starbucks-philadelphia-black-men-arrest.html; **6.** Weick, K. E. (1995). *Sensemaking in organizations* (Vol. 3). Sage; **7.** Sarasvathy, S. D. (2008). What makes entrepreneurs entrepreneurial? *SSRN Electric Journal*. https://doi.org/10.2139/ ssrn.909038.

THE VISTA

1. Yong, E. (2022). *An immense world: How animal senses reveal the hidden realms around us*. Knopf Canada; **2.** Boisot, M., & McKelvey, B. (2011). Complexity and organization-environment relations: Revisiting Ashby's law of requisite variety. In *The Sage handbook of complexity and management* (pp. 279–298). Sage.

CHAPTER SEVEN

1. Kish-Gephart, J. J., Detert, J. R., Treviño, L. K., & Edmondson, A. C. (2009). Silenced by fear: The nature, sources, and consequences of fear at work. *Research in Organizational Behavior, 29,* 163–193; **2.** Tomasello, M. (2014). The ultra-social animal. *European Journal of Social Psychology, 44*(3), 187–194; **3.** Klein, T., Siegwolf, R. T., & Körner, C. (2016). Belowground carbon trade among tall trees in a temperate forest. *Science, 352*(6283), 342–344; **4.** Turchi, P. (2011). *Maps of the imagination: The writer as cartographer.* Trinity University Press; **5.** Frith, C. D., & Frith, U. (2006). The neural basis of mentalizing. *Neuron, 50*(4), 531–534; **6.** Call, J., Hare, B., Carpenter, M., & Tomasello, M. (2004). "Unwilling" versus "unable": Chimpanzees' understanding of human intentional action. *Developmental Science, 7*(4), 488–498; **7.** Tomasello, M., & Vaish, A. (2013). Origins of human cooperation and morality. *Annual Review of Psychology, 64,* 231–255; **8.** Frith, U., & Frith, C. D. (2003). Development and neurophysiology of mentalizing. *Philosophical Transactions of the Royal Society of London. Series B: Biological Sciences, 358*(1431), 459–473; **9.** Warneken, F. (2013). The development of altruistic behavior: Helping in children and chimpanzees. *Social Research: An International Quarterly, 80*(2), 431–442; **10.** Tomasello & Vaish. "Origins of human cooperation and morality," 231–255; **11.** Warneken, F., & Tomasello, M. (2008). Extrinsic rewards undermine altruistic tendencies in 20-month-olds. *Developmental Psychology, 44*(6), 1785; **12.** Hepach, R., Vaish, A., & Tomasello, M. (2012). Young children are intrinsically motivated to see others helped. *Psychological Science, 23*(9), 967–972; **13.** Frith & Frith, "Development and neurophysiology of mentalizing," 459–473; **14.** Segal, N. L., Goetz, A. T., & Maldonado, A. C. (2016). Preferences for visible white sclera in adults, children and autism spectrum disorder children: Implications of the cooperative eye hypothesis. *Evolution and Human Behavior, 37*(1), 35–39; Tomalski, P., Csibra, G., & Johnson, M. H. (2009). Rapid orienting toward face-like stimuli with gaze-relevant contrast information. *Perception, 38*(4), 569–578; **15.** Provine, R. R., Cabrera, M. O., & Nave-Blodgett, J. (2013). Red, yellow, and super-white sclera: Uniquely human cues for healthiness, attractiveness, and age. *Human Nature, 24*(2), 126–137; **16.** Bielsky, I. F., & Young, L. J. (2004). Oxytocin, vasopressin, and social recognition in mammals. *Peptides, 25*(9), 1565–1574; **17.** Izuma, K., Saito, D. N., & Sadato, N. (2008). Processing of social and monetary rewards in the human striatum. *Neuron, 58*(2), 284–294; **18.** Tabibnia, G., & Lieberman, M. D. (2007). Fairness and cooperation are rewarding: Evidence from social cognitive neuroscience. *Annals of the New York Academy of Sciences, 1118*(1), 90–101; **19.** Rogers Flattery, C. N., Coppeto, D. J., Inoue, K., Rilling, J. K., Preuss, T. M., & Young, L. J. (2022). Distribution of brain oxytocin and vasopressin V1a receptors in chimpanzees (Pan troglodytes): Comparison with humans and other primate species. *Brain Structure and Function, 227*(5), 1907–1919; **20.** Berg, J., Dickhaut, J., & McCabe, K. (1995, July). Trust, reciprocity, and social history. *Games and Economic Behavior, 10*(1), 122–142; **21.** Kosfeld, M., Heinrichs, M., Zak, P. J., Fischbacher, U., & Fehr, E. (2005). Oxytocin increases trust in humans. *Nature, 435*(7042), 673–676; **22.** Eisenberg, N., & Miller, P. A. (1987). The relation of empathy to prosocial and related behaviors. *Psychological Bulletin, 101*(1), 91; **23.** Rilling, J. K., King-Casas, B., & Sanfey, A. G. (2008). The neurobiology of social decision-making. *Current Opinion in Neurobiology, 18*(2),

159–165; **24.** Cieri, R. L., Churchill, S. E., Franciscus, R. G., Tan, J., & Hare, B. (2014). Craniofacial feminization, social tolerance, and the origins of behavioral modernity. *Current Anthropology*, *55*(4), 419–443; **25.** de Waal, F. B., & Hoekstra, J. A. (1980). Contexts and predictability of aggression in chimpanzees. *Animal Behaviour*, *28*(3), 929–937; **26.** Wrangham, R. W., Wilson, M. L., & Muller, M. N. (2006). Comparative rates of violence in chimpanzees and humans. *Primates*, *47*(1), 14–26; **27.** Lane, J. D., Wellman, H. M., Olson, S. L., Miller, A. L., Wang, L., & Tardif, T. (2013). Relations between temperament and theory of mind development in the United States and China: Biological and behavioral correlates of preschoolers' false-belief understanding. *Developmental Psychology*, *49*(5), 825; **28.** Litvak, P. M., Lerner, J. S., Tiedens, L. Z., & Shonk, K. (2010). Fuel in the fire: How anger impacts judgment and decision-making. In *International handbook of anger* (pp. 287–310). Springer. **29.** Imbault, C., & Kuperman, V. (2018). Emotional reactivity and perspective-taking in individuals with and without severe depressive symptoms. *Scientific Reports*, *8*, 7634. https://doi. org/10.1038/s41598-018-25708-x; **30.** Gable et al., "Regulatory behavior and frontal activity"; **31.** Pobiner, B. (2016). Meat-eating among the earliest humans. *American Scientist*, *104*(2), 110–117; **32.** Mann, N. (2000). Dietary lean red meat and human evolution. *European Journal of Nutrition*, *39*(2), 71–79; **33.** MacLean, E. L., Hare, B., Nunn, C. L., Addessi, E., Amici, F., Anderson, R. C., Aureli, F., Baker, J. M., Bania, A. E., Barnard, A. M., Boogert, N. J., Brannon, E. M., Bray, E. E., Bray, J., Brent, L. J. N., Burkart, J. M., Call, J., Cantlon, J. F., Cheke, L. G., . . . & Zhao, Y. (2014). The evolution of self-control. *Proceedings of the National Academy of Sciences*, *111*(20), E2140–E2148; **34.** Newton, M. (2011). *Savage girls and wild boys*. Faber & Faber; **35.** Sánchez-Amaro, A., Duguid, S., Call, J., & Tomasello, M. (2019). Chimpanzees and children avoid mutual defection in a social dilemma. *Evolution and Human Behavior*, *40*(1), 46–54; **36.** Chernyak, N., Leimgruber, K. L., Dunham, Y. C., Hu, J., & Blake, P. R. (2019). Paying back people who harmed us but not people who helped us: Direct negative reciprocity precedes direct positive reciprocity in early development. *Psychological Science*, *30*(9), 1273–1286; **37.** Lee, K., Talwar, V., McCarthy, A., Ross, I., Evans, A., & Arruda, C. (2014). Can classic moral stories promote honesty in children? *Psychological Science*, *25*(8), 1630–1636; **38.** McAuliffe, K., Jordan, J. J., & Warneken, F. (2015). Costly third-party punishment in young children. *Cognition*, *134*, 1–10; **39.** Blake, P. R., & McAuliffe, K. (2011). "I had so much it didn't seem fair": Eight-year-olds reject two forms of inequity. *Cognition*, *120*(2), 215–224; **40.** Henrich, J., & Henrich, N. (2014). Fairness without punishment: Behavioral experiments in the Yasawa Island, Fiji. *Experimenting with Social Norms: Fairness and Punishment in Cross-Cultural Perspective*, 171–218; **41.** Baumeister, R. F., Zhang, L., & Vohs, K. D. (2004). Gossip as cultural learning. *Review of General Psychology*, *8*(2), 111–121; **42.** Sebastián-Enesco, C., Hernández-Lloreda, M. V., & Colmenares, F. (2013). Two-and-a-half-year-old children are prosocial even when their partners are not. *Journal of Experimental Child Psychology*, *116*(2), 186–198; **43.** Engelmann, J. M., Herrmann, E., & Tomasello, M. (2012). Five-year-olds, but not chimpanzees, attempt to manage their reputations. *PLoS One*, *7*(10), e48433; **44.** Sofer, C., Dotsch, R., Oikawa, M., Oikawa, H., Wigboldus, D. H., & Todorov, A. (2017). For your local eyes only: Culture-specific face typicality influences perceptions of trustworthiness.

Perception, 46(8), 914–928; **45.** Jordan, J. J., McAuliffe, K., & Warneken, F. (2014). Development of in-group favoritism in children's third-party punishment of selfishness. *Proceedings of the National Academy of Sciences, 111*(35), 12710–12715; **46.** Zhang, W., Liang, G., Guo, Z., Liu, Y., & Fan, W. (2021). The more familiar the others, the higher the morality: Children's preference for familiar others in moral expectations early appears in the negative moral context. *Early Child Development and Care,* 1–14; **47.** Swann Jr., W. B., Gómez, Á., Dovidio, J. F., Hart, S., & Jetten, J. (2010). Dying and killing for one's group: Identity fusion moderates responses to intergroup versions of the trolley problem. *Psychological Science, 21*(8), 1176–1183; Hester, N., & Gray, K. (2020). The moral psychology of raceless, genderless strangers. *Perspectives on Psychological Science, 15*(2), 216–230; **48.** Baumgartner, T., Götte, L., Gügler, R., & Fehr, E. (2012). The mentalizing network orchestrates the impact of parochial altruism on social norm enforcement. *Human Brain Mapping, 33*(6), 1452–1469; **49.** Moore-Berg, S. L., Ankori-Karlinsky, L. O., Hameiri, B., & Bruneau, E. (2020). Exaggerated meta-perceptions predict intergroup hostility between American political partisans. *Proceedings of the National Academy of Sciences, 117*(26), 14864–14872; **50.** Hart, A. J., Whalen, P. J., Shin, L. M., McInerney, S. C., Fischer, H., & Rauch, S. L. (2000). Differential response in the human amygdala to racial outgroup vs ingroup face stimuli. *Neuroreport, 11*(11), 2351–2354; **51.** Glover, J. (2012). *Humanity: A moral history of the twentieth century.* Yale University Press; **52.** Crespi, B. J. (2016). Oxytocin, testosterone, and human social cognition. *Biological Reviews, 91*(2), 390–408; **53.** De Dreu, C. K., Greer, L. L., Van Kleef, G. A., Shalvi, S., & Handgraaf, M. J. (2011). Oxytocin promotes human ethnocentrism. *Proceedings of the National Academy of Sciences, 108*(4), 1262–1266; **54.** Waytz, A., & Epley, N. (2012). Social connection enables dehumanization. *Journal of Experimental Social Psychology, 48*(1), 70–76; **55.** Samuni, L., Preis, A., Mundry, R., Deschner, T., Crockford, C., & Wittig, R. M. (2017). Oxytocin reactivity during intergroup conflict in wild chimpanzees. *Proceedings of the National Academy of Sciences, 114*(2), 268–273; **56.** Haslam, N., & Stratemeyer, M. (2016). Recent research on dehumanization. *Current Opinion in Psychology, 11,* 25–29; Khamitov, M., Rotman, J. D., & Piazza, J. (2016). Perceiving the agency of harmful agents: A test of dehumanization versus moral typecasting accounts. *Cognition, 146,* 33–47; **57.** Grant, A. (2013). *Give and take: A revolutionary approach to success.* Penguin; **58.** Barraza, J. A., & Zak, P. J. (2009). Empathy toward strangers triggers oxytocin release and subsequent generosity. *Annals of the New York Academy of Sciences, 1167*(1), 182–189; **59.** Procyshyn, T. L., Watson, N. V., & Crespi, B. J. (2020). Experimental empathy induction promotes oxytocin increases and testosterone decreases. *Hormones and Behavior, 117,* 104607.

CHAPTER EIGHT

1. Talbert, M. Moral responsibility. In E. N. Zalta (Ed.), *The Stanford encyclopedia of philosophy* (Winter 2019 ed.). https://plato.stanford.edu/archives/win2019/entries /moral-responsibility/; **2.** Simpson, B., Willer, R., & Harrell, A. (2017). The enforcement of moral boundaries promotes cooperation and prosocial behavior in groups. *Scientific Reports, 7*(1), 1–9; **3.** Balliet, D., Mulder, L. B., & Van Lange, P. A. (2011). Reward, punishment, and cooperation: A meta-analysis. *Psychological Bulletin*, *137*(4), 594; **4.** Baumeister, R. F., Bratslavsky, E., Finkenauer, C., & Vohs, K. D. (2001). Bad is stronger than good. *Review of General Psychology*, *5*(4), 323–370; **5.** Schrauf, R. W., & Sanchez, J. (2004). The preponderance of negative emotion words in the emotion lexicon: A cross-generational and cross-linguistic study. *Journal of Multilingual and Multicultural Development*, *25*(2–3), 266–284; Averill, J. R. (1980). On the paucity of positive emotions. In *Assessment and modification of emotional behavior* (pp. 7–45). Springer; **6.** Finkenauer, C., & Rimé, B. (1998). Socially shared emotional experiences vs. emotional experiences kept secret: Differential characteristics and consequences. *Journal of Social and Clinical Psychology*, *17*(3), 295–318; **7.** Brickman, P., Coates, D., & Janoff-Bulman, R. (1978). Lottery winners and accident victims: Is happiness relative? *Journal of Personality and Social Psychology*, *36*(8), 917; **8.** Tversky, A., & Kahneman, D. (1989). Rational choice and the framing of decisions. In *Multiple criteria decision making and risk analysis using micro-computers* (pp. 81–126). Springer; **9.** Higgins, E. T., & Liberman, N. (2018). The loss of loss aversion: Paying attention to reference points. *Journal of Consumer Psychology*, *28*(3), 523–532; **10.** Pratto, F., & John, O. P. (1991). Automatic vigilance: The attention-grabbing power of negative social information. *Journal of Personality and Social Psychology*, *61*(3), 380; **11.** Losada, M., & Heaphy, E. (2004). The role of positivity and connectivity in the performance of business teams: A nonlinear dynamics model. *American Behavioral Scientist*, *47*(6), 740–765; Bertoni, A., & Bodenmann, G. (2010). Satisfied and dissatisfied couples. *European Psychologist*, *15*(3), 175–184; **12.** Guglielmo, S., & Malle, B. F. (2019). Asymmetric morality: Blame is more differentiated and more extreme than praise. *PloS One*, *14*(3), e0213544; **13.** Pizarro, D., Uhlmann, E., & Salovey, P. (2003). Asymmetry in judgments of moral blame and praise: The role of perceived metadesires. *Psychological Science*, *14*(3), 267–272; **14.** Baumeister et al., "Bad is stronger than good," 323–370; **15.** Gilbert, E. A., Tenney, E. R., Holland, C. R., & Spellman, B. A. (2015). Counterfactuals, control, and causation: Why knowledgeable people get blamed more. *Personality and Social Psychology Bulletin*, *41*(5), 643–658; Siegel et al., "Inferences about moral character," 201–211; **16.** Burns, Z. C., Caruso, E. M., & Bartels, D. M. (2012). Predicting premeditation: Future behavior is seen as more intentional than past behavior. *Journal of Experimental Psychology: General*, *141*(2), 227; **17.** Gray, K., & Wegner, D. M. (2008). The sting of intentional pain. *Psychological Science*, *19*(12), 1260–1262; **18.** Kruger, J., & Gilovich, T. (2004). Actions, intentions, and self-assessment: The road to self-enhancement is paved with good intentions. *Personality and Social Psychology Bulletin*, *30*(3), 328–339; **19.** Arriaga, X. B., & Rusbult, C. E. (1998). Standing in my partner's shoes: Partner perspective taking and reactions to accommodative dilemmas. *Personality and Social Psychology Bulletin*, *24*(9), 927–948; **20.** Gordon, A. M., & Chen, S. (2016). Do you get where I'm coming from?: Perceived understanding buffers against the negative impact of conflict on relationship satisfaction. *Journal of Personality and Social Psychology*, *110*(2), 239; **21.** Tierney, W., Schweinsberg, M., Jordan, J., Kennedy, D. M., Qureshi, I., Somer, S. A., Thornley, N., Madan, N., Vianello, M., Awtrey, E., Zhu, L. L. , Diermeier, D., Heinze, J. E., Srinivasan, M. Tannenbaum, D., Bivolaru, E., Dana, J., Davis-Stober, C. P., du Plessis, C., . . . & Uhlmann, E. L. (2016). Data from a pre-publication independent replication initiative examining ten moral judgement effects. *Scientific Data*, *3*, 160082

(2016). https://doi.org/10.1038/sdata.2016.82; **22.** Anderson, S., & Cameron, C. D. (2023). How the self guides empathy choice. *Journal of Experimental Social Psychology*, *106*, 104444; **23.** Nichols, S., & Ulatowski, J. (2007). Intuitions and individual differences: The Knobe effect revisited. *Mind & Language*, *22*(4), 346–365; **24.** Orfali, K., & Gordon, E. (2004). Autonomy gone awry: A cross-cultural study of parents' experiences in neonatal intensive care units. *Theoretical Medicine and Bioethics*, *25*(4), 329–365; **25.** Janoff-Bulman, R. (1979). Characterological versus behavioral self-blame: Inquiries into depression and rape. *Journal of Personality and Social Psychology*, *37*(10), 1798; **26.** Reeder, G. D., Kumar, S., Hesson-McInnis, M. S., & Trafimow, D. (2002). Inferences about the morality of an aggressor: The role of perceived motive. *Journal of Personality and Social Psychology*, *83*(4), 789; **27.** Wikipedia. (n.d.) Death of Conrad Roy. Retrieved on May 1, 2022, from https://en.wikipedia.org/wiki/Manslaughter_of_Conrad_Roy; Nashrulla, T. (2020, January 23). Michelle Carter, who encouraged her boyfriend to kill himself, was released from prison early. Buzzfeed News. https://www.buzzfeednews. com/article/tasneemnashrulla/michelle-carter-prison-release-texting-suicide; **28.** Malle, B. F., Monroe, A. E., & Guglielmo, S. (2014). Paths to blame and paths to convergence. *Psychological Inquiry*, *25*(2), 251–260; **29.** Ross, N. E., & Newman, W. J. (2021). The role of apology laws in medical malpractice. *The Journal of the American Academy of Psychiatry and the Law*, *49*(3), 406–414; **30.** Paharia, N., Kassam, K. S., Greene, J. D., & Bazerman, M. H. (2009). Dirty work, clean hands: The moral psychology of indirect agency. *Organizational Behavior and Human Decision Processes*, *109*(2), 134–141; **31.** Lagnado, D. A., & Channon, S. (2008). Judgments of cause and blame: The effects of intentionality and foreseeability. *Cognition*, *108*(3), 754–770; **32.** Public Citizen. (2000, September 12). *Firestone Tire defect and Ford Explorer rollovers: Testimony of Public Citizen's President Joan Claybrook to the Committee on Commerce*. https://www.citizen.org/ article/firestone-tire-defect-and-ford-explorer-rollovers-testimony-of-public-citizens-president-joan-claybrook-to-the-committee-on-co/; **33.** Tennen, H., & Affleck, G. (1990). Blaming others for threatening events. *Psychological Bulletin*, *108*(2), 209; **34.** Leach, C. W., & Cidam, A. (2015). When is shame linked to constructive approach orientation? A meta-analysis. *Journal of Personality and Social Psychology*, *109*(6), 983; **35.** Gausel, N., Vignoles, V. L., & Leach, C. W. (2016). Resolving the paradox of shame: Differentiating among specific appraisal-feeling combinations explains pro-social and self-defensive motivation. *Motivation and Emotion*, *40*(1), 118–139; **36.** Leach, C. W. (2017). Understanding shame and guilt. In *Handbook of the psychology of self-forgiveness* (pp. 17–28). Springer; **37.** Bryan, C. J., Adams, G. S., & Monin, B. (2013). When cheating would make you a cheater: Implicating the self prevents unethical behavior. *Journal of Experimental Psychology: General*, *142*(4), 1001; **38.** Schein, C., Jackson, J. C., Frasca, T., & Gray, K. (2020). Praise-many, blame-fewer: A common (and successful) strategy for attributing responsibility in groups. *Journal of Experimental Psychology: General*, *149*(5), 855; **39.** Henderlong, J., & Lepper, M. R. (2002). The effects of praise on children's intrinsic motivation: A review and synthesis. *Psychological Bulletin*, *128*(5), 774.

CHAPTER NINE

1. Baghramian, M., & Carter, J. A. Relativism. In E. N. Zalta (Ed.), *The Stanford encyclopedia of philosophy* (Spring 2021 ed.). https://plato.stanford.edu/archives/spr2021/entries/relativism/; **2.** Putnam, H. (2004). *The collapse of the fact/value dichotomy and other essays.* Harvard University Press; **3.** Kelly, D., Stich, S., Haley, K. J., Eng, S. J., & Fessler, D. M. (2007). Harm, affect, and the moral/conventional distinction. *Mind & Language, 22*(2), 117–131; Quintelier, K. J., & Fessler, D. M. (2012). Varying versions of moral relativism: The philosophy and psychology of normative relativism. *Biology & Philosophy, 27*(1), 95–113; **4.** Oosterbeek, H., Sloof, R., & van De Kuilen, G. (2004). Cultural differences in ultimatum game experiments: Evidence from a meta-analysis. *Experimental Economics, 7,* 171–188; **5.** Tian, Q. (2008). Perception of business bribery in China: The impact of moral philosophy. *Journal of Business Ethics, 80*(3), 437–445; **6.** Rai, T. S., & Holyoak, K. J. (2013). Exposure to moral relativism compromises moral behavior. *Journal of Experimental Social Psychology, 49*(6), 995–1001; Vitell, S. J., & Paolillo, J. G. (2003). Consumer ethics: The role of religiosity. *Journal of Business Ethics, 46*(2), 151–162; **7.** Ruttan, R. L., & Nordgren, L. F. (2021). Instrumental use erodes sacred values. *Journal of Personality and Social Psychology, 121*(6), 1223–1240; **8.** Nichols, S. (2004). After objectivity: An empirical study of moral judgment. *Philosophical Psychology, 17*(1), 3–26; Goodwin, G. P., & Darley, J. M. (2012). Why are some moral beliefs perceived to be more objective than others? *Journal of Experimental Social Psychology, 48*(1), 250–256; **9.** Ayars, A., & Nichols, S. (2020). Rational learners and metaethics: Universalism, relativism, and evidence from consensus. *Mind & Language, 35*(1), 67–89; **10.** Sarkissian, H., Park, J., Tien, D., Wright, J. C., & Knobe, J. (2011). Folk moral relativism. *Mind & Language, 26*(4), 482–505; Schmidt, M. F., Gonzalez-Cabrera, I., & Tomasello, M. (2017). Children's developing metaethical judgments. *Journal of Experimental Child Psychology, 164,* 163–177; **11.** Skitka, L. J., Hanson, B. E., Morgan, G. S., & Wisneski, D. C. (2021). The psychology of moral conviction. *Annual Review of Psychology, 72,* 347–366; **12.** Skitka, L. J. (2010). The psychology of moral conviction. *Social and Personality Psychology Compass, 4*(4), 267–281; **13.** Skitka, L. J., Bauman, C. W., & Sargis, E. G. (2005). Moral conviction: Another contributor to attitude strength or something more? *Journal of Personality and Social Psychology, 88*(6), 895; **14.** Skitka et al., "Moral conviction," 895; **15.** Garner, R. (2007). Abolishing morality. *Ethical Theory and Moral Practice, 10*(5), 499–513; **16.** Condry, J., & Condry, S. (1976). Sex differences: A study of the eye of the beholder. *Child Development,* 812–819; **17.** Crary, A. (2007). *Beyond moral judgment.* Harvard University Press; **18.** Putnam, *The collapse of the fact/value dichotomy and other essays.*; **19.** Berlin, I. (2017). Two concepts of liberty. In *The liberty reader* (pp. 33–57). Routledge; **20.** Berlin, I. (2013). *The crooked timber of humanity: Chapters in the history of ideas.* Princeton University Press; **21.** Appiah, K. A. (2006). *Cosmopolitanism: Ethics in a world of strangers.* Norton; **22.** Epstein, D., & Pro Publica. (2017, February 22). When evidence says no, but doctors say yes. *The Atlantic.* https://www.theatlantic.com/health/archive/2017/02/when-evidence-says-no-but-doctors-say-yes/517368/; **23.** Smith, W. D. A. (1965). A history of nitrous oxide and oxygen anaesthesia part I: Joseph Priestley to Humphry Davy. *British Journal of Anaesthesia, 37*(10), 790–798; **24.** Wright, J. C., &

Pölzler, T. (2021). Should morality be abolished? An empirical challenge to the argument from intolerance. *Philosophical Psychology*, 1–36.

CHAPTER TEN

1. Litvak et al., "Fuel in the fire," 287–310; **2.** Crockett, M. J. (2017). Moral outrage in the digital age. *Nature of Human Behaviour*, *1*(11), 769–771; **3.** Kubin, E., & von Sikorski, C. (2021). The role of (social) media in political polarization: A systematic review. *Annals of the International Communication Association*, *45*(3), 188–206; **4.** Zhuravskaya, E., Petrova, M., & Enikolopov, R. (2020). Political effects of the internet and social media. *Annual Review of Economics*, *12*, 415–438; **5.** Milinski, M., Semmann, D., & Krambeck, H. J. (2002). Reputation helps solve the "tragedy of the commons." *Nature*, *415*(6870), 424–426; **6.** Turner, C. W., Layton, J. F., & Simons, L. S. (1975). Naturalistic studies of aggressive behavior: Aggressive stimuli, victim visibility, and horn honking. *Journal of Personality and Social Psychology*, *31*(6), 1098; **7.** Watts, D. P. (2006). Conflict resolution in chimpanzees and the valuable-relationships hypothesis. *International Journal of Primatology*, *27*(5), 1337–1364; Wittig, R. M., & Boesch, C. (2005). How to repair relationships: Reconciliation in wild chimpanzees (Pan troglodytes). *Ethology*, *111*(8), 736–763; **8.** Dechêne, A., Stahl, C., Hansen, J., & Wänke, M. (2010). The truth about the truth: A meta-analytic review of the truth effect. *Personality and Social Psychology Review*, *14*(2), 238–257; **9.** Atari, M., Davani, A. M., Kogon, D., Kennedy, B., Saxena, N. A., Anderson, I., & Dehghani, M. (2021, December). Morally homogeneous networks and radicalism. *Social Psychological and Personality Science*, *13*(6), 999–1009; **10.** Rathje, S., Van Bavel, J. J., & van der Linden, S. (2021). Out-group animosity drives engagement on social media. *Proceedings of the National Academy of Sciences*, *118*(26). **11.** Ward, A. F., Zheng, F., & Broniarczyk, S. (n.d.). I share, therefore I know? Sharing online content—even without reading it—inflates subjective knowledge. *Journal of Consumer Psychology* [Unpublished article]. Retrieved on May 1, 2022, from https://doi.org/10.1002/jcpy.1321; **12.** Gallup. (2019). *Gallup's latest global emotions report.* https://www.gallup.com/analytics/248906/gallup-global-emotions-report-2019. aspx; **13.** Huang, C. (2022). A meta-analysis of the problematic social media use and mental health. *International Journal of Social Psychiatry*, *68*(1), 12–33; **14.** Kross, E., Verduyn, P., Sheppes, G., Costello, C. K., Jonides, J., & Ybarra, O. (2021). Social media and well-being: Pitfalls, progress, and next steps. *Trends in Cognitive Sciences*, *25*(1), 55–66; **15.** Ironside, M., Kumar, P., Kang, M. S., & Pizzagalli, D. A. (2018). Brain mechanisms mediating effects of stress on reward sensitivity. *Current Opinion in Behavioral Sciences*, *22*, 106–113; **16.** Gray, J. R. (1999). A bias toward short-term thinking in threat-related negative emotional states. *Personality and Social Psychology Bulletin*, *25*(1), 65–75; **17.** Lazarus, R. S. (1991). Progress on a cognitive-motivational-relational theory of emotion. *American Psychologist*, *46*(8), 819; **18.** Cooper, A., Gomez, R., & Buck, E. (2008). The relationships between the BIS and BAS, anger and responses to anger. *Personality and Individual Differences*, *44*(2), 403–413; Wacker, J., Heldmann, M., & Stemmler, G. (2003). Separating emotion and motivational direction in fear and anger: Effects on frontal asymmetry. *Emotion*, *3*(2), 167; **19.** Lawrence, A. D., Goerendt, I. K., &

Brooks, D. J. (2007). Impaired recognition of facial expressions of anger in Parkinson's disease patients acutely withdrawn from dopamine replacement therapy. *Neuropsychologia, 45*(1), 65–74; **20.** Joyce, P. R., McHugh, P. C., Light, K. J., Rowe, S., Miller, A. L., & Kennedy, M. A. (2009). Relationships between angry-impulsive personality traits and genetic polymorphisms of the dopamine transporter. *Biological Psychiatry, 66*(8), 717–721; **21.** Gilam, G., Abend, R., Gurevitch, G., Erdman, A., Baker, H., Ben-Zion, Z., & Hendler, T. (2018). Attenuating anger and aggression with neuromodulation of the vmPFC: A simultaneous tDCS-fMRI study. *Cortex, 109,* 156–170; **22.** Wang, L., Restubog, S., Shao, B., Lu, V., & Van Kleef, G. A. (2018). Does anger expression help or harm leader effectiveness? The role of competence-based versus integrity-based violations and abusive supervision. *Academy of Management Journal, 61*(3), 1050–1072; **23.** Kelly, J. R., Iannone, N. E., & McCarty, M. K. (2016). Emotional contagion of anger is automatic: An evolutionary explanation. *British Journal of Social Psychology, 55*(1), 182–191; **24.** Brown, M., Keefer, L. A., Sacco, D. F., & Brown, F. L. (2021). Demonstrate values: Behavioral displays of moral outrage as a cue to long-term mate potential. *Emotion* [Advance online publication]. https://doi.org/10.1037/emo0000955; **25.** Barrett, L. F. (2017). *How emotions are made: The secret life of the brain.* Pan Macmillan; **26.** Troy, A. S., Willroth, E. C., Shallcross, A. J., Giuliani, N. R., Gross, J. J., & Mauss, I. B. (2023). Psychological resilience: An affect-regulation framework. *Annual Review of Psychology, 74,* 547–576; **27.** Duhigg, C. (2019, January/February). The real roots of American rage. *The Atlantic.* https://www.theatlantic.com/magazine/archive/2019/01/charles-duhigg-american-anger/576424/; Stapleton, C. E., & Dawkins, R. (2021). Catching my anger: How political elites create angrier citizens. *Political Research Quarterly,* 10659129211026972; **28.** Bodenhausen, G. V., Sheppard, L. A., & Kramer, G. P. (1994). Negative affect and social judgment: The differential impact of anger and sadness. *European Journal of Social Psychology, 24*(1), 45–62; **29.** Leith, K. P., & Baumeister, R. F. (1996). Why do bad moods increase self-defeating behavior? Emotion, risk tasking, and self-regulation. *Journal of Personality and Social Psychology, 71*(6), 1250; Keinan, G. (1987). Decision making under stress: Scanning of alternatives under controllable and uncontrollable threats. *Journal of Personality and Social Psychology, 52*(3), 639; **30.** Greenstein, M., & Franklin, N. (2020). Anger increases susceptibility to misinformation. *Experimental Psychology, 67*(3), 202–209. https://doi.org/10.1027/1618-3169/a000489; **31.** Zajenkowski, M., & Gignac, G. E. (2018). Why do angry people overestimate their intelligence? Neuroticism as a suppressor of the association between trait-anger and subjectively assessed intelligence. *Intelligence, 70,* 12–21; **32.** McDaniels, T. L., Axelrod, L. J., Cavanagh, N. S., & Slovic, P. (1997). Perception of ecological risk to water environments. *Risk Analysis, 17*(3), 341–352; **33.** Quigley, B. M., & Tedeschi, J. T. (1996). Mediating effects of blame attributions on feelings of anger. *Personality and Social Psychology Bulletin, 22*(12), 1280–1288; **34.** McTernan, E. (2021). Taking offense: An emotion reconsidered. *Philosophy & Public Affairs, 49*(2), 179–208; **35.** Solnit, R. (2014). *Men explain things to me.* Haymarket Books; **36.** Poggi, I., & D'Errico, F. (2018). Feeling offended: A blow to our image and our social relationships. *Frontiers in Psychology, 8,* 2221; **37.** McTernan, "Taking offense," 179–208; **38.** Rini, R. (2018). How to take offense: Responding to microaggression. *Journal of the American Philosophical Association, 4*(3), 332–351; **39.** Simester, A. P., & von Hirsch, A.

(2002). Rethinking the offense principle. *Legal Theory*, *8*(3), 269–295; **40.** Paul, S., Kathmann, N., & Riesel, A. (2016). The costs of distraction: The effect of distraction during repeated picture processing on the LPP. *Biological Psychology*, *117*, 225–234; **41.** Webb, T. L., Miles, E., & Sheeran, P. (2012). Dealing with feeling: A meta-analysis of the effectiveness of strategies derived from the process model of emotion regulation. *Psychological Bulletin*, *138*(4), 775; **42.** Lau, C. Y., & Tov, W. (2023). Effects of positive reappraisal and self-distancing on the meaningfulness of everyday negative events. *Frontiers in Psychology*, *14*. https://doi.org/10.3389/fpsyg.2023.1093412; **43.** Haines, S. J., Gleeson, J., Kuppens, P., Hollenstein, T., Ciarrochi, J., Labuschagne, I., Grace, K. & Koval, P. (2016). The wisdom to know the difference: Strategy-situation fit in emotion regulation in daily life is associated with well-being. *Psychological Science*, *27*(12), 1651–1659; **44.** Noddings, N. (2013). *Caring: A relational approach to ethics and moral education*. University of California Press; **45.** Tjosvold, D., Wong, A. S., & Feng Chen, N. Y. (2014). Constructively managing conflicts in organizations. *Annual Review of Organizational Psychology and Organizational Behavior*, *1*(1), 545–568; **46.** Gibson, J. L. (2004). Does truth lead to reconciliation? Testing the causal assumptions of the South African truth and reconciliation process. *American Journal of Political Science*, *48*(2), 201–217; **47.** Fehr, R., Gelfand, M. J., & Nag, M. (2010). The road to forgiveness: A meta-analytic synthesis of its situational and dispositional correlates. *Psychological Bulletin*, *136*(5), 894; **48.** Jha, A. (2021). *Peak mind: Find your focus, own your attention, invest 12 minutes a day*. Hachette UK.

CHAPTER ELEVEN

1. Argote, L. (1982). Input uncertainty and organizational coordination in hospital emergency units. *Administrative Science Quarterly*, 420–434; **2.** Friedman, L. (1999). Doubt & inquiry: Peirce and Descartes revisited. *Transactions of the Charles S. Peirce Society*, *35*(4), 724–746. http://www.jstor.org/stable/40320795; **3.** Wilson, T. D. (2011). *Redirect: The surprising new science of psychological change*. Little, Brown and Company; **4.** Wilson, T. D., Centerbar, D. B., Kermer, D. A., & Gilbert, D. T. (2005). The pleasures of uncertainty: Prolonging positive moods in ways people do not anticipate. *Journal of Personality and Social Psychology*, *88*(1), 5; **5.** Yoshida, W., Seymour, B., Koltzenburg, M., & Dolan, R. J. (2013). Uncertainty increases pain: Evidence for a novel mechanism of pain modulation involving the periaqueductal gray. *Journal of Neuroscience*, *33*(13), 5638–5646; Chou, E. Y., Parmar, B. L., & Galinsky, A. D. (2016). Economic insecurity increases physical pain. *Psychological Science*, *27*(4), 443–454; **6.** De Berker, A. O., Rutledge, R. B., Mathys, C., Marshall, L., Cross, G. F., Dolan, R. J., & Bestmann, S. (2016). Computations of uncertainty mediate acute stress responses in humans. *Nature Communications*, *7*(1), 1–11; **7.** Chernev, A., Böckenholt, U., & Goodman, J. (2015). Choice overload: A conceptual review and meta-analysis. *Journal of Consumer Psychology*, *25*(2), 333–358; McShane, B. B., & Böckenholt, U. (2018). Multilevel multivariate meta-analysis with application to choice overload. *Psychometrika*, *83*(1), 255–271; **8.** Durso, G. R., Briñol, P., & Petty, R. E. (2016). From power to inaction: Ambivalence gives pause to the powerful. *Psychological Science*, *27*(12), 1660–1666; **9.** Redelmeier,

D. A., & Shafir, E. (1995). Medical decision making in situations that offer multiple alternatives. *JAMA*, *273*(4), 302–305. **10.** McGregor, I., Zanna, M. P., Holmes, J. G., & Spencer, S. J. (2001). Compensatory conviction in the face of personal uncertainty: Going to extremes and being oneself. *Journal of Personality and Social Psychology*, *80*(3), 472; **11.** Cialdini, R. B., Borden, R. J., Thorne, A., Walker, M. R., Freeman, S., & Sloan, L. R. (1976). Basking in reflected glory: Three (football) field studies. *Journal of Personality and Social Psychology*, *34*, 366–375; **12.** Arndt, J., Solomon, S., Kasser, T., & Sheldon, K. M. (2004). The urge to splurge: A terror management account of materialism and consumer behavior. *Journal of Consumer Psychology*, *14*(3), 198–212; **13.** Landau, M. J., Solomon, S., Greenberg, J., Cohen, F., Pyszczynski, T., Arndt, J., Miller, C. H., Ogilvie, D. M., & Cook, A. (2004). Deliver us from evil: The effects of mortality salience and reminders of 9/11 on support for President George W. Bush. *Personality and Social Psychology Bulletin*, *30*(9), 1136–1150; **14.** Landau, M. J., Johns, M., Greenberg, J., Pyszczynski, T., Martens, A., Goldenberg, J. L., & Solomon, S. (2004). A function of form: Terror management and structuring the social world. *Journal of Personality and Social Psychology*, *87*(2), 190; **15.** Grieve, P. G., & Hogg, M. A. (1999). Subjective uncertainty and intergroup discrimination in the minimal group situation. *Personality and Social Psychology Bulletin*, *25*(8), 926–940; **16.** Fritsche, I., Jonas, E., & Fankhänel, T. (2008). The role of control motivation in mortality salience effects on ingroup support and defense. *Journal of Personality and Social Psychology*, *95*(3), 524; **17.** van Horen, F., & Millet, K. (2022). Unpredictable love? How uncertainty influences partner preferences. *European Journal of Social Psychology*, *52*(5-6), 810–818; **18.** Heine, S. J., Proulx, T., & Vohs, K. D. (2006). The meaning maintenance model: On the coherence of social motivations. *Personality and Social Psychology Review*, *10*(2), 88–110; **19.** Damisch, L., Stoberock, B., & Mussweiler, T. (2010). Keep your fingers crossed! How superstition improves performance. *Psychological Science*, *21*(7), 1014–1020; **20.** Wisman, A., & Koole, S. L. (2003). Hiding in the crowd: Can mortality salience promote affiliation with others who oppose one's worldviews? *Journal of Personality and Social Psychology*, *84*(3), 511; **21.** Taubman-Ben-Ari, O., Findler, L., & Mikulincer, M. (2002). The effects of mortality salience on relationship strivings and beliefs: The moderating role of attachment style. *British Journal of Social Psychology*, *41*(3), 419–441; **22.** McKimmie, B. M., Terry, D. J., Hogg, M. A., Manstead, A. S. R., Spears, R., & Doosje, B. (2003). I'm a hypocrite, but so is everyone else: Group support and the reduction of cognitive dissonance. *Group Dynamics: Theory, Research, and Practice*, *7*(3), 214–224; **23.** Pinel, E. C., & Long, A. E. (2012). When I's meet: Sharing subjective experience with someone from the outgroup. *Personality and Social Psychology Bulletin*, *38*(3), 296–307; **24.** Crimston, C. R., Selvanathan, H. P., & Jetten, J. (2021). Moral polarization predicts support for authoritarian and progressive strong leaders via the perceived breakdown of society. *Political Psychology*, *43*(4), 671–691; **25.** Murray, S. L., Lamarche, V., Seery, M. D., Jung, H. Y., Griffin, D. W., & Brinkman, C. (2021). The social-safety system: Fortifying relationships in the face of the unforeseeable. *Journal of Personality and Social Psychology*, *120*(1), 99; **26.** Bowles, D. (2007). Wrongfully accused: The political motivations behind Socrates' execution. *Hirundo*, *5*, 16–30; **27.** Abensour, M., & Breaugh, M. (2007). Against the sovereignty of philosophy over politics: Arendt's reading of Plato's cave allegory. *Social*

Research, *74*(4), 955–982. http://www.jstor.org/stable/40972036; **28.** Verhaeghen, P. (2021). Mindfulness as attention training: Meta-analyses on the links between attention performance and mindfulness interventions, long-term meditation practice, and trait mindfulness. *Mindfulness*, *12*(3), 564–581; **29.** Barton, M. A., Sutcliffe, K. M., Vogus, T. J., & DeWitt, T. (2015). Performing under uncertainty: Contextualized engagement in wildland firefighting. *Journal of Contingencies and Crisis Management*, *23*(2), 74–83; **30.** Edmondson, A. (1999). Psychological safety and learning behavior in work teams. *Administrative Science Quarterly*, *44*(2), 350–383; **31.** Cohen, S. L., Bingham, C. B., & Hallen, B. L. (2019). The role of accelerator designs in mitigating bounded rationality in new ventures. *Administrative Science Quarterly*, *64*(4), 810–854; **32.** Fox, B. C., Simsek, Z., & Heavey, C. (2022). Top management team experiential variety, competitive repertoires, and firm performance: Examining the law of requisite variety in the 3D printing industry (1986–2017). *Academy of Management Journal*, *65*(2), 545–576; **33.** Dew, N., Sarasathy, S., Read, S., & Wiltbank, R. (2009). Affordable loss: Behavioral economic aspects of the plunge decision. *Strategic Entrepreneurship Journal*, *3*(2), 105–126; **34.** Lipshitz, R., & Strauss, O. (1997). Coping with uncertainty: A naturalistic decision-making analysis. *Organizational Behavior and Human Decision Processes*, *69*(2), 149–163.

TOOLS APPENDIX

1. Arpan, L. M., & Roskos-Ewoldsen, D. R. (2005). Stealing thunder: Analysis of the effects of proactive disclosure of crisis information. *Public Relations Review*, *31*(3), 425–433; Williams, K. D., Bourgeois, M. J., & Croyle, R. T. (1993). The effects of stealing thunder in criminal and civil trials. *Law and Human Behavior*, *17*(6), 597–609; **2.** Freeman, R. E. (2010). *Strategic management: A stakeholder approach.* Cambridge University Press.

About the Author

BIDHAN (BOBBY) PARMAR is the Shannon G. Smith Bicentennial Professor of Business Administration and associate dean for faculty development at the Darden School of Business at the University of Virginia. He teaches courses on business ethics, collaboration, and creative and critical thinking. He is also a fellow at the Olsson Center for Applied Ethics and the co-director of the Darden Experiential Leadership Development Lab. He is a former fellow at the Safra Center for Ethics at Harvard University.

Parmar's unique research focuses on how managers make sense of uncertainty and collaborate to create value for stakeholders. His work helps executives better handle doubt in their decision-making. Parmar's scholarship has been published in leading journals, such as *Organization Science, Psychological Science, Journal of Applied Psychology, Journal of Experimental Psychology, Organizational Behavior and Human Decision Processes, Organization Studies, Business & Society,* and *Journal of Business Ethics.*

Parmar produced the documentary film *Fishing with Dynamite* about the role of business in society, featuring leading thinkers such as former Labor Secretary Robert Reich, Jim Collins (author of *Good to Great*), and Bethany McLean (author of *The Smartest Guys in the Room*).

He was named one of the top forty business school professors under forty in the world, and has won several awards for his teaching and research. Parmar lives in Charlottesville with his wife and two daughters.